Language, Intertext

Mary Talbot

Language, Intertextuality and Subjectivity

Voices in the Construction of Consumer Femininity

LAP LAMBERT Academic Publishing

Impressum/Imprint (nur für Deutschland/ only for Germany)

Bibliografische Information der Deutschen Nationalbibliothek: Die Deutsche Nationalbibliothek verzeichnet diese Publikation in der Deutschen Nationalbibliografie; detaillierte bibliografische Daten sind im Internet über http://dnb.d-nb.de abrufbar.

Alle in diesem Buch genannten Marken und Produktnamen unterliegen warenzeichen-, marken- oder patentrechtlichem Schutz bzw. sind Warenzeichen oder eingetragene Warenzeichen der jeweiligen Inhaber. Die Wiedergabe von Marken, Produktnamen, Gebrauchsnamen, Handelsnamen, Warenbezeichnungen u.s.w. in diesem Werk berechtigt auch ohne besondere Kennzeichnung nicht zu der Annahme, dass solche Namen im Sinne der Warenzeichen- und Markenschutzgesetzgebung als frei zu betrachten wären und daher von jedermann benutzt werden dürften.

Coverbild: www.ingimage.com

Verlag: LAP LAMBERT Academic Publishing GmbH & Co. KG
Dudweiler Landstr. 99, 66123 Saarbrücken, Deutschland
Telefon +49 681 3720-310, Telefax +49 681 3720-3109
Email: info@lap-publishing.com

Herstellung in Deutschland:
Schaltungsdienst Lange o.H.G., Berlin
Books on Demand GmbH, Norderstedt
Reha GmbH, Saarbrücken
Amazon Distribution GmbH, Leipzig
ISBN: 978-3-8433-5859-0

Imprint (only for USA, GB)

Bibliographic information published by the Deutsche Nationalbibliothek: The Deutsche Nationalbibliothek lists this publication in the Deutsche Nationalbibliografie; detailed bibliographic data are available in the Internet at http://dnb.d-nb.de.

Any brand names and product names mentioned in this book are subject to trademark, brand or patent protection and are trademarks or registered trademarks of their respective holders. The use of brand names, product names, common names, trade names, product descriptions etc. even without a particular marking in this works is in no way to be construed to mean that such names may be regarded as unrestricted in respect of trademark and brand protection legislation and could thus be used by anyone.

Cover image: www.ingimage.com

Publisher: LAP LAMBERT Academic Publishing GmbH & Co. KG
Dudweiler Landstr. 99, 66123 Saarbrücken, Germany
Phone +49 681 3720-310, Fax +49 681 3720-3109
Email: info@lap-publishing.com

Printed in the U.S.A.
Printed in the U.K. by (see last page)
ISBN: 978-3-8433-5859-0

Contents

Part 2   Practice: Critical Analysis of the Construction of Consumer Femininity in a Two-Page Feature from *Jackie* Magazine

2

1

Purpose and scope

Disciplinary context

In this book I propose an approach to doing critical linguistic analysis that focuses on the constitution of a language user's subjectivity in the act of reading. I shall begin by establishing the broad field within linguistics within which I locate the present work. First and foremost I associate it with some collaborative, synthesising work at Lancaster known as Critical Language Study (CLS), which has an explicit emancipatory objective. Romy Clark, Norman Fairclough, Roz Ivanic and Marilyn Martin-Jones (1987: 21) identify CLS as 'a resource for developing the consciousness and self-consciousness of dominated people'.

Clark et al. remark on 'strong family resemblances with other syntheses' (17), including in particular the Critical Linguistics developed by Roger Fowler and associates. As Fowler (1988) notes, the critical readings of newspaper articles etc. constitute attempts to turn the close grammatical analysis of specific texts into consciousness-raising activities. This body of work, with its attention to the interpretation of texts, especially from the mass media, is a background influence on this book. My more direct influences are other bodies of work in linguistics which have directly tackled the issue of how language constructs the subjectivities of its users: namely, discourse analysis (Michel Pêcheux 1978, 1982, Pêcheux and Christine Fuchs 1975), trends in the study of language as social semiotic (eg. Michael Halliday and Ruqaiya Hasan 1985, Gunther Kress 1985, Terry Threadgold 1987, 1988) and a contribution to Critical Language Study by Fairclough (1989) which shares their systemic linguistics approach to language description.

The work within linguistics devoting attention to subjectivity has of necessity turned to other fields. They all employ a conceptualisation of discourse from social theory, which, with the exception of Pêcheux, is explicitly referred to as Foucauldian discourse, after Michel Foucault. I will be making use of this view of discourse, with its accompanying view of the social subject, with specific reference to feminist appropriations (Dorothy Smith 1987, Valerie Walkerdine 1985, Chris Weedon 1987). Other disciplines which I have needed to range.into are literary semiotics (especially Julia Kristeva 1969,

1970), cultural studies (eg. Cynthia White 1970, Marjorie Ferguson 1983, Angela McRobbie 1978, Janice Winship 1987) and, to a lesser extent, psychoanalysis (Jacques Lacan 1966, Walkerdine 1985).

Critical language study

In the following I refer to Clark et al. (1987) and Fairclough (1989). This is by no means the only work in the field, but it is the most relevant here (other work includes, for example, Roz Ivanic' article (1988) focusing on foreign/ second language learning and issues relating to bilingualism). Fairclough (1989: 33) establishes the theoretical objective of his book on CLS as doing 'justice to the rich and complex interrelationships of language and power' 1 by setting actual discourse in place in history and society. He states the practical objective of CLS as the stimulation of critical awareness of language, in particular of how existing discourse conventions have come about as a result of relations of power and power struggle. This involves showing the social and historical constitution of 'common sense', i.e. naturalized conventions:

> Institutional practices which people draw upon without thinking often embody assumptions which directly or indirectly legitimize existing power relations. Practices which appear to be universal and commonsensical can often be shown to originate in the dominant class or the dominant bloc, and to have become *naturalized*.

Drawing attention to the ideological and constructed nature of naturalized 'commonsense' can involve showing that apparently natural kinds of interaction or representation are conventional social practices, and showing that they legitimize existing power relations.

CLS is intended to counter an increasing tendency for state and capitalist control through strategic language use (see chapter 2). Put simply, by providing a way for denaturalising discourse, CLS offers to 'arm' people against manipulation through discourse. It is intended to counter specific tendencies in discourse change upholding existing relations of power. It is a strategy for undermining existing power relations, which begins by offering language users critical positions as interpreters: empowerment through critical awareness: 'to help increase consciousness of how language contributes to the domination of some people by others, because consciousness is the first step towards emancipation' (Fairclough 1989: 1)

The sociolinguistic world bestows social identities and relationships on language users. Part of what CLS has to offer is awareness of these identities and relationships and how they are bestowed upon us; i.e. recognition of how people are constituted as subjects in/through language practices. Close

6

analysis of individual texts can contribute to stimulating critical awareness of positioning in relations of power as dominated subjects.

In common with other CLS practitioners, I have both theoretical and more practical objectives. On the theoretical side, I want to contribute to the development of a linguistic model of discourse which integrates linguistic and social theoretical perspectives, so that discourse can be analysed both as interaction between individuals and as socially reproductive and constitutive of subjectivity. I do this by bringing together anti-humanism, coherence and intertextuality. On the practical side, I want to locate points of focus for taking up a critical (specifically, feminist) reading position in discourse analysis. It is also my hope that this will provide others with the theoretical and analytical grounding for a critical pedagogy that will take attention to language and the construction of language users' subjectivities into the classroom.

My contribution to the resource of CLS is in two parts. Part 1 deals with the theoretical claim that social subjects are constituted in discourse and proposes the concept of 'intertextual coherence' as a way of examining this constitution. Part 2 puts this conception of intertextual coherence into operation in a sample analysis of a type of discourse that contributes to the formation of women as feminine subjects: the women's magazine. Parts 1 and 2 are outlined in the last two sections of this introductory chapter.

Feminism and the denaturalization of femininity

Women's emancipation, the political objective underlying feminism, can only begin with an understanding of the social construction of gender. Before change can take place or even be desired, what appear to be natural aspects of the everyday life of women and men have to be exposed as disadvantageous to women and culturally produced.

Gender differences in women and men are non-physiological differences. In our society, gender is constructed in patriarchal and capitalist social relations. Divisions are made, on the grounds of sex, relating to who does what kinds of labour, who is responsible for childcare, for keeping relationships going, and so on. For example, as Catherine Belsey (1985: 49) says: 'In patriarchal society women 'choose' to do the housework, to make sacrifices for their children, not to become engineers'.

Divisions are also made between the kinds of appearance and behaviour permissable for women and men. Women also 'choose' to cultivate a feminine appearance, to spend money on cosmetics and time learning how to wear it, to apologize, to read stories about 'relationships'. In other words, women tend to willingly behave in ways that are considered feminine. It is crucial therefore to distinguish

7

between sex, which is biological and natural, and gender, which is culturally produced. To stress cultural production rather than biology is to introduce the possibility of change.

Masculine and feminine gendered identities are not simply pre-given but constructed in social relations between people, in their enactments of social practices. The emancipatory aim of feminism must begin with the de-naturalization of these gendered identities, particularly those available for women which subordinate them. Naturalization concerns the degree of acceptance as natural of social practices and the identities and relationships of participants involved in them. A social practice is naturalized when it is no longer apparent that it has come into being as a result of specific needs of particular people and by means of specific strategies of exclusion, appropriation of rights, resources etc. What is natural is unarguable, beyond criticism and not open to change.

Femininity can never be completely 'natural' for women, since it has to be achieved. A feminine identity involves, among other things, a particular mode of consumption. In fact it requires work on women's part, the grooming and beauty work needed for a conventional feminine appearance. Yet this is work that most women are happy to do, since it is an everyday aspect of women's lives and through doing it they can hope to establish for themselves acceptable social identities as women. Being feminine is being an acceptable woman in patriarchal social relations. We must be careful not to alienate women from feminism by downgrading women's interests and activities (they'll probably agree with you anyway!) For instance, it is not sufficient to criticise women for attention to appearance in general because it is trivial or trivializing, or for wearing a particular kind of clothing because it sexualizes them. To do this is to criticize women for being women. Instead we must take care to value women's preoccupations and acknowledge their/our specialist knowledge and skills, while at the same time exposing the social conditions in which they are acquired.

Undermining consumer femininity

My aim is to stimulate critical awareness of consumer femininity, to 'arm' women, especially young women, against manipulation by the fashion and publishing industries, etc. My aim is to help young women to see how their sense of self, their identity as women, is tied up in the production of profit for others through the consumption of commodities, but I want to do this without attacking their self-esteem and making them feel stupid or duped. This is essential because for adolescents consumer femininity is an important part of claiming adult status and is important for female group membership and solidarity. For working-class girls, it is essential for strategies of resistance to the powerless positions assigned to them as working-class schoolgirls (see McRobbie 1978). It is also important to

8

them for entry into adolescent social relations between the sexes (numerous biographical accounts report the feeling of being 'left out' and learning about fashion and make-up in order to make male friends and keep female friends (e.g. Cohen 1984, Brownmiller 1986).

Women's and men's gendered identities are determined by capitalist and patriarchal social conditions and constructed in capitalist and patriarchal social relations. According to MacKinnon (1982: 530-1), femininity sexualizes women:

> Socially, femaleness means femininity, which means attractiveness to men, which means sexual attractiveness, which means sexual availability on male terms. What defines woman as such is what turns men on. ...Gender socialization is the process through which women internalize (make their own) a male image of their sexuality as their identity as women. It is not just an illusion.

In this view women are the sexualized sex; the need for a gendered identity forces women in patriarchal society to see themselves through men's eyes and to cultivate feminine characteristics which they expect men to want from them.[1] Coward (1984: 7) remarks that women's self-esteem is caught up in their appearance and desirability to others. As she says:

> However unconsciously, most members of this society get the message that there's a lot at stake in visual impact. Most women know to their cost that appearance is perhaps the crucial way by which men form opinions of women. For that reason, feelings about self-image get mixed up with feelings about security and comfort. Self-image in this society is enmeshed with judgments about desirability. And because desirability has been elevated to being the crucial reason for sexual relations, it sometimes appears to women that the whole possibility of being loved and comforted hangs on how their appearance will be received.

Conventional kinds of feminine appearance are shaped by the mass media, fashion and related industries. As I said above, being feminine involves women in particular patterns of consumption. In chapter 2, I present a view of femininity as a mass media construction and as a discursive phenomenon in which women actively participate.

Outline of part 1

Part I concerns the constitution of the social subject in discourse and endeavours to integrate linguistic method and an anti-humanist perspective for critical language study (CLS) I conclude by presenting a view of coherence as an intertextual phenomenon. This is offered as part of a critical discourse analysis and its purpose is to make accessible the process of being positioned as a subject: the critical awareness of subjectivity which is a necessary first step for 'changing the subject'.

I begin, in **chapter 2**, by examining the concepts of 'subject' and 'discourse', setting out the anti-humanist position taken. First I explain the term 'anti-humanist' and its significance for a linguistic investigation of subjectivity, then centre on the language user as social subject. I present first the anti-humanist conceptions of the subject in social theory and psychoanalysis. I then go on to show the absence of such a view of the language-using subject in linguistics (theoretical linguistics, sociolinguistics, pragmatics, discourse analysis) and its drawbacks. I then set out what I mean by 'discourse'. This involves establishing two complementary conceptions: discourse as linguistic activity, and discourse in the epistemological sense used by Foucault. A short section on discourse in linguistics establishes both a distinction between discourse-process and text-product and the general systemic-functional framework I intend to employ in analysis. It also introduces the view of discourse-production and -interpretation as cognitive processes related to social practices for which language users draw upon resources. I then turn to Foucauldian discourse and the discursive constitution of knowledge and practices.

Next I proceed to relate the issues covered in the previous sections specifically to feminine subjectivity and the critical analysis of texts. I illustrate how the conceptions of discourse and subjectivity have been operationalized in feminist social analysis and linguistics. First I deal specifically with the constitution of women as subjects, considering in particular how a consumerist femininity constructs women's subjectivities. Then I examine two approaches in linguistics working with both linguistic and Foucauldian senses of discourse and with an anti-humanist view of the subject. Here I outline Michel Pêcheux' view of discourse as 'ideological materiality' and Fairclough's model of discourse as historically constituted social practice. This section combines attention to societal and institutional levels of analysis with linguistic analysis and outlines specific tendencies in discourse change which CLS aims to counteract.

I close the chapter with the proposal that coherence may be used as a focus for examining the constitution of subjectivity. This section contains a selective review of work on coherence. After a general discussion of the field I review some useful contributions from Pêcheux (1982), Halliday and Hasan (1976), Halliday (1985), Thibault (1988) and Fairclough (1989), bringing out the potential their work offers for turning attention to the constitution of the subjectivity of language users in the act of constructing coherence.

Chapter 3 is an exposition of the concept of intertextuality. It culminates in a view of discourse as a social productivity and of text as a resource in this productivity, constructed by language users bringing together a tissue of 'voices' in the processes of production and interpretation. Taking an anti-humanist theoretical position, I consider discourse to be essentially intertextual or 'dialogic'. In an intertextual view of discourse, which stems from poststructuralist literary theory and, before that, Russian Poetics (Bakhtin's dialogism), a text consists of its relationships with other texts. It does not have a single originator, but multiple and indeterminate origins.

I begin by establishing what intertextuality has to offer for critical analysis and drawing out related concepts from chapter 2 in the work of Foucault, Pêcheux and Fairclough. This is followed in with a brief account of Bakhtin's dialogism, from which the actual concept of intertextuality was derived by Kristeva. The discussion of intertextuality itself begins with Kristeva's anti-humanist interpretation of Bakhtin's work on the novel, in which text-production is conceived as the reproduction of history and society. I also outline other applications of the concept in literary semiology, by Barthes, Culler and Bloom. A further section deals with how intertextuality has been adopted by linguists, focusing on contributions from textlinguistics (Beaugrande and Dressler) and systemic linguistics (Lemke, Halliday and Hasan, Kress).

I next establish three forms of intertextuality, on which the analytical framework in chapter 5 will be based. I then conclude the chapter by bringing out the intertextual view of discourse as dialogic and proposing the notion of 'intertextual coherence'. A dialogic text is a 'tissue of living voices' embedded in the social practice of discourse. It is not a single fixed object but traces of a productivity, containing an indeterminate 'text population'. In the act of producing and interpreting dialogic texts a language-user is embedded in intertextuality and multiply positioned as a subject. 'Intertextual coherence' is the focus for examining the constitution of subjectivity in discourse. The reader has an active part in constructing coherence, through which she[2] is constituted as a social subject.

Outline of part 2

Part 2 puts 'intertextual coherence' into operation in a critical discourse analysis that attends specifically to the constitution of subjectivity. It begins with a preliminary examination of aspects of the order of discourse in which the sample data was produced. This informs my selection of specific points of focus for examining its intertextuality and related 'text population'. The sample analysis is offered as an experiment in stimulating critical awareness of the tendencies in discourse change outlined in chapter

11

2; namely, the proliferation of synthetic personalization, of the subject position of consumer, and of subject shaping practices of discourse technologies.

Chapter 4 examines the social and discoursal context of the data I have chosen. It deals with some general considerations relating to mass media discourse, then turns specifically to women's magazines. First I discuss the asymmetrical quality of mass media discourse, the position of power it bestows on producers and the imaginary communities it constructs. Then I examine the women's magazine as a discourse-type with historical continuity and heterogeneous elements and go on to focus on *Jackie*, the teenagers' magazine chosen for analysis, presenting McRobbie's conception of the 'false sisterhood' this publication offers readers. This chapter introduces my view of *Jackie* as a 'synthetic sisterhood'.

In **chapter 5** I present the analytical framework for examining the 'synthetic sisterhood' offered by magazines. This chapter presents the points of focus for examining the intertextual connections readers need to construct coherence. I take the three forms of intertextuality in turn: Prior text, Interaction and Heterogeneity. Firstly, the Prior text section deals with the identification of Prior texts drawn in, or 'embedded', and their attribution. Then the Interaction section turns to a range of features for examining the simulation of reciprocal discourse in mass media texts. Finally, the Heterogeneity section focuses on ways of identifying the multiple subject positions assigned to the producer, and correspondingly to the interpreter, and the kinds of relationship established between them.

Chapter 6 contains the analysis of a sample 'consumer feature' from *Jackie*. I apply the framework given in chapter 5 for examining the intertextuality and 'text population' of mass media texts. I use it to substantiate and develop McRobbie's claim that *Jackie* synthesizes a female community, proposing that the feature establishes a consumption community based on lipstick to which readers are offered membership. After briefly introducing the component parts or texts of the sample data with some preliminary discussion, I attend to each text in turn. For each text in the sample first I examine prior texts and the characters producing them. Next I examine simulation of reciprocal discourse, if present in either one-way producer-audience interaction or representations of dialogue. Then I examine the construction of addresser-addressee identities; i.e. what kinds of subject position or 'voice' the mass media producer uses and the subject positions these 'voices' set up for the audience. I examine one specific 'voice' - editorial-as-friend - separately. This analysis chapter concludes with a reinterpretation of the notion of a sorority on the basis of the sample pages. Here I deal with McRobbie's claim that this sorority is 'unsisterly'.

The purpose of the practical half is not to offer a definitive analysis of *Jackie*'s contribution to the construction of girls' subjectivities. Research making such a claim would certainly need to add to

12

the text analysis of *Jackie* close attention to its interpretation by individuals. What the practical part is intended to provide is a way of helping girls to take up critical reading positions that, as members of the targeted readership of *Jackie*, they may find difficult. The approach to analysis then is offered as a strategy for resistance.

PART 1

Theory: the constitution of social subjects in discourse

2

Subject and discourse

Anti-humanism

'Anti-humanism' concerns a particular view of the nature of the human subject. This introductory section outlines briefly what an anti-humanist view consists of, and what it has to offer linguistics. Since the terminology is somewhat negative, I had better briefly mention what 'humanism' refers to. From a humanist viewpoint, there is something universally recognisable as human nature that exists irrespective of time and place. Human experience is shared by everyone - we have a common humanity and a shared reality. As thinking/speaking subjects, we are each, as individuals, a sovereign source of meaning, a 'transcendental ego'.[1] The 'transcendental ego' is a core of selfhood/identity that is assumed to exist outside or, better, prior to social relations (as though we should imagine individuals floating outside the social structures of which they are a part, i.e. 'transcending' them). Kristeva's rejection of the humanist conception of the human actor who produces meanings provides a useful starting point for outlining what an anti-humanist view of the subject consists of. Writing in the early seventies, in the heyday of Chomskian linguistics, Kristeva (1973: 28) describes the theory of meaning as standing at a crossroads:

> Either it will remain an attempt at formalizing meaning-systems by increasing sophistication of the logico-mathematical tools which enable it to formulate models on the basis of a conception ...of meaning as the act of a transcendental ego, cut off from its body, its unconscious and also its history; or else it will attune itself to the theory of the speaking subject as a divided subject (conscious/ unconscious) and go on to attempt to specify the types of operation characteristic of the two sides of the split.

Kristeva distinguishes between two kinds of assumption in philosophy about the production of meaning and its origin: 'one side argues for a transcendence with an immanent "human" causality while the other argues for an "ideology" whose cause is external and therefore transcendent' (25). Both of these kinds of assumption about the production and origin of meaning display an illusory 'transcendence'. In the first case 'immanent "human" causality' is where meanings come from; i.e. meanings are produced by individuals. In the second, meanings are produced by external social causes, implemented by individuals. She goes on to identify the first of these with a neglect 'of the historical socializing role of the symbolic', and the second with the views of 'the various sociological dogmatisms, which suppress the specificity of the symbolic and its logic in their anxiety to reduce them to an "external" determinant' (27). Neither position, she says, 'shows any awareness of the linguistic and, at a more general level, semiotic logic of the sociality in which the (speaking, historical) subject is embedded' (25-6). Kristeva identifies a possible anti-humanist perspective that will avoid either of these positions in semiology.[2] The route to this anti-humanist approach lies, she suggests, in a theory of meaning which is also a theory of the subject who produces it. The consequence of taking up an anti-humanist position is that the causality behind human actions is neither, in Kristeva's terms, quoted above, simply 'immanent' nor 'external'.

As I said above, Kristeva describes the theory of meaning standing at a crossroads. The route she indicates is certainly the 'lefthand path' of 'militant anti-humanism' (as it is described by Fredric Jameson (1972: 139), citing Althusser and Foucault), the path taken by that development of structuralism known as poststructuralism. A defining characteristic of poststructuralism is an explicit rejection of a 'transcendent' view of the human subject. The speaking subject is not 'unitary', which is to say it does not have some mysterious core or 'essence' from which meanings and intentions emanate, which remains intact regardless of the surrounding context. Instead the individual is multiply positioned as a subject. In Kristeva's writing, the theory of the meaning-producing subject is semiology, informed by psychoanalysis. Individuals are positioned as subjects in the symbolic order. As the poststructuralist feminist Walkerdine (1985: 238) says: 'There is, in this account, no lone individual, no single point of causality, but subjects created in multiple causality, shifting, at relay points of dynamic intersection'. In the anti-humanist view, subjects do not share a common nature or have access to a common reality. Diversity between subjects is not accounted for in terms of individual differences but in terms of positioning in symbolic and social orders.

Such a view is for the most part absent from linguistics, to its detriment. In structuralism, meaning is produced by structures, in systems of interrelated terms. Meaning resides in the conventional relation of one term to another. Following this structuralist pattern, the speaking subject of theoretical ('autonomous') linguistics is an abstraction, which is assumed to merely implement the meanings produced by systems. Systems not users are the object of analysis. Areas of linguistics examining language in operation have included the people producing language in their object of analysis. Pragmatics has explored how meanings depend crucially on speakers' intentions and hearers' recognition of them. In discourse analysis, language users are described as actors playing roles, operating rules and acting according to conventions. In these approaches meaning lies not only in the conventional relations between terms in a system but also in the actions of the language-using subject. However, they work with a humanist view of the language user as a 'unitary' subject, as I will go on to show. Speaking subjects are seen as role-playing actors who are individually responsible for their actions and able to freely pick and choose among options. These actors operate rules and act according to conventions, from which however they still remain detached. This view is not sufficient for an account of the construction of the language user as a social subject in the act of interpreting texts. There is no account of the interplay between the acting individual and the multiple conventions that construct her as a subject. This is what an anti-humanist view has to offer.

Subject

The anti-humanist subject

The social subject in an anti-humanist view is a subject-in-process, constructed in the process of interaction with the social world. This subject is fragmentary and lacks unity. It has a shifting, uncertain identity; it is the product of unconscious processes.[3] Althusser (1971: 163) has proposed a mechanism known as 'interpellation' by which individuals take up subject positions. He explains it as follows:

> interpellation ...can be imagined along the lines of the most commonplace everyday police (or other) hailing: 'Hey, you there!' The hailed individual will turn round. By this mere one-hundred-and-eighty-degree physical conversion, he becomes a subject. Why? Because he has recognized that the hail was 'really' addressed to him, and that 'it was really him who was hailed' (and not someone else).

People are constituted as subjects in ideology through the process of recognition and identification. It is through this mechanism of interpellation that people are brought into existence as social subjects whose identities appear self-evident to them. This self-evidentness gives subjects the illusion of self-determination, of being able to 'pull themselves up by their own bootstraps' - an illusion Michel Pêcheux (some of whose work I present later) calls the 'Munchausen effect': 'the necessary obliteration within the subject as "cause of himself" of the fact that he is the result of a process' (1982: 108). In order to avoid this 'Munchausen effect' we need to attend to how it is people, as subjects, accept meanings as obvious and self-evident.

19

A psychoanalytical version of the anti-humanist 'decentred' subject is given by Jacques Lacan. Lacan (1966) provides an account of the subject's constitution in language and in the symbolic order. According to his post-Freudian theorising, the subject is split between conscious and unconscious, and the unconscious structured like a language. What Lacan has done is 'inject' a subject into the signifier - signified pair of Saussurian linguistics. He has extended the basic tenet, that in language there are only differences, to the subject itself: the subject's identity is built (and constantly rebuilt) in the process of differentiation. In the action of producing a comprehensible world 'out there' by continuous acts of differentiation, the subject is also producing positions for itself in relation to that world and in so doing placing itself in the symbolic order. The symbolic order 'is a domain of position and judgment' (Moi 1986: 19). It can be rather crudely thought of as a set of cultural coordinates. Neither subjects, positions nor differentiations are stable. The meaning-producing subject is itself constituted in the act of producing meaning. The subject's sense of being a 'transcendental ego' with a fixed stable identity is an illusion.

Lacan works with both these senses of 'subject': an individual is both the source of rational intentions and the site of unconscious processes. Coward and Ellis (1977: 108-9) discuss Lacan's use of both these senses:

He sometimes emphasizes the importance of the subject proposed by Descartes in the formulation, 'Cogito ergo sum' ('I think therefore I am'). At the same time he insists that this is the most blatant form of the stupidity of thought which posits a subject completed and finished in its identity, knowing always exactly where it is going. He considers it to be important that the Cartesian subject should not be ignored out of philosophical pretensions. For the place man assigns for himself in knowledge is what makes possible communication and meaning, even if that place is ascribed to him long before he 'knows' anything about it.

In an anti-humanist view, the subject is the site of unconscious processes of meaning production. It is subject to contradictions Wendy Hollway (1984: 230) argues, for instance, that a woman's gendered subjectivity is not unitary:

'man' and 'person' have been synonymous in western, patriarchal thought, as is evidenced by the use of the terms 'man', 'mankind' and 'he/him' as universals. As women we can strive to be 'people' and 'women'. Logically there is no contradiction. However, because 'person' actually consists of all the attributes which are meant to be characteristic of men, there is an underlying contradiction.

20

Subjectivity is a site of conflict. In Hollway's chapter in *Changing the Subject*, from which I have quoted above, she refers to her own experiences of coping with conflict between her growing feminism, in thought and action, and her self-perception as female (since being female involves her in the need for heterosexual relations and femininity). She is caught between the aim of being like and 'as good as' a man and, as a woman, being different. Taking an example from Cathy Urwin's chapter of the same volume, a child, in her interaction with parents, experiences conflict between her desires for independence and for approval (1984: 310).

These contradictions are part of what constitutes the human subject. The 'decentred' subject harbours contradictory desires and aims etc. Contradiction is part of any individual's subjectivity; hence an important aspect of subjectivity is non-rationality. An example in Debbie Cameron (1985: 87), in which she discusses the bodily demands on women as workers, illustrates how contradictions between what people can see for themselves and what they believe to be true, or right: 'For instance, the notion that women cannot do heavy work (which carries high rates of pay) ought not to cut any ice with women who regularly lift heavy children and stones of shopping, but it does. Women who clean up after incontinent elderly relations ought not to entertain the oft-repeated observation that some jobs are too unpleasant and dirty for women to do, but apparently they accept it'. What Cameron attends to here is the irrational acceptance of a contradiction between what women do as domestic workers and what they are deemed capable of as paid workers. As domestic social subjects - as wives, mothers, daughters - they are expected to do whatever work is necessary in the maintenance of their families, regardless of how arduous and unpleasant it may be. But when it comes to the jobmarket, arduousness and unpleasantness are used as reasons for excluding women from doing what is traditionally men's work, on the basis of beliefs about femininity. The contradiction does not exist only in the minds of these women. It is present as a consequence of real relations within the family and the economic world. They may be unaware of the contradiction between the two subject positions imposed on them, or be aware of it but feel powerless to change the social conditions that bring it about.

I will now turn from the psychoanalytic subject to the subject in social theory. Numerous theorists of discourse and social theory, Foucault in particular, refer to 'double subjection'. According to Foucault's retrospective 'Afterword' to Dreyfus and Rabinow (1982: 212), a dual view of the subject is central to his analyses of power:

power applies itself to immediate everyday life which categorizes the individual, marks him by his own individuality, attaches him to his own identity, imposes a law of truth on him which he must recognize and which others have to recognize in him. It is a form of power which makes

21

individuals subjects. There are two meanings of the word subject: subject to someone else by control and dependence, and tied to his own identity by a conscience or self-knowledge. Both meanings suggest a form of power which subjugates and makes subject to.

Foucault argues that in analysing power the focus should be on what makes individuals subjects, and why. This necessarily involves examining the historical conditions bringing about relations of power between subjects. Social double subjection refers to subjection to others and the subject of selfhood. The social subject is constituted within relations of power. It is constrained in relations of power with others. It is also constrained in its own sense of identity, which has been/is formed in social power relations. These two kinds of subjection cannot be described as 'external' and 'internal'. This would perpetuate the artificial division between subject and social world that I am presenting here. The subject's sense of identity is not 'internal': it is constituted in social relations of power.

The language-using subject in linguistics

The language user in linguistics is a 'unitary' rather than a 'decentred' subject. A 'unitary' subject has a certain detachment and independence from the world she inhabits; she is assumed to be already in existence as a knowing subject prior to her entry into the social world. Language users have a common pool of language conventions at their disposal; they are free agents who can pick and choose what 'roles' to play in language. These conventions and roles are external to them; language users implement them voluntaristically and 'transcend' them. As Fairclough (1989: 245) remarks, linguistics is one of social sciences which contributes to sustaining this conception of the autonomous subject. In linguistics, where the concept of the speaking subject itself is not problematised, a language user tends to be viewed as such a unitary subject: as an abstract asocial entity in 'autonomous' linguistics, as rational individual and role-player in areas of language study attending to language use.

I begin this examination of the language using subject in linguistics by presenting briefly the notion of an abstract speaker-hearer in theoretical linguistics (Noam Chomsky), and then outline the sociolinguistic view opposing it (Dell Hymes and Ronald Wardhaugh). For sociolinguists, who focus on actual performance rather than some abstract competence, the language using subject is no longer an abstraction but a social actor who takes on a wide range of roles in interaction. I will demonstrate that, while potentially useful for examining language users' multiple and possibly contradictory subject positioning in interaction, in practice this approach tends to over-emphasize language-users' autonomy and shared experience of reality. I will turn to some work in pragmatics to substantiate the claim that the capacity for deliberation and means-end reasoning is greatly overstated. The goal of pragmatics is a

22

full account of the conditions of production of speech acts, according to Helmut Haberland and Jacob Mey (1977) in their editorial to the first issue of *Journal of Pragmatics*. Such an account cannot ignore the constitution of subjectivity in discourse. After a short discussion of rationality as the essential quality of the language user in linguistics, with specific reference to Dan Sperber and Deirdre Wilson's *Relevance*, I will conclude by critically discussing in some detail the notion of means-end reasoning as a method for identifying the functions of speech acts (William Downes and Geoffrey Leech for examples). I will refer to observations by social theorists Jurgen Habermas and Anthony Giddens in this discussion.

According to Chomsky (1965), a 'grammar of a language purports to be a description of the ideal speaker-hearer's competence'. Chomsky's dissatisfaction in *Syntactic Structures* (1957) with the use of only 'observed utterances' as data, led him to make the distinction between corpus and language. In this early model, language is taken as the sum of sentences generated by a grammar; corpus as the available observational data. This he developed later into the concepts of competence and performance (cf. langue - parole) by which he distinguishes between 'the speaker-hearer's knowledge of his language' and 'the actual use of language in concrete situations' (*Aspects* 1965: 4).

Chomsky employed this concept of an abstract capacity of linguistic competence so that he could write a grammar with which he could deduce new structures from the data of existing ones, and eliminate the disturbance factors, which Chomsky felt made the evidence of performance 'restricted and degenerate' (1968: 27). So, by hypothesising the competence of an idealised speaker-hearer, Chomsky was avoiding factors like memory lapse, distractions and variations in non-linguistic knowledge of the world, which he considered to be extraneous elements:

Linguistic theory is concerned primarily with an ideal speaker-listener, in a completely homogeneous speech community, who knows its language perfectly and is unaffected by such grammatically irrelevant conditions as memory limitations, distractions, shifts of attention and interest, and errors (random or characteristic) in applying his knowledge of the language in actual performance (1965: 3).

Ultimately, Chomsky's model was intended to explain the human cognitive capacity to acquire language. Within this model, this capacity is a set of universals - invariant properties of the human mind. Chomsky's idealised subject is incompatible with the sociolinguistic goal of describing the interaction/ interrelation of social factors with language (as in William Labov's studies of phonological

23

and syntactic variation, for example). For sociolinguists and the analysis of speech in its social setting the focus of attention is performance.[4]

One move away from the idealised speaker-hearer was Dell Hymes' ethnographic work on aspects of the speech situation. Hymes (1972: 272) is critical of the detachment from social reality of Chomsky's theory of linguistic competence (ironically given the epithet 'noble') which renders all social considerations irrelevant: 'the controlling image is of an abstract, isolated individual, almost an unmotivated cognitive mechanism, not, except incidentally, a person in a social world'.

Speaking subjects, participants in a speech event, are one component in Hymes' ethnography of speaking. The subject is an individual who plays different roles according to the speech situation. Downes (1984: 257) summarizes the Participant component as follows: 'Whom the act is addressed to, and who it is uttered by, are significant. In various situations, participants are allocated communication roles by the culture, for example, "a chairman", "therapist", "a patient", "a client", "a teacher", "a pupil", "an interviewee"'. Meanings are produced in the situated action of a speech event by the role-playing individuals who are participating.

Since there are many situation-types, there is a wide variety of social roles available for language users. This potentially offers an alternative to the humanist view of the language user as integral individual. For example, in Michael Halliday (1978)'s conception of the language user as an aggregate of social roles an individual's identity is constructed in a synthesis of these roles. As Threadgold (1987: 117) observes:

Halliday sees the individual as derived from his participation in the social group, which enters the individual by way of his interaction with others through language... Being a 'member of society' means occupying a social role or, more normally, several social roles. These are defined by the relationship into which one enters with others and through semiotically mediated language. The individual's 'personality' is a synthesis of these social roles.

However, this view is undeveloped in studies of language in use. There is a theatrical metaphor with unfortunate consequences behind the representation of a human subject as an aggregate of different roles. This is a metaphor used by J.R.Firth (1950) and widely taken up by linguists. It is used explicitly in Wardhaugh's (1985) introductory text to the analysis of spoken language. This text will serve as an example of the prevailing view in discourse analysis and pragmatics of role-playing actors who are autonomous individuals in full control of their actions: unitary subjects. His discussion of the concept of 'Face' from Goffman's work on rituals of everyday interaction[5] has the metaphor of 'talk as

24

unconscious theatre' running through it (Wardhaugh 1985: 44). He presents the metaphor most fully in the following passage:

It [a conversation] is a piece of theatre. There is a real sense in which each of the participants in conversation plays out a part in an ongoing action or drama. Each consciously or unconsciously plays a role. Each must have a sense of both character and event. Each must choose a self or 'face' to present and relate to the selves and faces of others (38).

Elsewhere he talks about the 'stage of life', 'scenes' and 'performances'. This metaphor however distorts its user's view of what it is intended to represent. While it is the case that actual theatrical actors take on stage-roles irrespective of their social identities offstage, a speaking subject is not simply a collection of different 'roles' appropriate to each situation, with a kernel of self which remains intact.

The role-playing actor is presented as an integral individual who chooses what part to play in a given situation. Although Wardhaugh several times states the unconscious nature of talk-as-theatre, his discussion is set in terms of conscious deliberation. For instance, after a warning about the dangers of 'over-acting', Wardhaugh continues, 'while you must play your chosen role with a certain amount of detachment (or awareness), too much distancing from it may prove to be just as ineffective as too great an involvement' (38-9).

The effect of this sustained 'thespian' metaphor is to produce a text which reads like a guide to social skills.[6] There is a sustained vagueness surrounding the matter of whether or not the speaking subject is conscious of 'playing roles'. The language-using subject in this view is in full control of her actions, rather than having her actions constrained by the nature of the situation. She takes on roles in interaction which appear to be freely chosen, when they may be assigned to her, irrespective of her wishes. She is presented as the performer of intentional actions, with a capacity for deliberation that seems greatly overstated. The diverse social roles she takes up in interaction are not viewed as diverse subject positions in which she is 'called into existence' but as accomplishments to be acquired by a free agent.

Wardhaugh's sustained use of this metaphor provides a particularly clear example of the conception of the language user as autonomous subject in linguistics. It is perhaps unfair to use what is after all an introductory text for lay readers as the main example (however, bear in mind this is many students' first or only contact with linguistics). In the field of pragmatics, the essential quality of the language-using subject is rationality. Working in pragmatics, Brown and Levinson (1978) have used Goffman's 'face-work' concept as the basis for a detailed descriptive model for politeness phenomena

25

across cultures. They propose a 'Model Person' (MP) which is a "rational face-bearing agent". It has the properties of i. being rational: able to work form desired ends to the means of achieving those ends, and ii. two wants: to be liked and to be left alone. The MP's wants are the motivation for it to employ its capacity for 'practical reasoning'. Rationality is elevated to the status of an overriding principle for social actions.

A contribution to pragmatics/cognitive psychology, Sperber and Wilson's *Relevance*, combines the speaking subjects of both Chomskian and pragmatic linguistics. As in Brown and Levinson's collaborative work, reason is favoured as the key property of the subject. They also employ a sense of the subject as an abstraction (an 'information-processing device'). Their model is intended to account for cognition and communication. In brief: language-using subjects are the possessors of identical 'processing devices' and individually varying sets of assumptions grounded in a common view of reality. What the subject as human-information-processing-device does in Sperber and Wilson's model is 'explicate' and 'manipulate' the conceptual content of assumptions (1986: 103). This device has access to assumptions from various sources. The assumptions are submitted to the device for processing by its owner. Together all these assumptions make up the device-owner's total cognitive environment. The device analyses and manipulates the conceptual content of assumptions; it operates automatically. When focusing on the information-processing element of their model, Sperber and Wilson's subject is the owner of a 'device': the site of automatic operations. The device-owning language user in Sperber and Wilson's model of meaning-production is a 'unitary subject': a rational being. One of the functions of the "device" is to resolve any contradictions between incoming data and between existing and new data:

> Before writing down an assumption in its memory, it [the system] checks to see whether that assumption or its negation is already there. If the assumption itself is there, the device refrains from writing it down again, and marks the theses and deductive rules used in deriving it so that the derivation will not be repeated. If the negation of the assumption is already there, the device halts, and the deductive process is suspended until the contradiction is resolved. (95)

There is no place in this account for a social subject beset with conflict and contradiction. When focusing on the communicative element, the subject in Sperber and Wilson's model of meaning-production is the possessor of intentions/ recogniser of the intentions of others. Communication, in Sperber and Wilson's model, relies in essence on the intention to inform. It rests on speaker's intentions and hearer's recognition of intentions. The informative intention is the 'commonsensical' conception

26

(23) underlying communication for Sperber and Wilson: i.e. that a speaker intends a hearer to recognise S's intention to inform H of something: H recognises S's intention to communicate, and tries to recognise S's intended information. Since Sperber and Wilson's communication model hinges on the intention to inform, the model stops at the level of conscious assumptions, intentions, motivations, goals. There is no place here for discussion of contradictory subject positioning or the unconscious.

In identifying the function of an utterance a connection must be made between the act and the actor's intention or reason for doing it, i.e. a teleological explanation for the speech act must be constructed. This kind of explanation, rather than causal explanation, is considered by most discourse analysts to be the one that is appropriate in an account of human actions. See for instance Downes (1984: 341):

> In a causal explanation, we say, 'This happened, *because* that had occurred.' In a teleological explanation we say, 'This happened, *in order that* that should occur' ...So we can give a causal account in answer to the question, 'Why did the window open?' - someone applied physical pressure to it. But this is very different from the appropriate answer to the question, 'Why did that man open the window?' A teleological explanation is that he opened it in order to cool the room.

Downes describes the relation between 'the volitional-cognitive complex behind a basic act, and the act itself', that is, between action and intention, as a matter of logical means-end reasoning. This activity is mirrored by the analyst, who infers S's intentions, thus constructing a teleological explanation of S's action:

> Just as a hearer constructs a teleological explanation of an utterance, so can an observer of the exchange ...He tries to reconstruct the intentionality from the evidence of the outer aspect of the act. We are in this position when we do discourse analysis ...When we interpret utterances as illocutionary acts, we are constructing teleological explanations of S's behaviour (345)

Downes sees the ability to label speech acts as evidence for the appropriacy of teleological explanation: 'The mere fact that we can appropriately label utterances as speech acts tells us that teleological explanation is ...applicable to verbal behaviour' (342). It follows from this that, in inferring a connection between a verbal act and S's reason in uttering it, the one who provides the label for a speech act is producing a 'packaged' teleological explanation on the utterer's behalf.

Analytic theories of action, of which speech act theory is an example, are set in a philosophical tradition which, Habermas (1984: 275) argues, conceptualizes action asocially in terms too general for

27

social-theoretical use. He sees the limitation of models of action oriented to consequences as a failure to 'keep in view the problem of how the actions of several actors ...can be interlaced in social spaces and historical times'.

Some comments by Habermas on intentionalist semantics are useful here for identifying the drawback of this approach (labelling speech acts as pre-packed teleological explanations). For if, he says, a meaning X is 'what S means by X, or indirectly gives to understand by X', then H needs to recognise the intention of a certain meaning and the meaning itself for S to accomplish her intention, i.e. H must: i) understand what S means by X (ie. X's meaning), ii) be aware of S's intention in using S (including the intention to convey a certain meaning). But i), understanding meaning, cannot be derived from ii), recognising S's intention: 'Solely on the basis of knowing that S has the intention of achieving understanding, H will not be able to infer what S means and wants to communicate to him' (275).

The ability to understand a meaning is not dependent solely on recognition of S's apparent intentions - it is crucially dependent on the 'social spaces and historical times' in which S and H are differently embedded. The origin of a meaning cannot reside in S's intentions. Meaning must be seen to originate in culture, not the individual. An extreme intentionalist position leads to a Humpty Dumpty attitude to language: 'Words mean what I want them to mean, no more and no less'. The ability to supply another's action with a teleological explanation is not solely dependent on the recognition of S's apparent intentions - it is inferred on the basis of the observer's own knowledge of practices.

Downes does not specify whether these intentions are conscious, sub-conscious, accessible to S on reflection, or whatever. But as he describes actions involving complexes of intentionality (primary, secondary intentions etc) we must assume that some of these at least are meant to be subconscious intentions which are assumed to be perceived by the analyst in assessing an actor's reasons for an action The analyst is assumed to have access to an actor's thought processes to an extent that the actor herself is not normally capable: 'The analyst's interpretation takes the same form as everyday understanding. However, the explicitness itself leads to insights about what people are doing and why they are doing it at a level of self-consciousness beyond that we normally have in everyday life' (350).

The inappropriacy of an intentionalist model of human agency is discussed by Giddens (1976: 156), providing a useful counter-argument:

'Intention', 'reason' and 'motive' ...are all potentially misleading terms, in that they already presuppose a conceptual 'cutting into' the continuity of action, and are aptly treated as expressing an ongoing reflexive monitoring of conduct that 'competent' actors are expected to maintain as a routine part of their day-to-day lives. The reflexive monitoring of conduct only becomes the statement of intentions, or the giving of reasons, when actors either carry out retrospective enquiries into their own conduct or, more usually, when queries about their behaviour are made by others.

Retrospective reflection on an act, leading to for instance, the stating of intentions behind an act, is not an element of that act but a speech act upon it. The 'ongoing reflexive monitoring of conduct' with which Giddens contrasts this accounts for the more general assumption that people have intentions in doing things, i.e. that they 'commit' acts for reasons which they could retrospectively provide if asked. Giddens also points out a tendency in writing on action to 'assimilate "action" with "intended action", and "meaningful act" with "intended outcome"' (156). Neither actions nor meanings can be accounted for solely by their producers' intentions in producing them. As speech act analysts, we are looking at what an utterer is doing, which cannot be simplistically equated with what she intends in so doing, or even with what she might conceivably tell us she intended if we asked her.

For a concrete example to illustrate the shortcomings of an intentionalist approach to the interpretation of actions, consider the following scene. A visitor to Wakefield maximum security prison is in a cell at the local police station, being strip-searched by a constable.

Visitor: This is rather humiliating, isn't it?
Constable: It's not humiliating. It's procedure.

The strip-search is a non-verbal interrogation, which 'reminds' the visitor of his subordinacy in that situation - it puts him in his place. His powerlessness is made manifest to him, and he comments on the relational and expressive meanings in the act of the strip search, although he obediently complies with this imposition. The PC denies the visitor's reading of the interpersonal element. Through his reflexive monitoring he *knows* he is not humiliating him - he is 'just doing his job'. As Giddens (1987: 66) says: 'There is a sense in which lay agents must always "know what they are doing" in the course of their daily activities. Their knowledge of what they do is not just incidental but is constitutively involved in that doing'.

In an important sense, the intentions of both the participants in this encounter are irrelevant. You could even say that it makes no difference whether they 'know what they're doing' at all. What matters is that they know *how* to act. There is a rigid code of practices in police interaction. This is known in police discourse as 'procedure' (non-count noun, general noun) and includes specific practices of 'apprehension', 'strip-search' etc. (I presume this is accessible in writing to police, and is taught to new members, but not to non-members.) In the process of interaction, interactants are constrained by these conventional practices, and placed by them in their respective subject positions; as interrogator and suspect, for instance, as in the example above. Whatever the PC is conscious of doing or intending to do in enacting the search, he is acting in an agentive capacity as dominor in an unequal encounter. He denies the interpersonal meaning ascribed by the suspect but it really makes little difference to the suspect whether the PC is intending to humiliate or even conscious of the interpersonal meanings embodied in the episode at all - either way he gets to sit in a cell, in his underpants, for two hours (from which we may sympathetically assume, I think, that he experienced humiliation).

The practice in which searcher and suspect are engaged is demanded and defined by the rules of police procedure, a code of practices. In the production of the act of the search, they are re-producing the practice itself, the procedure determining that practice and the specific relations of power enabling it. The affirmation of the specific relations of power may not be explicitly oriented to in the encounter but that encounter nevertheless affirms those relations.

Intentionalist models of human agency are looking at only half the picture of language. A theory of social action, whether for language or any other form of behaviour, needs an account of the actions of individuals and the enactments of conventions by social subjects; that is, it needs a theory of the subject. Paradoxically, people act conventionally at the same time as they act uniquely. Every social action carried out by an individual is made possible by convention. Actions are not adequately explainable in terms of teleology. In an intentionalist model, an actor is a spontaneous individual consciously working on unique problems, rather than a social agent working within pre-existing conventions with given resources available to her, which she cannot be assumed to be aware of.

Within pragmatics, coherence construction is seen as a problem-solving exercise confronting individuals for which they employ interpretive rules as strategies. For instance, Leech (1983: 31-2) presents hypothesis formulation as 'an informal rational problem-solving strategy':

This kind of strategy is a general strategy employed by human beings for solving interpretative problems. It is found on the one hand in highly abstract and complex scientific theorizing, and on the other hand in homely examples, such as the following. If an electric light fails when the switch is turned on, the first and most likely hypothesis is that the bulb is broken; if the bulb is replaced, and the light still does not go on, the next most likely guess is that the lights have fused, or perhaps that the connection is faulty. The process goes on until a solution (i.e. a hypothesis consistent with the observed facts) is found.

Leech explicitly avoids the term 'intentions' as 'suggesting a degree of conscious or deliberate planning of discourse which the model does not necessarily imply' (40). However, he does appear to imply the presence of some kind of sub-conscious intentionality. Note the lack of attention to where the hypotheses about the cause of light failure come from. Leech is talking about culture-specific knowledge which he has access to, being a competent member of our technologized culture who has been forced by the hypothetical event of light failure into becoming an amateur electrician. This electrician's formulation of hypotheses is a routine procedure. We cannot assume that it is always worked out uniquely by all electricians, even amateur ones.

As Giddens (1987: 60) says, 'in those approaches which treat human agents as purposive, reasoning beings, the notion of action is often understood as though it were composed of an aggregation of intentions. That is to say, the agent is not placed in the unfolding of the routines which constitute day-to-day life'. Actors' procedural knowledge can be accounted for by the phenomenological concept of 'practical consciousness', as Giddens has called it, 'intervening between the unconscious and the conscious is practical consciousness, the medium of human practical activity' (63). People must know *how* to do a certain act, its 'routine', in order to engage in doing it, but they are not constantly working out problems in engaging in actions. People draw upon practical consciousness in accounting for actions, stating intentions etc., but this does not mean that they can give a full account of what they do when called upon to do so:

Agents can sometimes express their reasons for what they do in verbal or discursive form. Human beings can in some degree - fluctuating according to historically given social circumstances - give accounts of the circumstances of their action. But this by no means exhausts what they know about why they act as they do. Many most subtle and dazzlingly intricate forms of knowledge are embedded in, and constitutive of, the actions we carry out. They are done knowledgeably, but without necessarily being available to the discursive awareness of the actor. To speak a language, an individual needs to know an enormously complicated range of rules, strategies and tactics involved in language use. However, if that individual were asked to give a discursive account of what it is that he or she knows in knowing these rules etc., he or she would normally find it very difficult indeed. Any analysis of social activity which ignores practical consciousness is massively deficient (63)

In speaking of human agents one should of course say 'we' not 'they', for analysts' actions are also constituted in practical consciousness. Our knowledge of procedures is used in analysis. An

31

analyst draws on her own knowledge of practical consciousness of an activity in any account of its enactment by others: 'To be able to generate veridical descriptions of social activity means in principle being able to 'go on' in that activity, knowing what its constituent actors know in order to accomplish what they do' (66).

So, in looking at the strip-search example, we must acknowledge that 'there is a sense in which lay agents must always "know what they are doing" in the course of their daily activities. Their knowledge of what they do is not just incidental but is constitutively involved in that doing' (66). Dominors cannot be viewed simplistically as the source of initiative for the 'strategic' acts they produce. In their assessment and control of subordinates they embody, manifest bodily, the power bestowed on them as dominant subjects positioned in an institution. A speech act always does more than a speaker can intend. The notion of individualized, fully accountable speakers hides from view the fact that a speech act is a socially defined act of which speakers have practical knowledge. The enactment of social practices, of which actors are knowledgeable on the level of practical consciousness, both positions speaker and hearer as subjects within discourse and reproduces its own conditions of production, thereby reinforcing, and tending to naturalize, existing asymmetries. When we take into account interactants' constitution as subjects within interaction they can no longer be seen as conscious actors.

An intentionalist approach cannot account for the ideological construction of subjectivity and the determination of meanings according to the position of the interactants within a complex of institutions. Such an account cannot be given if an utterance is seen solely as a purposive action performed by an individual, requiring some kind of means-end analysis of its actor's intentions. Rather than looking for intentional strategies, attention should be turned to discursive practices. This is not just a matter of terminology, but a broadening of scope to account for the non-intentional production of utterances, which includes an account of the institutional and societal conditions of production and interpretation - their broader origins in discourse as social practice.

Summary

I outlined the anti-humanist 'decentred' subject as it appears in psychoanalysis and social theory, concluding that the subject, from an anti-humanist view, is i. a site of non-rational conflict and contradiction in the process of which subjectivity is constituted; ii. the inmate of its own identity who is subjected to the conventions and authority of others. The language using subject can be seen as an active producer and also as agent unknowingly constituted in the act of using it. As the autonomy of the subject's identity and agency is diminished, automatically stress is placed instead on conventions. The extent of the subject's autonomy as a producer of meaning is diminished by focusing on the enactment of language conventions which mediate between society and individuals. As the part played by these conventions is foregrounded, the importance of the individual consciousness of subjects diminishes; or rather, it is seen as a function of those conventions, not developed independently of them.

I presented views of the language using subject in linguistics, showing that they work with a humanist conception of the subject as fully rational actors individually responsible for their actions. In Chomskian linguistics, the subject is completely asocial, an abstraction from the social world, with which it does not connect at all. In sociolinguistics, and pragmatics, the subject is role-player and bearer of intentions, a rational individual who acts according to existing conventions. Subject and convention exist side by side in these accounts, without the relation between them being made explicit. There is no account of the subject's construction in the symbolic order in the act of producing meaning. Nor is there any account of the social and historical conditions forming language-users and bringing about relations of power between them.

Rather than just talking of roles, means-end reasoning and intentions, we need to turn attention to subject positioning. An individual's subjectivity is constructed at every moment through subject positions. These positions are taken up by the language-user in the enactment of discourse practices and are constantly shifting. From this view of subjectivity as a process it is evident that a person's sense of identity is an 'effect of discourse' which is therefore changeable. This view is put forward by Chris Weedon (1987) in her offer of a post-structuralist feminist perspective: 'A poststructuralist position on subjectivity and consciousness relativizes the individual's sense of herself by making it an effect of discourse which is open to continuous redefinition and which is constantly slipping' (106).

Subject positions are imposed by the specific social conditions impinging on practices. I will conclude this section on the subject with 3 points:

1.   subjects do not experience a common reality, but diverse realities;
2.   diversity between subjects is not accounted for in terms of individual differences but in terms of differences in the social determinants shaping them (enacted in the conventions of discourse);
3.   an individual's subjectivity is not fixed and 'unitary' but diversified and potentially contradictory.

My next focus of attention is discourse: the social practices which are sites of the enactment of conventions and the constitution of subjectivity.

33

Discourse

Discourse in linguistics

In linguistics, the term 'discourse' is frequently used interchangeably with 'text' (e.g. Stubbs 1983). More often the two are set in opposition, to make some kind of distinction between two views or aspects of language. (An account of all the different applications of the two terms would be confusing without helping the present discussion.) The usage I will present here is the one I intend to follow.

I use 'text' to mean the observable product of interaction: a cultural object; and 'discourse' to mean the process of interaction itself: a cultural activity. The distinction between 'text' and 'discourse' I am making is an analytical one between the observable materiality of a completed product and the ongoing process of human activity (Widdowson 1979; Brown and Yule 1983; Halliday 1985). I do not use the terms to distinguish between spoken and written language, nor between dialogue and monologue. 'Text' is the fabric in which 'discourse' is manifested, whether spoken or written, whether produced by one or more participants.

So the distinction is between product and process. As I said, 'text' here refers to the observable product of interaction (whether language -production or -interpretation). A 'text' may be either written or spoken, since spoken language can be tape-recorded and thereby transformed into an object of analysis. In the actual production and interpretation of a stretch of language (a simple example being a conversation) the interactants have access to historically prior texts. These are products of previous interaction, which make up the conversants' interactional history. In reporting previously uttered speech, for instance, a fragment of an earlier text is embedded in the current text. 'Text', then, is a 'frozen' observable substance, a concrete cultural object. This does not mean that the text-product actually exists as marks on paper or impulses on magnetic tape. It may only exist in the possibly mistaken memories of people; indeed with the texts of previous conversations this is almost always the case.

Discourse is not a product but a process. To analyse it we need to look at both the text itself and the interaction in which it is embedded. A text is part of the process of discourse. It is the product of a writer/speaker and a resource for a reader/hearer. A text consists of cues for interpretation processes and traces of production processes. As Fairclough (1989) says: 'This process includes in addition to the text the process of production, of which the text is a product, and the process of interpretation, for which the text is a resource'. As a resource for the interpreter, the text consists of lexico-grammatical realisations of three kinds of meaning relating to three basic language functions (the ideational, interpersonal and textual functions of systemic linguistics). These lexico-grammatical cues to

34

ideational, interpersonal and textual meanings are interpreted with the help of other resources beyond the text.

Discourse is produced and interpreted by specific people in specific institutional and broader societal contexts. I have already given attention to people, the language-using subjects, who produce and interpret discourse. I have argued that language-users should not be seen only as 'unitary' subjects who produce intended meanings in discourse, but also as 'decentred' subjects who are constituted by their actions. In presenting the decentred subject I suggested that there is in fact no clear division between a person and her actions and she is not their inventor or sole creator. In producing discourse, she is constrained by what has gone before.

In production and interpretation people draw upon a wide range of what Fairclough (1989: 24-5) refers to as 'members' resources', or MR. These MR include: 'their knowledge of language, representations of the natural and social worlds they inhabit, values, beliefs, assumptions, and so on'. In this view, MR are both cognitive and social:

The MR which people draw upon to produce and interpret texts are cognitive in the sense that they are in people's heads, but they are social in the sense that they have social origins - they are socially generated, and their nature is dependent on the social relations and struggles out of which they were generated - as well as being socially transmitted and, in our society, unequally distributed. (25)

Production and interpretation, then, are cognitive processes related to social practices. To conclude this chapter, I examine approaches to the concept of coherence which take into account the social constitution, and asymmetrical distribution, of the MR language users draw upon to produce and interpret coherent discourse.

Foucauldian discourse

Discourses in Foucault's work are structures of possibility and constraint which impinge on, and indeed bring about social practices. This sense of discourse from social theory is used by a number of linguists; I will outline some of them later in this chapter. Fairclough employs the term 'discourse' in a Foucauldian sense, to mean systematically-organized sets of conventions forming practices, in accounting for how language use is socially conditioned (see later in this chapter). A similar, apparently unacknowledged conception underlies the work of Pêcheux (also outlined later). A third linguist, Gunther Kress, refers to the work of Foucault in characterising discourse as sociocultural

35

practice. Kress (1985: 6-7) draws upon Foucault in describing the defining and delimiting quality of discourse:

Discourses are systematically-organized sets of statements which give expression to the meaning and values of an institution. Beyond that, they define, describe and delimit what it is possible to say and not possible to say (and by extension - what it is possible to do or not to do) with respect to the area of concern of that institution, whether marginally or centrally. A discourse provides a set of possible statements about a given area, topic, object, process that is to be talked about. In that it provides descriptions, rules, permissions and prohibitions of social and individual actions'.

Discourses for Foucault are historically-constituted social constructions in the organisation and distribution of knowledge. Knowledge does not arise out of things and reflect their essential truth: it is not the essence of things in the world. Discourses are constituted in history and society; what is included as truth, access to that truth, who may determine it, depends on relations of power in institutions. Foucault argues that dominant members of institutions maintain control through discourses by creating order, i.e. by being the ones who make boundaries and categories.

Foucault produced historical analyses of discourse and power. He investigated the exercise of social power in/through discourses, through the definition of objects and social subjects themselves. His approach is anti-humanist. As post-structuralist feminist, Weedon (1987: 107), says:

It is in the work of Michel Foucault that the poststructuralist principles of the plurality and constant deferral of meaning and the precarious, discursive structure of subjectivity have been integrated into a theory of language and social power which pays detailed attention to the institutional effects of discourse and its role in the constitution and government of individual subjects.

In Foucault's work, in fact, he attends to discourses of the social sciences, which he argues have contributed substantially to what people are. That is, practices and relations between people are brought into being as a result of the socially-constructed bodies of knowledge which are the social sciences. He writes about how the discourses of the social sciences have impinged physically on people, constructing them as patients, legal subjects, sexual subjects and so on. He shows in his archaeologies that the domains of knowledge, which form social subjects in taking human beings as their subject, are not timeless but historical constructions. In *The History of Sexuality*, for instance, his focus is the discursive constitution of sexual subjects in the juridical system, in medical texts etc. In *The Birth of*

36

the Clinic, he examines medical writing, exploring shifts in what it is to 'do medicine', what illness is, both clinically and socially.

'Unities' of discourse. In contrast with the analysis of discourse in linguistics, Foucault does not analyse concrete text samples (see Fairclough (1988)). However, in *The Archaeology of Knowledge* (1972: 23) he makes brief but interesting observations about the notion of a concrete whole text. 'The materiality of the book', he says, is only one kind of 'unity', and not the most significant; for example, a missal and an anthology of poems are both books but the unity each derives from discourse is what constitutes them as missal and anthology. The unity a single actual text has is weaker than the 'discursive unity of which it is the support'. The 'discursive unity' is not homogeneous; to illustrate this point he contrasts the relation between Balzac's novels with the relation between Joyce's *Ulysses* and the *Odyssey*. There is more to a text than the concrete book; it only exists in relation with other texts: 'The frontiers of a book are never clear-cut ...it is caught up in a system of references to other books, other texts, other sentences: it is a node within a network. ...It indicates itself, constructs itself, only on the basis of a complex field of discourse' (23).

Foucault proposes that discourses consist of sets of statements whose unity is based on objects, 'style', concepts and themes; but with an important proviso: their unity is not fixed but constructed through dispersion and discontinuity. In this way, Foucault avoids presenting a discourse as though it were a single continuous book, naturally unfolding through time. For instance, in saying that a set of statements has unity in terms of the objects/referents it describes we cannot assume a 'well defined field of objects' (37) outlined in discourses. In discourses on madness, for example, madness is not a single object: it is constructed in an interplay of conditions enabling its appearance as an object and subject of constant displacement. Objects are shaped in social practices: 'shaped by measures of discrimination and repression ...differentiated in daily practice, in law, in religious casuistry, in medical diagnosis ...manifested in pathological descriptions ...circumscribed by medical codes, practices, treatment, and care' (33).

Foucault's other proposed bases for the unity of sets of statements - 'style', concepts and themes - are also constructed through dispersal and discontinuity. By 'style' Foucault means connection between statements in terms of shared types of normative, descriptive statement, vocabulary used - these are not fixed but constantly displaced. In that large group of statements we call medicine, for instance, deriving information by clinical testing has not only changed the objects described but also the doctor's position as observer and the whole 'lexicon of signs and their decipherment' (33). Kind of vocabulary and descriptive statement has only partial effectiveness as the basis for a connection between statements. Discourse is as much to do with hypotheses about life and death and with making ethical choices and following regulations as it is to do with sets of normative statements.

Unity of concepts provides another kind of connection between statements. But these cannot be seen as a 'well-defined alphabet of notions' (37) since they are not permanently established and cannot be fitted into orderly overarching structures. Rather than looking for an illusive overall coherence among groups of concepts, Foucault proposes examining their discontinuity: 'One would no longer seek an architecture of concepts sufficiently general and abstract to embrace all others and to introduce them into the same deductive structure; one would try to analyse the interplay of their appearances and dispersion' (35).

Theme too cannot be seen as a permanent or well-defined basis for accounting for the unity of a discourse. Foucault points out that the theme of evolution for instance has shifted from the discourse of philosophy/cosmology to biology. The pre-Darwinian evolutionist theme 'directed research from afar rather than named, regrouped, and explained results' (35). The emergent discourse of biology forced a transformation in this earlier discourse and in the evolutionist theme. The philosophical/ cosmological discourse had to 'transform into discursive knowledge' its hypotheses. What does he mean by 'transform into discursive knowledge'? Both 'to talk and write about' and develop knowledge configurations.

A necessary condition for any statement is an associated field. A statement can only exist in connection with other statements that it repeats, opposes, comments on etc.:

> The associated field is made up of all the formulations to which the statement refers (implicitly or not), either by repeating them, modifying them, or adapting them, or by opposing them, or by commenting on them; there can be no statement that in one way or another does not reactualize others (ritual elements in a narrative; previously accepted propositions in a demonstration; conventional sentences in a conversation). (98)

Foucault then, proposes the examination of discourses as systematically organised sets of statements by locating discontinuity and dispersion. He refers to a particular system of dispersion between a group of statements and to a specific regularity between object, types of statement, concepts and thematic choices as a 'discursive formation' (38).

Delimitation and control of discourses. In 'The Order of Discourse', Foucault accounts for how discourses are 'externally' and 'internally' delimited. The delimitation and external control of discourses is imposed by strategies of prohibition (in taboos, rituals, privileges) and rejection (valid contributors to

38

discourse are delimited on grounds of falsity, lack of authority, madness). Access to discourse is controlled by entrance rituals and qualification.

'Internal' control of discourses according to Foucault is imposed by/through various principles of classification and ordering by which actual texts are distributed. One of these principles by which groups of texts are bound together is the author: 'Not, of course, in the sense of the speaking individual who pronounced or wrote a text, but in the sense of a principle of grouping of discourses, conceived as the unity and origin of their meanings, as the focus of their coherence' (116).

Opposed to the author-principle is organisation according to discipline, which is 'defined by a domain of objects, a set of methods, a corpus of propositions considered to be true, a play of rules and definitions, of techniques and instruments' (118). This is opposed to the author-principle because it 'constitutes a sort of anonymous system at the disposal of anyone who wants to or who is able to use it, without their meaning or validity being linked to the one who happened to be their inventor' (118). Author and discipline are organising principles by which texts are classified and put in order within a discourse (echoed by principles of organisation operative in libraries). The domains of these contrasting principles have not remained historically constant. Foucault refers to the importance in the Middle Ages of substantiating scientific discourse by attribution to an author: 'A proposition was considered as drawing even its scientific value from its author. Since the seventeenth century, this function has steadily been eroded in scientific discourse: it now functions only to give a name to a theorem, an effect, an example, a syndrome' (116-7).

Another fundamental principle is commentary, which Foucault says is complementary to the author-principle. A text is bound to a previous text in that it imitates, repeats and comments on it. This organising principle provides a point of contact between linguistic and Foucauldian conceptions of 'discourse'. Unlike author and discipline, commentary is a clearly dialogical, interactive principle, where the relation is between one text and a specific earlier text, as in the intertextual relation of summary to original in Beaugrande and Dressler's textlinguistics (see Chapter 3). This interactive element is rarely explicit in Foucault's writing but is an essential part of the associated field of a statement. Foucault expresses uncertainty about commentary as an organising principle, but as a point of contact between linguistic and social theoretical senses of 'discourse' I find it particularly interesting.

Value for linguistics. Foucault's use of the term 'discourse' is difficult to square with the use of the term in linguistics to mean situated action between people. He only considers what have been called 'serious speech acts' (by Dreyfus and Rabinow (1986)), by which he means statements/propositions put forward in seminal texts. The sets of statements in a given discourse are only possible because of an associated field with which they interact. He does not attend directly to the 'ordinary' language of interaction at all. He does however use structuralist, linguistic terminology. Brief examination of this will underline the combination of interaction and knowledge in his conception of discourse. In *The Archaeology of Knowledge* Foucault (1972) argues for a conception of 'discourse' as an intermediary level that allows us to 'slide' culture between thought and speech. Discourses are defined by social institutions. Individual speech is both made possible and constrained by discourses. Foucault schematises this relationship as: speech (discourse) thought. Discourse is the middle term that provides the discontinuity between speech and thought, the 'hole' through which ideology can creep. Foucault here is discussing the inadequacy of the distinction between langue and parole without a third, mediating conception. The postulation of intermediary discourses produces a shift in focus:

no longer ...treating discourse as groups of signs (signifying elements referring to contents or representations) but as practices that systematically form the objects of which they speak. Of course, discourses are composed of signs; but what they do is more than use these signs to designate things. It is this more that renders them irreducible to language (langue) and to speech. It is this 'more' that we must reveal and describe'. (49)

Foucault himself is not making an artificial division between an abstract language-in-itself and language-use. He states that signs are 'irreducible' to these notions alone. As Paul Rabinow (1984: 9-10) says:

Although Foucault was temporarily caught up in some of the structuralist vocabulary of the moment, he never intended to isolate discourse from the social practices that surround it. Rather, he was experimenting to see how much autonomy could legitimately be claimed for discursive formations. His aim, then as now, was to avoid analyses of discourse (or ideology) as reflections, no matter how sophisticatedly mediated, of something supposedly 'deeper' and more 'real'. In this sense, Foucault has been consistently materialist.

Foucault, then, does not make a false division between convention and action, such as that embodied in the langue/parole distinction. What he does is to examine the social constitution in language of accumulated conventions related to bodies of knowledge, by investigating how power is exercised through conventions, including how they define subjects.

The value of Foucault's conception of discourses for linguists lies in his detailed historical and social account of their definition, delimitation and control. His approach can be summarized in the following set of questions he poses at the end of 'What is an Author?': 'What are the modes of existence of this discourse? Where has it been used, how can it circulate, and who can appropriate it for himself? What are the places in it where there is room for possible subjects? Who can assume these various subject functions?' (120) The anti-humanism of Foucault's approach - attention to the social constitution of subjects in discourse, rather than the individual - is underscored by the final question he poses: 'And behind all these questions, we would hear hardly anything but the stirring of an indifference: What difference does it make who is speaking?' (120)

Summary

In this third section, I have presented discourse as both action and convention. This double use of the term 'discourse' collapses the artificial division between an individual action and a conventional practice, since the one cannot exist without the other. Actions are only possible because of the conventions for enacting them. Conventions only exist insofar as they are performed.

I briefly outlined a systemic-functional view of discourse as process in which people produce and interpret meanings with the help of textual and other resources. I then undertook to outline as briefly as possible the Foucauldian view of discourse, concentrating on his fracturing of the boundaries between texts and his attention to the internal and external delimitation and control of types of discourse.

Discourse and subjectivity

It has been necessary to treat Subject and Discourse as separate issues but, as I have already indicated, they are intimately related. Having introduced the two terms separately, in order to present the contrasting conceptions they refer to in linguistics and in psychoanalytical and social theory, I will now bring discourse and subject together and focus on their relationship.

An individual can only act from a position as a social subject. People are constantly being constituted as subjects in the act of producing meaning in discourse. So discourse is the site of the constitution of the subject. The subject is constituted in the process, the enactment, of social practices.

From an anti-humanist perspective, the language using subject can only be described in conjunction with the concept of discourses, which bestow meanings, organize institutions and subjectivity. Foucault (in Rabinow, ed. 1986: 118) avoids the 'traditional problem', as he calls it, of the 'unitary' subject 'originating'" meaning ('transcendence'): 'How can a free subject penetrate the substance of things and give it meaning? How can it activate the rules of a language from within and thus give rise to the designs which are properly its own?' He avoids this problem by presenting instead a different set of questions centred on the view of the subject as a 'function' of discourse:

How, under what conditions, and in what forms can something like a subject appear in the order of discourse? What place can it occupy in each type of discourse, what functions can it assume, and by obeying what rules? In short, it is a matter of depriving the subject (or its substitute) of its role as originator, and of analysing the subject as a variable and complex function of discourse.

For specific accounts of discourses forming women as subjects I refer to Walkerdine (1985) and Smith (1988). Walkerdine's examination of the contradictions placed on women, as nurturers of children, and on girls, as learners, is presented first. Active learning, in this view, imposes masculine subject positions on girls, so that they need to construct their femininity in other ways. This is followed by Smith's account of a discourse of femininity proliferating in the mass media and based on consumption patterns which is of particular relevance for the sample analysis in Part 2.

Without a linguistic sense of 'discourse' as process, an activity carried out by individuals at specific times and places, it is difficult to look at the production or interpretation of specific texts. This is not present in the work of Walkerdine or Smith. In dealing with discourses shaping women as subjects they use the term 'discourse' in the sense of conglomerations of themes, concepts, practices of classification, conventional modes of interaction, kinds of belief, etc. They cannot engage with the specific problem of accounting for how these discourses can be said to position a reader or writer as a subject through a particular text at a particular point. We are not given any workable way of pinpointing particular resources needed for interpretation which originate in a given discourse. For example, part of the global coherence of the following extract (from my sample consumer feature) is dependent on a bridging assumption:

...the trend is towards subtler shades rather than the brilliant reds of previous generations, to reflect the natural look of the 80s.

The bridging assumption is that 'the natural look is achieved by using subtler shades': knowledge likely to be readily available to interpreters who are proficient in feminizing practices.

In the remainder of this section I go on to inspect two attempts to combine social-theoretical and linguistic perspectives on 'discourse' and 'subject', picking out aspects which I intend to incorporate into my sample analysis.

Women's subjectivity (Walkerdine)

Foucault provides a useful framework for examining the constitution of subjectivity in relations of power and in orders of discourse. It has been taken up by feminists examining the institutions impinging on women and the kinds of knowledge which shape the practices of those institutions. Valerie Walkerdine (1985) investigates the position of women as mothers and girls as learners. Her work rests upon a view of practices in psychiatry, medicine, education etc. as historically produced for the surveillance and control of conflict in the family and primary school. She argues that practices of classification in psychiatry etc. determine the normal and the deviant and thereby regulate the constitution of children as social subjects.

The young learner is assumed to be rational, independent, autonomous, with a natural developmental sequence dependent only on the presence of the mother/teacher. This child becomes a rational adult citizen as a natural consequence of passive, facilitative maternal nurturance. Walkerdine demonstrates that the concept of the autonomous individual is itself a construction crucial to the production of the self-regulating citizen. She does this by 'deconstructing' [i] the autonomy of the 'unitary' subject (the 'autonomous individual') using two psychoanalytic conceptions: the 'Mirror stage' and 'identification with the other'.

The Mirror stage: a metaphor for the infant's illusion of control. The mother, the apparent source of power, offers the child the illusion of having power. She does this in so far as she develops practices with the child in which it knows how to act in the required way, thereby feeling both empowered and attaining Other-identification.

Identification with the Other: being the object of the mother's desire (i.e. being what its mother wants it to be, the object she most desires.)

The infant in this view is not autonomous. Nevertheless, it is in the child's relationship with a facilitative mother that the illusion of autonomy is produced. The institution of the family, and later the primary school, are sites of the production of the modern conception of the autonomous individual.

In Walkerdine's account, people are constituted by the practices produced by discourses. The key position in which women are placed as passive facilitators in the production of the illusion of autonomy presents particular problems for women themselves, both as adults and as children. Contradictions in different discourses have specific consequences for women. They are normalized as passive nurturers. Walkerdine shows the historical constitution of this position for women and the intervention necessary to impose what was believed to be normal:

43

Women's bodies were both the place where the production of reasoning beings as children was assured and yet a constant source of danger. For example, educating women inasmuch as it might adversely affect their productive capacities, was discouraged as endangering the future of the species. Women had therefore to become both the producer of reason through child rearing, and its opposite. Passive, receptive and nurturant femininity became the obverse of reasoning or masculinity, itself made possible through active exploration ...the pathologization of passion, activity, on the part of the women regulated their fitness for motherhood. (208-209)

'Passion and activity' must be displaced onto passive motherhood.

Beliefs about the naturalness of women as the producers, or rather passive facilitators, of children's development into rational adults carry over into presentday practices in schooling, medicine and so on. Mothers who do not provide the facilitative environment necessary are pathologized. Such mothers are women who go out to work, women who use overt displays of positional power in regulating their children's conflictual behaviour. Difficulties in the regulation of conflict in school are put down to the absence of the necessary facilitative environment at home: ie. to 'maternal deprivation'. This 'maternal deprivation' is seen as evidence of the need for intervention by educational medical and welfare institutions.

As a result of this construction of motherhood embodied in the practices of the social sciences, women are also placed in contradictory positions as learners at school. Girls are caught between contradictory needs for masculinity, as active learners, and femininity. They have to 'cross over' into masculinity to be what the teacher wants them to be (identification with the Other) and thus to be 'empowered', i.e. given the illusion of control. A girl who becomes empowered by successfully mastering[n] the practices in which she is embedded in school has to find practices elsewhere in which she can construct her femininity.

Femininity (Smith)

Here I will examine femininity: a particular structuring of social space which spans across institutions and which is a key factor in the constitution of women's subjectivities. Femininity refers to an indeterminate conglomeration of concepts and themes, social relations and practices. It discursively organizes women's lives, even in impinging on their bodies. This discursively organized social space called femininity is articulated in commercial and mass media discourses - especially in the magazine, clothing and cosmetics industries. These discourses shape social practices forming subjects and relations. Social conditions bestow upon women feminine social identities, specific kinds of social

44

relationship with other women, and with men. Consumer femininity enters into women's daily lives in the MR they draw upon in their involvement in spoken and written discourses, and in non-linguistic practices.

For an approach to femininity as discursive I turn to a paper by Smith (1988). She uses the conception of femininity as discourse to connect together diverse phenomena in the economic and symbolic world: resources, women's work and standards of appearance. Femininity informs the production and distribution of resources (such as clothes and cosmetics particularly, but also non-material resources). Part of femininity as discourse relates to women's skills and work: 'beauty work' and the activities surrounding it (planning, shopping for materials etc.). Most women are non-professional practitioners; their work, on themselves, has the status of a 'hobby'.[n]

According to Smith, femininity is a mass media construction: 'a social organization of relations among women and between women and men which is mediated by texts, that is, by the materially fixed forms of printed writing and images' (39)[n] This 'textually mediated' discourse is realized through/on women's bodies. She stresses that femininity is not simply imposed on women by the mass media or by patriarchal social relations, but something in which they actively and creatively participate. It is manifested in women's activities, that is in practical skills cultivated, expenditure of money and 'free time', and also in patterns of friendship, especially among adolescents (see e.g. McRobbie 1978, Cohen 1984, both of whom are cited by Smith). Women are actively involved in the construction of femininity; manufacturers and the mass media must be responsive to them. Their active participation is shaped by what manufacturers and the media have to offer:

Women aren't just the passive products of socialization; they are active; they create themselves. At the same time, their self-creation, their work, the uses of their skills, are coordinated with the market for clothes, make-up, shoes, accessories, etc., through print, film, etc. This dialectic between the active and creative subject and the organization of her activity in and by texts coordinating it with the market is captured here using the concept of a textually-mediated discourse (39)

Manufacturing, advertising, fashion and magazine industries between them shape the 'paradigms for women's production of appearances' (43). These symbolic 'materials' are the fashion and beauty standards set in images of women in the mass media: 'A woman active in the discourse works within its interpretive circles, attempting to create in her own body the displays which appeal to

45

the public textual images as their authority and depend upon the doctrines of femininity for their interpretation' (44).

Women's bodies, as Smith says, 'always need fixing', since they cannot approximate the kinds of appearance offered by images in the mass media without work. Femininity constructs the feminine social subject's relation to self as an object of work: 'Participation in the discourse of femininity is ...a practical relation of a woman to herself as an object' (48). In the process of her practical efforts, the woman becomes the object defined by the image. She feminizes herself. Smith insists that this is more than a matter of sexualization. In participating in feminine discourse, women are constructing their identities as women, not sex objects for the male gaze.

Put in the sense of discourse being used in this chapter, this 'feminine discourse' is a conglomeration of activities and social relations, concepts and themes, which shape women's experience in diverse institutions (in their daily domestic activities, their friendship relations, in the workplace etc.). Femininity is not a discourse-type in its own right, but is articulated in discourse in different discourse-types.

Discourse as "ideological materiality" (Pêcheux)

Pêcheux' work is by his own definition 'linking the question *of the constitution of meaning* to that of *the constitution of the subject*' (1982: 105). He grounds the conception of 'discourse' he works with in both society and subjectivity by drawing on Althusser and Foucault. Discourse is presented as the point of articulation between ideological processes and linguistic phenomena. In Pêcheux' work we can see what I have presented as two senses of 'discourse' being used. 'Concrete' discourse, i.e. situated language use, is a complex of processes from different sources. It not just the production and interpretation of utterances by the 'unitary' subject; nor is it only a set of conventions, principles of organisation etc.. Discourse is 'one of the material aspects of ...ideological materiality' (1975: 11).

What I think is particularly interesting about Pêcheux' work is the way he tries to look at how elements from outside a current utterance are brought into it. He is attempting to pinpoint the 'raw material' in which people are constructed as subjects in using language.

Discourse formations. Following Foucault, discourses in his account are both historically constituted and consisting of practices enacted by subjects. The substance of 'concrete' discourse is not spontaneously created, but pre-determined by 'discourse formations', which are described as follows in Haroche Henry and Pêcheux (1971: 102): 'discourse formations ...determine what can and must be said (articulated in the form of an argument, a sermon, a pamphlet, a paper, a political statement etc.) from a

46

given position at a given conjuncture'. This concept of 'discourse formation' relates to Foucault's 'discursive practice'.

Pêcheux's social theoretical grounding is materialist/ Marxist; he does not work with an unexamined humanist conception of a 'unitary' language-using subject (as is more usually the case in the field of linguistics. The discourse formation is the site of the constitution of meaning and also the site of the constitution of the subject. He explains this with the mechanism of interpellation, which I introduced in the section on the subject: '"individuals are "interpellated" as speaking-subjects (as subjects of their discourse) by the discursive formations which represent "in language" the ideological formations that correspond to them' (1982: 112).

Pêcheux works with a dual view of the language-using subject. At the outset of this chapter, I quoted Kristeva on the need for a theory of the production of meaning which includes a theory of the production of the subject. Similarly, Pêcheux argues that separating theory of the production of meaning from theory of the production of subject has the effect of naturalising meaning, since to ignore the necessity for meaning to be produced by someone in a specific utterance in concrete discourse gives the illusion that meanings can somehow exist 'in themselves' or 'of themselves' outside the process of production.[n]

Inter-discourse and intra-discourse. The meaning of words, propositions etc is derived from the discourse formation producing them. These discourse formations embody socially constituted 'domains of thought' (1982: 112). That is, they correspond to ideological formations. Both discourse formations and ideological formations are part of larger structures which are 'complex wholes in dominance'. Pecheux refers to the 'complex whole in dominance' of discourse formations as 'interdiscourse' (113). It is from/in this interdiscourse that subjects and discourse formations are constituted. Pêcheux examines the constitution of the subject in discourse further by seeing how interdiscourse is drawn into the linear sequence or 'intradiscourse' produced by the language-using subject.

In examining the intersection with the linear sequence of a speaker's utterance, Pêcheux distinguishes two types of element. He calls these the 'preconstructed', an element is presented as pre-determined or taken for granted, as if it has already been thought. Pêcheux refers to this as the 'unthought in thought' and relates it to syntactic embedding. As an example of an utterance where there is a 'discrepancy' between what is thought elsewhere and what is being asserted, Pêcheux gives the following:

He who saved the world by dying on the cross never existed.

In this case the preconstructed element (belief in someone who saved the world by dying on the cross) is drawn in from a religious discourse in order to be denied. As Pêcheux says, there is 'a *separation, distance or discrepancy* in the sentence between *what is thought before, elsewhere or independently and what is contained in the global assertion of the sentence*' (64)

The other element Pêcheux distinguishes from preconstruction in examining the intersection of interdiscourse and intra-discourse is 'articulation'. This concerns the relations set up between propositions within a sentence. While pre-construction addresses what is put in the background as already given, articulation refers to what is being asserted. Here Pêcheux is looking at relations of substitutability (paraphrase) between elements, where two elements are seen to 'mean the same thing' in a given discourse formation. The crux of Pêcheux' argument is that relations between propositions are more than psycho-logical; they require 'an 'accessary' construction' (117) (i.e. bridging assumption) through which interdiscourse is brought into intra-discourse.

Pêcheux considers two basic forms that relations of substitutability may take. The first, equivalence, is an identity relation; the second, implication, covers other relations resulting from concatenation. Outlined briefly, Pêcheux gives the following examples of equivalence and implication: **equivalence.** There is a relation of equivalence between 'triangle with one rectangle' and 'rectangular triangle'. These elements are paraphrases of one another. They can only enter into a syntactic construction as identical: 'A triangle with one rectangle is a rectangular triangle'.

implication. By contrast, the two substitutable elements 'passage of an electric current' and 'the deflection of the galvanometer' cannot be placed in a relation of equivalence or identity. In order to place them in a syntactic relationship, we need to bring in a bridging assumption, 'an "accessory" construction of the type:

We observe a deflection of the galvanometer, which indicates the passage of an electric current'

(117).

This permits the concatenation of the two substitutable elements as either 'The passage of an electric current *causes* the deflection of the galvanometer' or 'The deflection of the galvanometer *indicates* the passage of an electric current'. Pêcheux refers to this process by which an implication is drawn into intra-discourse from inter-discourse as the 'syntagmatisation' of inter-discourse.[n]

What Pêcheux is looking at here is how elements from outside a current utterance are brought into it. He perceives the preconstructed and articulation as the 'raw material' in which people are constructed as language-using subjects. The exteriority of these elements are not apparent to the language-user. Inter-discourse is forgotten by the subject.

'Discourse formations' as Pêcheux presented them in the body of work presented above are static and homogeneous constructions (Courtine 1981; Fairclough 1992). This homogeneity masks the heterogeneity and dis-unity of texts. Another limitation of his anti-humanist linguistic work outlined here is that it only attends to grammatical constructions, and has nothing to say about interaction or the interpretation process. In the next section I present Fairclough's model of discourse as social practice, which compensates for both these omissions.

Discourse as Social Practice (Fairclough)

A linguistic combination of the two senses of discourse - as action and convention - is found in Norman Fairclough's presentation of critical language study in *Language and Power* (1989). He remarks on the 'felicitous ambiguity' of the term 'discourse', and the more general 'practice', to refer both to an actual enactment and to a social convention governing actions: 'the individual instance always implies social conventions - any discourse or practice implies conventional types of discourse or practice' (28). He also plays on this ambiguity to underline the way social practices, including discourse, are both enabling and constraining, providing the social conventions within which it is possible to act:

> The ambiguity also suggests social preconditions for action on the part of individual persons: the individual is able to act only in so far as there are social conventions to act within. Part of what is implied in the notion of social practice is that people are enabled through being constrained: they are able to act on condition that they act within the constraints of types of practice - or of discourse.

The importance placed on the category 'subject' in Fairclough's model is evident in the detailed consideration of interpersonal meaning and his emphasis on the subject positioning of language-users. Social positions are set up in discourse-types and subjects are constrained to act within them. These constraints are what make action possible; subjects are enabled by being constrained. Fairclough points out another 'felicitous ambiguity' in the term 'subject'. The subject is both an active agent and passively shaped: 'In one sense of subject, one is referring to someone who is under the jurisdiction of a political authority, and hence passive and shaped: but the subject of a sentence, for instance, is usually the active one, the 'doer', the one causally implicated in action' (39).

49

Fairclough splits the Interpersonal dimension of meaning into two closely related but distinct considerations: the social identities of interactants and their social relationships. These enter into the process of discourse as in features with expressive and relational value respectively. These two aspects of interpersonal meaning are closely related but it is sometimes useful to distinguish between them and I intend to employ the two terms in my analysis.

Subject positions and relations between them are set up in discourse-types. A single individual is placed in a wide range of subject positions. She is not an autonomous entity who exists independently of these positions and social relations, but constituted in the act of working within various discourse-types. From the beginning of her entry into social life she is positioned within varied institutional and societal structures, which bestow upon her specific social 'roles':

The social process of producing social subjects can be conceived of in terms of the positioning of people progressively over a period of years - indeed a lifetime - in a range of subject positions. The social subject is thus constituted as a particular configuration of subject positions. A consequence is that the subject is far less coherent and unitary than one tends to assume (103).

Fairclough is aiming to account for how it is people are constituted in social struggle through discourse, i.e. he is ultimately interested in social subjects; discourse is the focus of attention because that is what subjects are constituted *in*. Like Foucault, he attends to how the practices of the social sciences have shaped, and continue to shape, the institutional discourses forming subjects. His contribution is to construct a model of discourse as social practice allowing detailed linguistic analysis of the interaction of individuals as realisations of these subject-shaping practices. It is an attempt to operationalize a social theoretical view of discourse as socially constitutive.

He refers to the development of 'discourse technologies', which are 'types of discourse which involve the more or less self-conscious application of social scientific knowledge for purposes of bureaucratic control' (213). His Foucauldian perspective on the development of 'discourse technologies' for the control of populations informs a linguistic analysis of specific discourse-types. Interviewing and form-filling, for instance, are viewed as bureaucratic technologies. His dual perspective (both linguistic and social theoretical) enables him to attend on the one hand to concrete texts and production- and interpretation- processes and on the other to the social conditions determining processes and their consequences for social subjects.

Order of discourse and discourse-type. 'Order of discourse' and 'discourse-type' in Fairclough's account correspond to some extent to Pêcheux's 'interdiscourse' and 'discourse formation', the key difference

50

being in the extent to which they allow for an account of heterogeneity and disunity. In chapter 4 I will examine the mass media and the women's magazine using these concepts.

A social order is 'a structuring of a particular social 'space' into various domains associated with various types of practice' (29). From a discoursal perspective, a social order is an 'order of discourse'. It is here we can see the Foucauldian sense of discourses as conventional, as systematically organized sets of conventions forming practices. Just as a social order determines types of practice (conventions) which in turn determine actual practices (actions), orders of discourse determine the types of discourse that determine actual discourses.

Discourses, then, are structured in orders of discourse. This emphasizes the shaping of actual discourse production and interpretation by higher-level structures beyond the immediate situation of utterance and amounts to an expansion of the notion of context to include the social formation. This three 'level' structuring relating orders of discourse, types of discourse and the actual activity of discourse also enables Fairclough to account for the presence of more than one discourse-type in discourse. He emphasizes that discourses are not simply mechanical implementations of discourse-types but 'the creative extension-through-combination of existing resources'.[n] Indeed, actual discourses which draw on a single discourse-type are 'limiting cases rather than the norm' (31).

Resources for production and interpretation All discourse is determined by the social conditions in which it is produced and interpreted. Institutional and societal structures always impinge upon discourse, bestowing specific social identities and power relations upon interactants and giving them different access to language, to representations of knowledge/beliefs, etc. (MR). These MR then are not mutually accessible to all; they are not to be compared with 'mutual knowledge'.

In discourse interpretation, features of text and context serve as cues which activate specific MR. Interpretation is achieved in the dialectical interplay of cues and MR. It is a complex of different processes in which MR serve as interpretive procedures for both the language-user and the analyst. Fairclough identifies six major elements of MR functioning as interpretive procedures which relate to features of text and context. He distinguishes between MR for interpreting the situational context, for which subjects need knowledge of social orders, and MR for interpreting the intertextual context, for which knowledge of interactional history is needed.

The situational context provides external cues which have to be interpreted on the basis of MR:

Participants arrive at interpretations of situational context partly on the basis of external cues - features of the physical situation, properties of participants, what has previously been said: but also partly on the basis of aspects of their MR in terms of which they interpret these cues -

51

specifically, representations of societal and institutional social orders which allow them to ascribe the situations they are actually in to particular situation types (144).

Participants' interpretations of what the situation is determine the discourse-types drawn upon. These in turn determine the kinds of procedure drawn upon for interpretation of the text. Fairclough distinguishes between situational and intertextual context. In addition to 'what has previously been said' in the same stretch of discourse, interactants also need to refer explicitly or implicitly to previous discourses:

> we also need to refer to intertextual context: participants in any discourse operate on the basis of assumptions about which previous (series of) discourses the current one is connected to, and their assumptions determine what can be taken as given in the sense of part of common experience, what can be alluded to, disagreed with, and so on (145).

In my view, 'what has previously been said' in the same stretch of discourse can be seen as part of the intertextual context, there to be alluded to, disagreed with etc.

The four remaining elements of MR functioning as interpretive procedures relate to the text. Conventions of phonology, grammar and lexis are resources which provide procedures for interpreting the surface of utterance. Other kinds of resource are semantics, pragmatics and cohesion, which provide procedures for interpreting the meaning of utterance and its local coherence. Other resources are schemata, which provide procedures for interpreting a text's structure and 'point': its global coherence.

These six domains of interpretation are interdependent. At any given point, among the resources for interpretation are previous interpretations; for example, interpretation of 'higher level', global elements of text are dependent on interpretation of local elements: 'for instance, to interpret the global coherence and 'point' of a text, you draw upon interpretations of the local coherence of parts of it; and to arrive at these, you draw upon interpretations of utterance meanings; and to arrive at these, you draw upon interpretations of the surface forms of utterances (145). The interdependency of interpretation in different domains is not one directional: it is 'top-down' as well as 'bottom-up' (as in the example above): 'For instance, interpreters make guesses early in the process of interpreting a text about its textual structure and 'point', and these guesses are likely to influence the meanings that are attached to individual utterances, and the local coherence relations set up between them' (145).

Intertextual context. Interpretation of the intertextual context involves the historical series to which a text belongs. Here the interpreter draws upon MR relating to interactional history. Fairclough's interest in this part of the context stems from the critical focus on naturalization in his work; he attends to the establishment or imposition through presupposition of common ground among participants:

the interpretation of intertextual context is a matter of deciding which series a text belongs to, and therefore what can be taken as common ground for participants, or presupposed. As in the case of situational context, discourse participants may arrive at roughly the same interpretation or different ones, and the interpretation of the more powerful participant may be imposed upon others. So having power may mean being able to determine presuppositions (152).

Producers of mass media texts are placed in a position of power in having to construct an 'ideal reader'. Through presupposition, they are able to present specific intertextual experiences as common ground, thus postulating an audience with shared moments in interactional histories which are taken as given rather than asserted. As well as presupposing elements of the intertextual context, producers can contest them. By refuting or negating assertions in a text, a producer can assume that these assertions 'are to be found in antecedent texts which are within readers' experience (155). As an illustration of this Fairclough cites this negative assertion in a magazine:

Treatment isn't the equivalent of a week listening to Nana Mouskouri albums and your dentist isn't there to give you nightmares and inflict unnecessary pain on you

which presuppose the 'corresponding positive assertions' that these things are so.

Fairclough describes the extract from which the example above was taken as a kind of '"dialogue" between the text producer and (the producers of) other texts' (155). These texts are taken to be part of the intertextual context. He notes a dialogic quality 'of a less dynamic sort' (155) in presuppositional phenomena in texts, adding that 'dialogism', or intertextuality, can be said to be a property of all texts, since texts always have an intertextual context. Intertextual context adds a historical dimension to discourse as social practice by placing a single text, a product of discourse, in a historical series with other texts: 'The concept of intertextual context requires us to view discourses and texts from a historical perspective, in contrast with the more usual position in language studies which would regard a text as analysable without reference to other texts, in abstraction from its historical context' (155).

Tendencies in discourse change. Fairclough points to certain tendencies in discourse in contemporary society which I think are of particular import for women. There is a high degree of integration among social institutions in modern capitalist society and these institutions collude in legitimising certain kinds of social identity and relationship. This is significant because particular kinds of social identity

53

and relationship are likely to appear commonsensical and natural when they span across institutional orders of discourse; i.e. when people are placed in them in all kinds of situations in diverse institutions. Some general tendencies are an increasing sophistication of discourse technologies, the use of synthetic personalization in addressing mass audiences and an increasing tendency for the formation of subjects as consumers. I intend to draw upon these observations in my sample analysis.

In examining how discourse practices shape subjects, Fairclough points to an increasing tendency for subject formation through strategic, manipulative discourses.[n] This tendency is marked by a sophistication of subject-shaping practices, informed by discourses of the social sciences: the development of discourse technologies for the management of populations, referred to last section. Discourse technologies are discourse-types which span across institutional orders of discourse, 'colonising' new areas (key examples being interviewing and counselling). These scrutinising discourses construct the object of their scrutiny, bringing into being the social subjects defined by the expertise of the human sciences, such as psychology. A characteristic of these forms of discourse is to present the interests of the dominant bloc as the interests of the population as a whole, so that existing social conditions are legitimized. One such manipulative kind of discourse which is spreading is advertising. As Fairclough says, 'advertising ...firmly embeds the mass of the population within the capitalist commodity system by assigning them the legitimate and even desirable role of "consumers"' (36). Social subjects are positioned as consumers in an increasing variety of social situations as commodification expands into new areas of social life:

> the capitalist economic domain has been progressively enlarged to take in aspects of life which were previously seen as quite separate from production. The *commodity* has expanded from being a tangible 'good' to include all sorts of intangibles: educational courses, holidays, health insurance, and funerals are now bought and sold on the open market in 'packages', rather like soap powders (35).

An increasingly common feature of types of discourse used to address mass audiences is 'synthetic personalization': 'a compensatory tendency to give the impression of treating each of the people "handled" *en masse* as an individual' (62). This synthetic personalization is extremely common in the mass media: in magazine advertisements and articles, leaflets, front page headlines, etc.. It involves the construction of an ideal subject as if it were an actual individual and also the construction of a persona or ideal subject for the producers.

Summary

In this section I have taken the two elements of the model of discourse I am building - subject and discourse - and worked them together. I began with specific attention to discourse and the constitution of women's subjectivities. Then for the rest of the section I presented and assessed two approaches to language analysis incorporating a Foucauldian sense of discourse and attention to the constitution of subjectivity.

Starting with some work in French discourse analysis by Pêcheux and associates, I examined his attempt to put into operation in language analysis the concept of discourse formation from Foucault. I outlined some of the kinds of grammatical construction Pêcheux attended to in his examination of the intersection of inter-discourse ('the complex whole in dominance' of discourse formations) and intra-discourse (the linear sequence of discourse). I went on to outline elements of Fairclough's model of discourse as social practice that I intend to use: order of discourse and discourse-type, the power of mass media producers in postulating an audience with shared intertextual experiences, the distinction between relational and expressive value, and specific tendencies in discourse (the use of discourse technologies, synthetic personalisation, the proliferation of the subject position of consumer).

Coherence as a focus for examining the constitution of subjectivity

I have already touched upon coherence as a focus for attention to the constitution of subjectivity. Local and global coherence were among the resources for production and interpretation in Fairclough's model of discourse as social practice. His reason for attending to discourse is because it is the site of the constitution of the subject. Coherence and subject-construction are implicit in Pêcheux' treatment of 'preconstruction' and 'articulation'.

The notion of coherence is used to cover a wide range of topics in linguistics in general and I cannot exhaustively review them all.[n] I shall therefore limit myself to a general discussion of the field and some useful contributions (principally: Pêcheux 1982; Halliday and Hasan 1976; Halliday 1985; Thibault 1988; Jarrett 1984 and Fairclough 1989), bringing out the potential their work offers for examining the constitution of subjectivity in the act of constructing coherence.

Stubbs (1983: 15) identifies discourse analysis as the study of the principles governing coherence: 'People are quite able to distinguish between a random list of sentences and a coherent text, and it is the principles which underlie this recognition of coherence which are the topic of study for discourse analysts'. He refers to discourse analysis as 'the study of connected discourse in natural situations' (7). Like other linguists he sees the objective of discourse analysis as an explanation for the possibility of 'well-formed' discourse beyond the scope of theoretical linguistics. As a result the tendency is to approach the problem in terms of how to account for meaningful discourse when textual cues cannot be found. Many approaches to studying coherence in discourse analysis explicitly use a distinction between 'surface' and 'underlying' coherence (e.g. Stubbs 1983; Widdowson 1979; Craig and Tracy, eds. 1983; Tannen, ed. 1984). This distinction is implicit in Brown and Yule (1983: 223-4), in their contrast between coherence that can be discussed in terms of formal linkage providing grammatical 'wellformedness' and 'the other extreme' where formal linkage is absent. As an example of the second 'extreme', Brown and Yule refer to Sinclair and Coulthard's (1975) model of classroom discourse. Starting with the inability to account for coherence grammatically Sinclair and Coulthard pose the problem of how language users can identify sequences of utterances as coherent discourse despite the absence of formal linkage. Formal properties are given a kind of primacy, as though what is in need of explanation is how coherence is possible in their absence.[n]

In approaches to 'underlying' coherence, then, the problem is posed as how people can identify sequences of utterances as coherent discourse in the absence of formal cues. Brown and Yule quote Labov's much-quoted statement (1970) that there are 'rules of interpretation which relate what is said to what is done'. As Brown and Yule say, 'it is on the basis of such social, but not linguistic, rules that we interpret some conversational sequences as coherent and others as non-coherent (226). In this view, connections between the actions performed in utterances are what make discourse coherent. In discourse analysis and pragmatics, which identify the functions of utterances and how they connect together to form coherent discourse, these actions are interpreted as the intentional actions of individuals; actions tend to be viewed solely as purposive interventions in the world.

I find this distinction between 'surface' and 'underlying' coherence used by discourse analysts misleading, since it suggests that we only need to have recourse to context to interpret a text in the case of texts which do not provide explicit cues to coherence. This distinction misleadingly implies the appropriacy of an 'economy principle' in accounting for coherence; i.e. an assumption that you only look as far as you have to in order to make any sense at all. What this would mean is looking at 'surface' coherence first, at the most explicit cues, and then, if explicit 'surface' cues are not to be found in the text, turning to some solitary element of the surrounding context (such as a writer's intention, or a reader's inference) for 'underlying' coherence.

The work on coherence I turn to demonstrates how misleading this distinction is. I will begin by attending to the contribution of formal linkage (grammar, cohesion) to coherence, with specific attention to Pêcheux, Halliday and Hasan, Halliday and Thibault on causal relations in texts. These bodies of work demonstrate that in accounting for coherence by focusing on observable textual

56

properties contributing to it, we rely heavily on the ability to fill in details not provided by textual cues themselves (i.e. 'surface' coherence is not a purely textual phenomenon) and for both 'surface' and 'underlying' coherence we need to consider other resources needed by a reader for interpreting discourse as coherent.

I will then turn to the characterisation of 'world-knowledge' brought in for interpretation in work on coherence. First I will present a distinction made by Fairclough between sequential 'text-text' connections and other 'text-world' connections made for coherence. Fairclough gives specific attention to prior knowledge of frames, to presupposition, automatic 'gap-filling' and inferencing, which he refers to as part of an interpreter's 'discoursal commonsense'. Lastly, I refer to other work on coherence using the concepts of schema, frame and script.

'Surface' coherence is sometimes referred to as 'cohesion' (e.g. Stubbs 1983; Tannen, ed. 1984). Halliday and Hasan (1976) use the term to refer to the following range of features which bind together clauses and sentences:

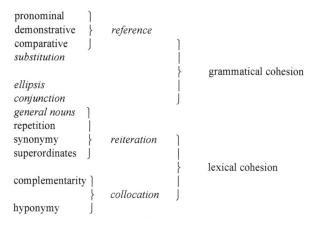

This kind of cohesion in general is characterized as a 'presuppositional' relation. The presence of a cohesive tie 'presupposes' something to which it connects:

Cohesion occurs where the INTERPRETATION of some element in the discourse is dependent on that of another. The one PRESUPPOSES the other, in the sense that it cannot be effectively decoded except by recourse to it. When this happens, a relation of cohesion is set up, and the two elements, the presupposing and the presupposed, are thereby at least potentially integrated into a text' (4)

Cohesive ties are 'directives indicating that information is to be retrieved from elsewhere' (31). The cohesive cues in Halliday and Hasan's inventory are presented as 'systematic resources' from which speakers/writers select options (from the textual element of MR). I want to stress the view implicitly held here that these formal features do not create the continuity that texts display, but cue it. Halliday and Hasan do not go into the implications of this. They give no indication of where (or who) the 'directive' in the cue comes from, or how/why it leads to one connection rather than another.

My next few pages demonstrate this point; namely that the interpretation of a textual cue to coherence requires text-subject and text-world considerations. Causal relations for instance are not purely textual even when a 'surface' cohesive cue is present (e.g. *because*: a formal feature with certain connective and experiential values). Sometimes *because* cues a relation of effect-cause between the content of two adjoining clauses, as it does in a Hillaire Belloc poem quoted by Halliday (1985: 380):

She died because she never knew
These simple little words and few.

However, even in the case of a hypotactic clause complex in which a conjunction provides an explicit cue to a causal relation between two clauses, the reader has to bring in additional information to coherently combine them. The 'reversed causal' connector, *because*, can serve all kinds of different functions in utterances. Consider the following example, which I have taken from a Jackie magazine interview with a soap opera star:

...I use ...Clinique and Almay which are good for my skin because it's quite sensitive.

In order to achieve a coherent interpretation of this clause complex, we need to know that skin is classified into different types, that some products have harmful effects on 'sensitive' skin, others are 'hypo-allergenic' etc.. We also have to fill in what kind of causal relation is being cued by the conjunction *because*. In the soap-star interview example it cues the grounding of an assertion (compare it with a promotion of Simple products: 'They have no added perfume or colour so they're ideal for even the most sensitive skins', *Jackie* 18.3.89: 35). Elsewhere it may be functioning to cue a reason for, for instance, a request for information (e.g. 'What's the time because I have to leave at eight'.)

Halliday groups all these functions together as types of expansion (see chapter 5). Subordinate clauses with connectors cuing a causal relation (and some non-finites) are grouped together in a subcategory of *enhancements: Cause*, which covers a range of reasons and purposes. The structural generalisation is functional, but not sufficient alone to interpret what kind of causal relation is cued. For this we need to draw on other resources. For the contextual information about discourse conventions, such as the classification schemes and act of grounding assertions needed for the Almay example above, we need knowledge not of grammar but of the world.

A causal relation within a clause complex may not be formally cued and depend entirely upon the reading subject's complicity. Some observations by Pêcheux (1982: 74) about a sentence containing an enhancing clause of the cause type are relevant here, focusing specifically on the constitution of a reader's subjectivity. He considers an example containing an implied causal relation:

Napoleon, *who recognized the danger to his right flank*, himself led his guards against the enemy position.

He says that this hypotactic clause complex has the 'necessary' interpretation:

Napoleon, *because* he recognized the danger to his right flank himself led his guards against the enemy position

rather than the "contingent" interpretation:

It happens that Napoleon (*of whom I say in another connection that* he recognized the danger to his right flank) himself led his guards...etc.

In other words there is an additional element drawn into the narrative on Napoleon's deeds - a causal relation which is assumed on the basis of conventions about the motivations of 'great generals'. The inferred relation takes the form of 'some connections of precondition and consequence', which enforce the 'necessary' rather than the 'contingent' interpretation. This comes from an ideologically constituted heroic code of conduct/ noblesse oblige specific to military leaders, which Pêcheux formulates as follows:

If (being a general, or being Napoleon) one recognizes a danger threatening, one must oneself lead the attack to ward it off.

His point is that the coherence of the clause complex depends on the reader's complicity. The reader draws upon a specific belief to causally connect the two clauses. In the act of doing this she is interpellated as a subject: 'So we see the emergence of a kind of complicity between the speaker and his addressee as a condition of existence of a meaning for a sentence. This complicity in fact presupposes an identification with the speaker in other words the possibility of thinking what he is thinking in his place'. 'Surface' coherence, then, is dependent on the language-user's ability to make connections 'outside' the text. In her act of constructing coherence by making these connections the reader is herself constructed as a subject.

In some work in systemic linguistics, Thibault (1988) extends the functional grammar description of the cause type of enhancement within a clause complex to cover connections in activity-structure manifested across groups of clause complexes. Thibault's article consists of an analysis of a letter and response from the problem page of a magazine for young women. He applies the function of enhancement to a 'discourse-level' relation between the actions: Reason for Request - Request, realized by three clause complexes. (We have already seen a single clause complex which can be interpreted as a sequence of two causally related acts of this kind: *What's the time* (Request) *because I have to leave at eight* (Reason for Request)) On the analogy of grammatical enhancement, Thibault describes a causal relation between actions manifested in groups of clause complexes. The first two clause complexes of the letter realize the Reason for Request:

> I am a 17 year old virgin and very scared. I have never been brave enough to try sexual intercourse.

The third clause complex realizes the Request itself:

> Could you please give me some idea as to how I will feel, what will happen and what to expect when I finally share my body with another?

Like the enhancing clause *because I have to leave at eight*, the first two clause complexes realize an act which functions as an 'enhancement' in an activity-structure. The Reason for Request qualifies the Request. As Thibault says, 'the clause complex relations ...contribute to the major structural boundaries of the text as social activity structure' (211). Prior knowledge of a conventional kind of activity is needed to read the passage as coherent; i.e. a reader needs MR to interpret as a coherent activity the actions embodied in the discourse. Thibault observes that the correspondent writes for advice about some condition seen as a 'problem'. The 'problem' condition is established in a confession: some kind of divulgence before (or alternatively, after) the request for advice. Problem page letters and replies contain conventional activity-structures such as this and constitute a generic activity-type. Thibault observes that Problem page letters offer specific kinds of social identity and relationship to writers and readers:

> They are a distinct sub-genre which both invites women to confess their 'inner' feelings and sexual problems ...as well as co-opting this genre in the service of a normative matching of the

positions of social agents with dominant schemas of actions, knowledge and belief about gender-differentiated heterosexual relations' (205).

The 'variations on a causal theme' above demonstrate that both textual properties and actions depend heavily on MR for interpretation. A text is only the trace of the meaningful action of discourse. This action is only meaningful because the reader has expectations about who people are, what they are like and the kinds of social practices they engage in. Knowledge and expectations about human actions in and surrounding discourse are needed for coherence globally and locally. All discourse takes place in a social context and has a history.

I will continue to refer to the sample text from Thibault's article as a way of presenting the specific points of focus for examining the coherence of discourse that are proposed by Fairclough; namely, frames, presuppositions, automatic 'gap-filling' and inferencing.

Fairclough uses the term coherence to cover two broad kinds of connection made by an interpreter; namely '(i) between the sequential parts of a text; and (ii) between (parts of) a text and "the world"' (78). He uses the notion of frames to account for the second of these: 'text-world' connections. We have already noted Thibault's observation that the discourse-level causal relation between the Reason for Request and the Request itself can only be interpreted given specific knowledge relating to the kinds of activity enacted in Problem pages in the press. In text interpretation, drawing on schemata, cognitive representations of conventional kinds of activity, is a form of 'top-down' processing (see the section on discourse as social practice), which a reader does to build both global and local coherence. In other words, we draw on knowledge of the world to make sense of a text 'as a whole' as well as to make connections between adjacent sentences in it. Other resources drawn upon for top-down processing are assumptions and expectations. In Fairclough's model of discourse these assumptions and expectations are elements of socially /discursively constituted knowledge that are drawn upon for coherent interpretation. They are represented cognitively in frames.

The correspondent writes for advice about some condition seen as a 'problem'. We need to draw upon implicit frames to know that her problem is fear of sexual involvement and her own perceived cowardice (and we probably have no difficulty in doing so). These frames relate to a range of assumptions and expectations about 'normal' behaviour among young people; the pressures of teenage 'bravado', etc. To highlight how much of our recognition of the writer's problem relies on 'unspoken' knowledge in frames, try imposing a fictional frame relating to the sacrifice of virgins as the root of her problem. This would, among other things, impose a causal connection (in this case more explicitly realisable by 'so') between the first and second clauses of her opening sentence. (This was my own

61

perverse first reading of it.) Other 'unspoken' knowledge contributing to coherence is more explicitly established in intertextual context by presupposition 'triggers'. For recognition of the 'problem', one of the resources available to a reader is an assumption which is set up as presupposed: 'you have to be brave to try sexual intercourse'.

The first kind of connection for coherence Fairclough refers to relates to local coherence between segments of text: 'text-text' connections.[ii] Along similar lines to those followed by Brown and Yule, he attends to this local, linear coherence using the notions of automatic 'gap-filling' and inferencing. Unlike them, he stresses that the distinction between the automatic provision of a 'missing link' and a connection requiring inferential work on the part of the interpreter is not clearcut. The amount of inferential work required of an interpreter depends on who she is (what discourses she has access to).

We can return to Thibault's sample text, and his analysis, for an example of this. There is a connection between the propositions in the first clause complex which is not made explicit. The additive connector and on its own is not sufficient to account for what I take to be a reader's likely interpretation; namely that the two clauses form part of what Thibault calls a 'set of circumstantial relations' (1988: 211) preceding the writer's request for advice. Following Fairclough's approach, this interpretation would be accounted for using the notion of automatic 'gap-filling' between explicit propositions. A reader who is unfamiliar with Problem pages (such as the perverse reader I pretended to be earlier) would need to engage in a good deal of inferential work to make this kind of connection.

I think the twin notions of automatic connections and inferencing need to be used in conjunction with conceptions intended to capture text-world considerations, such as frames and activity-types. Turning to the Problem page letter for an example again: the connection between the Reason for Request and the Request is likely to be commonsensical for a regular reader of Problem pages: an 'automatic' connection a reader makes by drawing on knowledge of a specific activity-type. For a less expert reader it might require inferential work.

Fairclough argues that frames, presupposed ideas, automatic connections and inferences are each part of the 'discoursal commonsense' a reader needs to draw upon in order to construct coherence. They are 'features of discourse which are taken for granted as matters of common sense' (77). They are assumptions about the social world that are set up in such a way that they are not asserted, but readers still need to supply them to read a text as coherent. Fairclough observes that persuasive discourse and propaganda make use of these features, but stresses that readers are not deterministically positioned by them. He gives an example of a writer attempting to position her reader as someone with a particular commonsensical assumption that is easy to spot and disagree with; viz: a journalist beginning an article with 'The Soviet threat to western Europe...', thus presupposing that 'there is a Soviet threat to western Europe'. A reader is necessarily complicit in constructing a text's coherence, since she needs to draw upon MR. But she can resist interpellation, i.e. positioning as a person with certain beliefs, schemas of action etc, if she has access to an oppositional discourse. Common sense assumptions attributed to a reader in presuppositions are probably more readily retrievable, and hence contestable, than those in 'missing links' or frames, as Fairclough implies.[n] Nevertheless the manipulative presupposition is only "obvious" to someone already critical of dominant cold war discourse (or a linguist accustomed to picking out presuppositions!), who is able to resist interpellation.

The interrelated concepts of *activity, schema, frame* and *script* have been proposed to account for 'world-knowledge' contributing to coherence. Cavalcanti (1983) has already provided an extensive and detailed review of these and other related concepts, with particular attention to prior knowledge-based research on text comprehension. As she remarks, there is 'a plethora of terms used variously in the literature, namely SCHEMA, FRAME, SCRIPT, SCENARIO, inter alia' (25). These are used in a variety of ways. Working in Artificial Intelligence, Shank and Abelson (1977) devised the notion of *script* to refer to stereotypical knowledge of an action structure. These scripts simulate a language user's expectations about sequences of action. They provide the encyclopaedic background information necessary to make inferential leaps from one sentence to another. We can think of this encyclopaedic knowledge as part of language users' 'practical consciousness' of activities; of what it is to go into a restaurant, take a bus ride, travel by train etc. According to Abelson (1981: 3) scripts involve two kinds of constraint: event sequence, 'the causal chaining of enablements and results for physical events and of initiations and reasons for mental events', and a notion of 'stereotypy and familiarity'.

In this approach, the bare minimum of cultural context is introduced to fill in gaps in the 'surface' text. As Holland and Quinn (1987: 20) say, they tend to attribute their own culture-specific knowledge of action sequences to 'pan-human experience of how the world works'. Since the objective of AI is to simulate human language processes on a machine (and not critical language awareness!), their view of people's 'standard' expectations is commonsensical and not subjected to critical examination. As I said earlier, in recognising an action (such as an utterance), an inferential connection is made between the action and its actor's intention or reason for doing it: a teleological explanation is constructed for it. In constructing teleological explanations for another's action, an interactant or an analyst is commonsensically assuming access to the same MR as the actor.

Minsky's (1975) notion of a *frame*, from which Shank and Abelson developed their *script*, suffers from similar problems. It has been fruitfully applied by linguists, however. Among these are

Tannen (1979, 1984) and Jarrett (1984), who use the concept of frame to examine the cultural variability of language users' expectations about activities.

Jarrett (1984) for instance examines the pragmatic coherence of blues lyrics, requiring knowledge of oral traditions in the blues and in other genres: 'one must be familiar with a number of Afro-American folk traditions, some of which mainly exist in speech-community activities other than the blues, others of which are commonly found in blues lyrics' (163). The coherence of blues lyrics is constructed by listeners drawing on frames relating to knowledge of genres. Ethnocentric white listeners lack the necessary frames to interpret the lyrics as coherent. This implies that the ability to construct coherence is dependent on the social identity of the interpreter, which I have referred to as subject positioning. The claim I wish to make goes one step further: people take up subject positions in constructing, or failing to construct, coherence and are thereby constituted as social subjects.

Coherence, then, offers a focus for attending specifically to the constitution of subjectivity in discourse. It provides this focus because subjectivity is constituted as coherent interpretation is made, i.e. the reader is positioned as a subject in the act of interpreting discourse. It is the points at which a reader needs to construct coherence which provide a focus of attention for a critical language analysis.

3

Intertextuality

Introduction

In Chapter 3 I examine the concept of intertextuality in semiology and linguistics. It is intended to enhance the examination of the constitution of subjectivity in reading texts. It provides a view of a text as 'multi-voiced', from which to examine the language-user's relation to a text as an anti-humanist 'decentred' subject. I intend to work with the concept of intertextuality as an extension to existing critical discourse analysis. By adding an intertextual or 'dialogic' perspective to analysis I want to demonstrate that any text is necessarily a tissue of voices. This chapter also underlines two key points made in chapter 2. Texts are not isolated cultural artifacts but embedded in history and society. A coherent text is constructed, not pre-given: writers/ readers need knowledge from beyond the text itself for production/ interpretation. I conclude the chapter with a proposal for how we might go about examining a text within this theoretical framework.

As far as I can determine, the term 'intertextuality' was coined by Kristeva in her development of Bakhtin's work on 'heteroglossia' and the dialogic 'literary word' (briefly outlined in the next section). This work is contained in her *Semiotike* (1969) and *Le Texte du Roman* (1970), which were written at about the same time (1966 to 1967, according to Moi (1986)).[1] In this chapter I present Kristeva's conception of intertextuality and then examine how intertextuality has since been interpreted and applied in diverse ways, each offering its own insights but losing some if not all of its anti-humanist flavour. (There are of course noteworthy applications of the concept of intertextuality which I have not had space to include. A particular omission is the typology of 'intertexts' for literary studies in Sebeok, ed. 1986. Another, which has appeared too late for inclusion, is Hatim and Mason 1990.) All the work looked at here shares a common theme of 'suspending unities' (to use Foucault's expression): some way of fracturing traditional boundaries and emphasising the heterogeneity of discourse. I had better note at the outset that there are terminological difficulties involved in this interdisciplinary endeavour. In particular, the terms 'text' and 'discourse' are used in different ways. Kristeva uses 'text' to refer to what I have established in chapter 2 as 'discourse', as I hope will be apparent in the discussion below.

Related concepts from chapter 2

In this introduction I begin by drawing out aspects of the work of Foucault, Pêcheux and Fairclough, looked at in Chapter 2, which suggest the concept of intertextuality. I will start by repeating Foucault's early remarks in *The Archaeology of Knowledge* on suspending the unity of a text:

> The frontiers of a book are never clear-cut: beyond the title, the first lines, and last full stop, beyond its internal configuration and its autonomous form, it is caught up in a system of references to other books, other texts, other sentences ...it indicates itself, constructs itself, only on the basis of a complex field of discourse (23).

This suspension of the unity of a text is for Foucault little more than part of a preamble to the main theme: a large-scale historical perspective on discourses as socially constituted, in which he attends to the development and inter-relationship of knowledge configurations. Knowledge is discursive: a necessary condition for its existence is interaction. Knowledges are developed and transformed in dialogue. Commentary is a fundamental principle for organising texts. Although possibly doubtful as an explicit classification principle internal to discourse by which texts are distributed, commentary connects one text to another. Statements in a text according to Foucault depend for their sense on relationships of an intertextual kind: statements depend on an associated field of other statements. They are always in a complex mesh of relationships. Statements are always in functional relationships with other statements: opposing, repeating etc.

The discursive unities based on objects, style, concepts and themes that Foucault speaks of cut across the physical boundaries of actual books. These unities also suggest an intertextual kind of connection, this time not between specific texts in dialogue but between texts sharing conventional configurations of concepts etc. Foucault does not provide a method of operation for examining specific texts, but he does provide a guiding principle: the discursivity of knowledge. This discursivity is intertextual.

Pêcheux has a linguist's view of discourse as socially constitutive. His perspective differs from Foucault's, since he attends to how knowledge is reproduced discursively by looking at how it enters into the sentence, the text. Pêcheux examines the intersection of intra-discourse (the linear sequence of an utterance) and inter-discourse (the 'complex whole in dominance' of discourse formations). From

Althusser, he has taken the conception of something-external-being-made-internal, drawn into a sequence. It is this conception that he expresses and explores with the terms inter-discourse and intra-discourse. I presented earlier the two kinds of sentential element in which Pêcheux examines the intrusion into the sentence of already constructed knowledge. The 'discursivity of primary matter' of words is lost to the speaking subject. In other words, the fact that what someone says is attached to some external discourse is not apparent to them. This chapter addresses this phenomenon using the concept of intertextuality. With the intertextuality concept, an observable product (text) of a process (discourse) is exposed in its mesh of relations with other texts and with discourse conventions. Exposing this mesh of relations shows that a text lacks unity: it exists only in relations with texts and conventions, being by nature inherently dialogic.

Fairclough (1989: 1590 points to this 'inherent dialogism' of texts. He himself uses the notion of intertextuality in a more delimited sense, to extend the context of discourse to include its interactional history. In his model of discourse as social practice, outlined briefly in Chapter 2, an interpreter draws upon MR of interactional history from the intertextual context. He refers in passing to a broader sense of intertextuality, a pervasive sense in which all discourse is inherently dialogic. A pervasive kind of intertextuality can be read in the notion that every discourse is embedded in a mesh of relations in which it is constituted at every moment in production and interpretation; the view that 'a single discourse implies a whole society' (156). The emphasis placed on the potential heterogeneity of a given discourse, in terms of the discourse-types that may occur in it and the diversity of resources it requires for interpretation, can also be read as attention to its intertextuality. In this chapter, I examine the concept of intertextuality in order to explore both these applications. I conclude by drawing out three distinct forms of intertextuality that can be used to examine coherence as an intertextual phenomenon.

Bakhtin's "dialogized heteroglossia"

Kristeva was one of the people who introduced the work of Bakhtin to the Western academic world in the mid sixties. She saw in his work a view of language which combined attention to the interaction and identity-construction of language-users at one and the same time. Her interpretation and development of his work in the concept of intertextuality are presented in this chapter. Before I begin on intertextuality, I need to outline briefly his variety-and-dialogue view of discourse as 'dialogized heteroglossia':

The living utterance, having taken meaning and shape at a particular historical moment in a socially specific environment, cannot fail to brush up against thousands of living dialogic threads, woven by socio-ideological consciousness around the given object of an utterance; it cannot fail to become an active participant in social dialogue (1981: 276).

In Bakhtin's writing on dialogism, he argues that we need to study discourse as a fundamentally social phenomenon. Discourse cannot be detached from its uses by people interacting in social life:

Discourse lives, as it were, beyond itself, in a living impulse toward the object; if we detach ourselves completely from this impulse all we have left is the naked corpse of the word, from which we can learn nothing at all about the social situation or the fate of a given word in life. To study the word as such, ignoring the impulse that reaches out beyond it, is just as senseless as to study psychological experience outside the context of that real life toward which it was directed and by which it is determined. (292)

Bakhtin observes (151-152) that we need to study not only what makes dialogic relations possible (i.e. language 'in itself' as it is conceived in 'autonomous' theoretical linguistics: in studies of grammar etc) but also the relations themselves. Subsequent advances in pragmatics etc. are doing just this, working with a humanist conception of the language-using subject.

What Bakhtin was proposing was, however, more than a shift of attention from language in the abstract to language as it is used in interaction. In his view of language, the concepts of interaction and linguistic diversity overlap - language is 'dialogized heteroglossia' (272). Language is always dialogic and never 'unitary', except as an ahistorical grammatical abstraction (288). (From this view, there is not one English language, but many Englishes.) Language and therefore language description are not dissociable from interaction and context.

Heteroglossia. Through Bakhtin's examination of literary language we can see his distinctive view of varieties/styles of social dialogue. Social varieties conceal "heteroglossia", a term coined for the context-dependency, ambivalence and diversity of meanings. The external determinants of a social variety, its 'alien context', are repressed:

Style organically contains within itself indices that reach outside itself, a correspondence of its own elements and the elements of an alien context. The internal politics of style (how the elements are put together) is determined by its external politics (its relationship to alien discourse). Discourse lives, as it were, on the boundary between its own context and another, alien, context. (1981:284)

The different 'styles' of literary language embody particular views of the world, or wordings of the world: 'forms for conceptualizing the world in words, specific world views, each characterized by its own objects, meanings and values' (292). Literary language is an imposed 'unitary' language. This apparent unity is achieved by the establishment of apparently discrete literary genres - poetry, the novel etc - which 'contain' diversity, without having recourse to the non-literary (288-289). He attends to the heteroglossic quality of literary texts, arguing that they are not discrete but contain non-literary varieties (see his example of 'skaz' below). Bakhtin attends to the interior of the novel, arguing that the 'novel as a whole is a phenomenon multiform in style and variform in speech and voice' (1981:261). But he stresses that dialogism and the external determination of social varieties in dialogical relationships are properties of all discourse.

An article on genre by Kress and Threadgold (1988) provides me with illustrations of the pervasiveness of 'dialogized heteroglossia' as a property of discourse. They discuss three texts in this article, one of which is a feminist short story by Audrey Thomas which rearticulates patriarchal narratives in a feminist 'voice', or counter-discourse. For example, the religious narrative of the annunciation is retold by a resistant Mary ('No, really, some other time...' line 51; 'I never accept free gifts' line 58) who is forced to comply (like '...the servant summoned to the bedchamber ...honoured ...afraid. Or perhaps like Leda.' lines 75-76). A little later the writer comments unfavourably but resignedly on the patriarchal nativity narrative in which women's experience of childbirth is absent: 'Unfair to gloss that over ...to make so little of the waiting ...the months ...the hours. They make no mention of the hours; but of course, men wrote it down. How were they to know?' (lines 85-89) The text is realized in interactive conversational mode; quotation marks, questions, etc. The conversation genre is paradoxically what gives the 'short story' genre its generic status (235).

They also observe multiple genres and discourses in a non-literary text: a transcription of recorded voices of two children who are supposed to be having their afternoon nap. They identify a 'let's pretend' genre, the topic of which is feeding puppies; this draws on a discourse of dog-breeding which the children (Threadgold's own) apparently participate in with their mother. They also find an 'instructional genre', as the sister is training her younger brother in 'let's pretend', that is, teaching him how to be a participant in the 'let's pretend' genre. For this she uses the discourse of parental control, as used by her mother. Other genres in this multi-genre text are a 'negotiation' genre (for possession of a

69

toy rabbit to take to bed with her), a 'bedtime story' genre, a 'nap genre' and others. The sense of genre that emerges is of topics and ways of speaking related to situation- and activity-types:

There is ...dialogism at work here, not merely in the usual sense of a dialogue between the participants in a conversation, but dialogism in Bakhtin's sense whereby this text dialogues with the other 'voices' of the culture, by referring to them intertextually and also constructing, for the participants in this dialogue, positions of compliance or resistance with respect to those other 'voices', It is also a text which dialogues with fictionality, a text which paradoxically, in constructing a fictional world, constructs the 'real' and constructs places for apprentice subjects within that 'real' (234-235)

Single- and double-voiced words. In language description we cannot dissociate words from the people producing them for specific purposes on particular occasions. Their meaning depends on the interaction and context in which they come into being. Logical and semantic relationships, as Bakhtin (1973: 151) says, do not exist in vacuo: 'they must clothe themselves in the word, become utterances, and become the positions of various subjects, expressed in the word'. In describing dialogic relationships in the novel's interior, Bakhtin anthropomorphizes the 'dialogic word'. By means of metaphorically 'animating' words (so that they 'cringe in anticipation' of criticism etc, see below), his description highlights the relational and expressive values which are attributed to words in addition to their experiential values.

He classifies words in the novel into two broad categories: single- and double- voiced. In the first category he distinguishes two sub-categories: 'object-oriented' and 'objectivized'. The object-oriented word is the direct denotative word of the author, which 'does not encounter in its path toward the object the fundamental and richly varied opposition of another's word, no one argues against it' (1981: 276). The objectivized word is the direct speech of a character represented by the author without alteration or comment. It is subordinate to the narrative. The character's utterance is subsumed by the narration; it is not at odds with it. So, as Bakhtin (1973: 154-5) explains, although there are two voices present in the writing, it is univocal:

Where there appears within the author's context the direct speech of, let us say, a certain hero, we have before us two speech centers and two speech unities within a single context: the unity of the author's utterance and the unity of the hero's utterance. But that second unity is not independent, it is subordinate to and included in the first as one of its elements. The stylistic treatment is not the same for both utterances. The hero's word is treated as the word of another person, as the

70

word of an individual whose character and type are pre-determined, i.e. it is treated as the object of the author's understanding, and nòt from the point of view of its own object-oriented directedness.

So, these two different types of word are distinguished because the first is the author's own and the second is someone else's subsumed under the author's own, being made its object. They are however both single-voiced in the sense that neither the direct authorial word nor direct speech representation contains an external voice which is 'foreign' to the author's own. The form of narrative known as 'skaz' contains such a foreign voice. Bakhtin explains skaz in the following way: 'Skaz - narrative told by a fictitious narrator in the language typical to him, containing the distinctive peculiarities of his own (as opposed to the author's) speech. (239n). The author's purpose in introducing this voice, which is foreign to him, is to draw in the values and attitudes of another person who is speaking from a different standpoint socially.

The distinction Bakhtin is making between single- and double-voice concerns the author's intention with the word, the presence or absence of a strategic position taken up in relation to the external voice in the word. He divides the double-voiced word into three sub-categories: single-directed, hetero-directed and active. The distinguishing trait of the first sub-category he gives is 'that the author's intention makes use of another person's word in the direction of its own aspirations' (160). An example of this kind of word would be speech reportage which retains the quality of the original without being direct quotation: 'Having penetrated into another person's word and having made itself at home in it, the author's idea does not collide with the other person's idea, but rather follows the direction of that idea, merely making that direction conditional' (160). Bakhtin calls this 'stylization'.

In the second sub-category the author introduces a signification which is opposed to the other's word; as in parody, which Bakhtin sees as a form of conflict between two voices:

As in stylization, the author speaks through another person's word, but in contrast to stylization, he introduces a semantic direction into that word which is diametrically opposed to its original direction. The second voice, which has made its home in the other person's word, collides in a hostile fashion with the original owner and forces him to serve purposes diametrically opposed to his own. The word becomes the arena of conflict between two voices. (160)

There are other ambiguous uses of another's word, which are similar to parody. In ironic or mocking repetition of someone else's speech for instance 'the other person's word is being used to

71

communicate aspirations which are hostile to it' (161). As Bakhtin says, this type of word is not found only in the novel, but is very common in everyday speech. So is the 'active' type, discussed below.

In the single- and hetero- directed word the external voice is 'passive'. It is being used against its will, as it were, and is at the mercy of the author. The third sub-category of double-voiced word is active. In this sub-category Bakhtin includes aggressive 'cutting remarks' and defensive 'self-deprecating, florid speeches' (163). These inner polemical words are acutely aware of the words of another and cast a 'sideward glance' at them:

In practical everyday speech all cutting remarks – 'jabs' and 'needles' - belong to this category. But all self-deprecating, florid speeches which repudiate themselves in advance and have a thousand reservations, concessions, loopholes, etc belong to this category, too. Such a speech as it were cringes in the presence or in the anticipation of another person's word, answer, or objection. The individual manner in which a person constructs his speech is to a large degree determined by his characteristic awareness of the other person's word and his means of reacting to that word. (163)

Distinct from, but similar to, the 'sideward glance' is the dialogical word which responds to the voice of another by answering it in anticipation: 'Such a word envelops and draws into itself the speeches of the other people and intensely reworks them' (163).

Now, in his principal distinction between single- and double-voiced words, Bakhtin is attending to whether or not the author is intending to interfere with the words of others. It is an approach to describing authorial alignment in which the narrative is peopled with voices. In terms of systemic components of meaning in discourse, Bakhtin is attending to interpersonal meaning. In the single-voiced objectivized word, as I said earlier, there are two voices present (two subjects to which the text connects); but they are univocal. In the direct object-oriented word there are also two voices, but the word is not 'conscious' of it:

The direct object-oriented word recognizes only itself and its object, to which it seeks to conform in the highest degree possible. If in the process it imitates or takes a lesson from someone else, nothing is changed in the slightest: it is like the scaffolding which is not part of the architect's plan, although it is indispensable and is taken into consideration by the builder. The fact that another person's word is imitated and that the words of other persons, clearly recognizable to the literary historian and to every competent reader, are present is not of concern to the word itself. (155)

Readers can be aware of this double voice even when writers are not, contrary to their intentions. The direct word imitates without intending imitation to be apparent and without commenting on the voice being imitated: 'it takes it seriously, it makes it its own, it seeks to master another person's word. The voices merge completely, and if we do hear the other voice, it is by no means because the imitator intended us to do so' (157).

The 'sphere of the genuine life of the word' is discourse. Yet again, it is best to quote Bakhtin himself:

The word is not a thing, but rather the eternally mobile, eternally changing medium of dialogical intercourse. It never coincides with a single consciousness or a single voice. The life of the word is in its transferral from one mouth to another, one context to another, one social collective to another, and one generation to another. In the process the word does not forget where it has been and can never wholly free itself from the dominion of the contexts of which it has been a part (167).

All words are intertextual, but this intertextuality is not always recognized. To use the anthropomorphic metaphor one last time: people forget where words have been, but words do not.

Intertextuality in semiology

Kristeva

In this section I will present Kristeva's interpretation of dialogism as 'intertextuality', and then outline her explicitly anti-humanist application of this dialogic view of language.

For Kristeva, Bakhtin is mingling the concepts of subjectivity and communication as the single phenomenon of intertextuality. In 'Word, Dialogue and Novel', she interprets his literary word as a dialogue among writer, addressee and cultural context. She also views his 'word' as the minimal structural unit in the intersection of texts, and not as a fixed meaning existing independently of its status as dialogue. This permits her to posit the writer as reader of the intersecting texts, and to capture the immediate presence of these exterior texts in the text the writer is producing: hence to present the writer's text-production as the reproduction of living history and society. As Kristeva (1980)[2] explains: 'By introducing the status of the word as a minimal structural unit, Bakhtin situates the text within history and society, which are then seen as texts read by the writer, and into which he inserts himself by rewriting them' (65). In the act of doing this, 'Diachrony is transformed into synchrony', as Kristeva says. In other words, disparate elements from different cultural sources 'read' by the writer coexist

73

within the same text so that 'History and morality are written and read within the infrastructure of texts' (65).

She expresses Bakhtin's dialogue and heteroglossia ('ambivalence' in Kristeva's writing) as two axes on which the word is defined: 'horizontally', according to the writing subject and the addressee, and 'vertically', according to exterior texts. The vertical axis concerns the orientation of the 'word' towards an anterior or synchronic text or corpus of texts. Kristeva describes these two axes in the following way: 'horizontal axis (subject-addressee) and vertical axis (text-context) coincide, bringing to light an important fact: each word (text) is an intersection of word (texts) where at least one other word (text) can be read' (66). It is in this doubly intersected word that Kristeva reads the concept of intertextuality, and on which she builds her own approach to texts as the intersection of semiotic practices:

In Bakhtin's work, these two axes, which he calls dialogue and ambivalence, are not clearly distinguished. Yet, what appears as a lack of rigor is in fact an insight first introduced into literary theory by Bakhtin: any text is constructed as a mosaic of quotations; any text is the absorption and transformation of another. The notion of intertextuality replaces that of intersubjectivity, and poetic language is read as at least double' (66).

I will now go on to outline Kristeva's formalisation, on the basis of these two axes, of the anti-humanist concept which she called intertextuality. Kristeva views a text as an intertextuality, embedded in history and society, where culture is seen as a macrotext. Culture (history and society) becomes text. For Kristeva a text is a productivity which relates communicative speech (the immediate/current text) to kinds of anterior or synchronic utterances (prior/external texts). As a productivity, a text is destructive and constructive: it re-arranges. This is its condition as an intertextuality, a permutation, a mesh of intersecting utterances.

This conception is enormously broad. However, unlike Jonathan Culler (see below), I do not conclude that this makes Kristeva's conception of intertextuality unusable.

Here is what I like about it. According to Kristeva, intertextuality is the essential property of a text which makes possible the constitution of subjectivity. An individual is constituted by past practices as a subject in her current act of writing or reading. Texts position writers and readers in the symbolic order. It is through the intertextuality of a text, its condition as a textual dialogue, that past practices can be brought into it. Intertextuality is pervasive, at the core of an individual's relation with the culture producing her. For Kristeva, culture itself is intertextual.

74

Culler complains that in practice Kristeva's application of the concept of intertextuality is limited to the predictable: citations, misquotations, fragments. I assume that he is referring to her analysis of a French Medieval short story in 'The Bounded Text',[3] where citation among other things is discussed. But Kristeva is not only referring to embedded concrete texts drawn into the narrative - she is describing the intersection of semiotic practices.

One practice occurring in the story is the 'blazon', or boastful public proclamation. Another is a conventional representation of female treachery. This second convention is itself 'double' since it non-disjunctively combines the idealization of woman (the deification of the Lady in courtly poetry, an existing literary tradition) with the infamy and disloyalty of the 'actual' woman which is antithetical to it. These opposites, Kristeva tells us, are contained within the single text without being semically opposed.[4] The treachery of the 'actual' woman alters the effect of the boastful 'blazon', so that it functions in the story in a double-voiced way, not only as the character's self-praise, but also as blame: 'Blazons are recorded into the book as univocally laudatory. But they become ambiguous as soon as they are read from the point of view of the novelistic text's general function: the Lady's treachery skews the laudatory tone and shows its ambiguity. The blazon is transformed into blame' (53). The intertextuality of the story does not begin and end with the blazon itself or the contemporary literary conventions for representing women. The story is an intertextuality, formed both from these things and their specific effects in intersection.

Kristeva also explores the text's intertextuality in the different kinds of 'temporality' in its narrative sequences. Its 'discursive temporality' is the linear chain of utterances being written. This in itself, according to Kristeva, involves two distinct semiotic practices: both spoken 'discursivity' and scriptural form: 'The succession of "events" (descriptive utterances or citations) obeys the motion of the hand working on the empty page' (54). This course of discursive time is interrupted by devices signalling the sequencing of the narrative - Kristeva cites as examples: 'To return to my point', 'to put it briefly', 'as I will tell you' and 'here I will stop speaking for a bit of Madame and her Ladies to return to little Saintre'. These topic coherence devices are meta-linguistic. They construct (signal the construction of) the 'temporality' of the story within the narrative. Kristeva refers to them as 'junctives': 'Such junctives signal a temporality other than that of the discursive (linear) chain: the massive present of the inferential enunciation (of the scriptural work)' (54).

In addition, the entire story is presented as a letter. So the whole written text, an intertextuality formed of utterances by its implied author and foreign texts (the citations, etc), its dual nature as spoken and written, its concealed contradictions and 'double-voiced' qualities, the 'temporalities' of linear and non-linear narrative - this intertextual totality of the text is intersected by yet another element: its function as a letter. The presence of the practice of letter-writing makes the text an exchange object. (Kristeva limits her analysis to the fictional 'interior' of novels. Hence she doesn't go on to discuss the discourse structure beyond the novel, in which the concrete novel is embedded - also as an exchange object.)

Having opened up the text as an intertextuality, the matter arises of what fills it and constitutes its intertextuality. Kristeva fills the novel as an intertextuality with meta-linguistic elements interweaving threads of narrative, discourse structure, coexisting novel conventions which contradict one another, the double-voiced word, and the most obviously intertextual: fragments of external texts, such as citations. For her, intertextuality is total, pervasive; another word for subjectivity and interaction. Following Bakhtin, her intertextuality includes the dialogic. Interaction and convention are blurred because conventions only come about as the cumulative result of past interactions. Intertextuality expresses this crucial element; the public quality of every interaction, the continuity of practices from one mouth to another.

Culler complains that Kristeva formulates intertextuality too all-encompassingly so that it could come to mean the 'sum of knowledge that makes it possible for texts to have meaning' (1983: 103), and says that in practice she looks only at the obvious citations. While the first complaint could be justified, I suggest that the second is not.

Barthes

As we have seen, Kristeva aims to analyse the process of the text's production, rather than approaching it as a product with a fixed structure. For this she suggests the term 'intertextuality': 'So as to study the structuration of the text as transformation, we shall picture it as a DIALOGUE of many texts, as a TEXTUAL DIALOGUE, or better, as an INTERTEXTUALITY' (1970: 68). Roland Barthes gives a rather different conceptualisation which retains the pervasiveness of Kristeva's. In Barthes' use of intertextuality, a text is tissue of voices, which he conceives as echoes of other texts. In this version of intertextuality, these external voices are expressed as 'codes'. In *S/Z* (1970), and later in 'Textual Analysis of Poe's 'Valdemar'' (1972), Barthes unpacks the codes of realist texts. He does this by examining, not their structure, but their 'mobile structuration', so that rather than looking at what texts share a basic story structure, he is looking at how they differ, how disparate elements from outside the texts are loosely combined.

What Barthes produces is, as Coward and Ellis call it, a '"slowmotion reading", watching the production of meaning' (1977: 55). This is a reading of the text as a process, rather than as a product, where the text is opened up to expose the weaving together of a tissue of codes. He insists that these codes must not be seen as rigorous categories but 'simply as associative fields, a supra-textual organization of notations which impose a certain idea of structure' (1972:).

In 'unpacking' the codes of a realist text, Barthes exposes the productivity of language behind the realist illusion of objective representation. This illusion is the effect of the mimetic use of language, used as if it were a transparent medium for imitating the world, and hence repressing its own productivity. In the production of a text, signifiers are fixed by codes through the 'mechanism' of connotation. Denotation, where a word is taken to denote a given fixed meaning is the effect of naturalisation: 'denotation is not the first of sense, but it pretends to be; under this illusion, it is ultimately only the last of connotations (that which seems at once to found and close the reading), the superior myth by which the text pretends to return to the nature of language, to language as nature' (1970: 16). A realist text appears real and natural and conceals its intertextual 'circular recollection' of text and 'the impossibility of living outside the infinite text - whether this be Proust, the daily newspaper or the television screen: the book makes sense, sense makes life'.

The codes, of which Barthes distinguishes five, are hidden voices which he characterizes as 'forces that can take over the text' (1972: 135). Coward and Ellis (1977) describe Barthes' 'proairetic' narrative code and 'hermeneutic' code of mystery and suspense as the codes 'responsible for giving text its forward movement' (55). The proairetic code consists of models of action which help the reader to place details into plot sequences. In the novella 'Sarrasine' which Barthes unpacks in S/Z, it includes stereotyped models of 'kidnapping' and 'falling in love'. The hermeneutic code presents and develops the plot's enigma - the gradual, delayed release of information leading to the final revelation of 'truth'. The semic code is concerned with character and atmosphere; for example, it constructs loose models of character as aggregates of semes 'fastened' by a Proper name. With the symbolic code Barthes' focus is on psychoanalytic interpretation. It is, according to Coward and Ellis, the 'field in which the basic positionality of the text and the reader is charted' (56). 'Sarrasine' contains a tale within a tale about a castrato, the sexually ambiguous Zambinella. Unsurprisingly perhaps, the principal semic oppositions Barthes unearths relate to the positionality of sexual subjects.

Lastly, the cultural code draws in bodies of knowledge, public opinions, and a host of received knowledge not covered by other codes about human nature and situation-types. Barthes presents these assorted knowledges as though they were anonymous Books: a metaphor for the ready-made quality of assumptions about human nature etc. in the text: 'the didactic material set in motion in the text (often ...as foundation for reasonings or as written authority for sentiments) corresponds rather to the play of 7 or 8 handbooks which could be at the disposal of a dutiful student in classical bourgeois education' (1970: 201). These include a Literary History, an Art History, a Practical Medicine, a treatise on psychology, morals, logic, a book of maxims, and so on. In 'Sarrasine', one source of the main character's self-deception is the Book of Woman, which is the collection of cultural knowledge about what women are like. The deceived character mistakenly takes soft skin, a high voice, women's clothing, fear of snakes, fainting and a general frailty to signify femaleness. In the automatic quotations of the cultural code are vanished history and tradition. When the text is looked at from this perspective, the speakers of these automatic quotations are ventriloquizing for bodies of knowledge.

Barthes tackles a text as a tissue of codes giving the impression as he does so of a work in progress. The meaning of 'Sarrasine', the novella under analysis, is not neatly tied up by the criticism but left open and incomplete, to be finished by the reader. This shows up an interesting relationship between reader, critic and text, precisely reflecting Kristeva's view of subjectivity being constituted in the intertextuality of a text: '*I* is not an innocent subject that is anterior to texts...The *I* that approaches the text is itself already a plurality of other texts, of infinite or, more precisely, lost codes (whose origins are lost)' (16).

The works of Barthes and others caused a rift in French literary criticism. In the critical climate of Barthes' contemporaries it appears positivism was rampant, Barthes took issue with the priestly posture of the critic as guardian and servant of the text's 'true meaning' and with the critics' insistence that they were on the outside of what they studied. This is reported by Annette Lavers:

> The Quarrel had revealed the contrast between critic and writer to be a veritable myth, a morality play where the cardinal sins of the nouveau critique were listed as ignorance, obscurity, presumption and mendacity. The good critic instead was erudite, clear, modest and sincere ...it became increasingly clear, at least to those not overwhelmed by their sense of being threatened, that the term 'critic' could denote other attitudes, which were also positive However, the scholarly work carried out in universities purported to discover the meaning of a text once and for all. (1982: 33)

Barthes' S/Z was clearly antithetical to this belief that a single interpretation can be achieved. In it he makes a point of showing his own hand in the creative process by, as Lavers remarks, 'adopting a stylistic strategy to focus the immediacy of a text, its ultimate opacity and irreducibility. And the critic who can do this surely has every right to consider himself in turn as a 'subject of writing', whose text is at par with that which gave rise to it". Actually Lavers gives the impression that a critic's productive involvement with a text is some kind of stylistic option only, rather than an unavoidable concommitant of criticism. This suggests that Barthes was advocating 'creative writing' for literary critics, which he certainly wasn't, and shows how insidiously a 'unitary' view of the subject can replace a 'decentred' one. Barthes was establishing the inevitability of productive involvement in any encounter with a text and the essential ambivalence and openness to interpretation of texts themselves.

Culler

In *The Pursuit of Signs* Culler introduces intertextuality by inviting his reader to consider how difficult it would be to explain the purpose of reading his or any critical theory text to a complete outsider, and that it would involve explaining the kinds of expectations readers bring to it and the 'body of discourse' to which it is a new addition. He goes on to consider how difficult it would be to explain precisely what these expectations are:

and how such a discussion is rendered intelligible and significant by a whole body of already existing discourse ...In saying that my discussion is intelligible only in terms of a prior body of discourse - other projects and thoughts, which it implicitly or explicitly takes up, prolongs, cites, refutes, transforms - I have posed the problem of intertextuality and asserted the intertextual nature of any verbal construct. (101)

Culler presents two different foci contained in the concept of intertextuality. He uses it to account for two kinds of continuity and dependency between texts: i) to destroy the illusion of a text's autonomy, he considers the importance of texts sequentially prior to it; ii) with a very loose and eclectic use of the term 'code' (which appears to refer both to codes in Barthes's sense and to formal linguistic codes) he considers the prior texts 'as contributions to a code' (103). Intertextuality refers to both of these things, but the point of interest for Culler is the second:

Intertextuality becomes less a name for a work's relation to particular prior texts than a designation of its participation in the discursive space of a culture: the relationship between a text and the various languages or signifying practices of a culture and its relation to those texts which articulate for it the possibilities of that culture. (103)

Culler rather grudgingly acknowledges Kristeva's invention of the term and then dismisses her treatment of the concept as too all-encompassing and loose in theory and too limited in application. Culler himself limits intertextuality in practice to presupposed prior texts and existing literary conventions. In doing so, he avoids attending to what I take to be the crucial point of the semiological concept of intertextuality: that it is pervasive, not an additional aspect of a text, but central to what constitutes it.

In practice, Culler restores intertextuality to a comfortable hunt for presuppositions. This 'modest intertextuality' (112), as he calls it, is limited, but nevertheless useful (recall Fairclough's observations about the way mass media producers can use presuppositions to postulate an audience with shared interactional histories). A presupposition is said to refer back to a prior sentence present in a current one as an 'intertext'. A presupposition in a poem may function as 'an intertextual operator which implies a discursive context and which, by identifying an intertext, modifies the way in which the poem must be read' (113). It is of considerable literary importance which propositions are presupposed (that is, placed in an 'intertext') and which are asserted; the 'intertext' invoked can bring in another voice. In other words, the author presents a previous text in using a presupposition. Culler draws an example from Blake's 'The Tyger'. In asking:

What immortal hand or eye
Could frame thy fearful symmetry?

Blake presupposes an earlier discourse, which may not necessarily have existed as a specific text, where it is taken as given that an immortal hand or eye framed the tiger's fearful symmetry and so on. He uses the presupposition to presuppose the existence of a text, on which he can voice his attitude. Through the presuppositional cue, the poem's interpreter can work out the prior discourse that is sedimented and commented on in the two lines of the poem extract. Contained in the lines are two voices; the poet's own, and a presupposed 'voice' whose expressed belief he is questioning. So, sedimented in the poem are 'sentences as part of a discourse or mode of discourse already in place, as a text or set of attitudes prior to the poem itself. Thus the problem of interpreting the poem becomes essentially that of deciding what attitude the poem (sic) takes to the prior discourse which it designates as presupposed' (114). In addition to the sedimentation of logical presupposition as an 'intertextual operator', Culler discusses pragmatic and rhetorical/ literary 'presupposition'.[5] As an example of pragmatic 'presupposition' he gives the speech act 'request': 'Open the door', where the request 'presupposes' the conditions which would make possible the request's satisfaction. The point of interest here intertextually is not, I assume, in the presence or absence of doors which are closed and people who are capable of closing them, nor, as in the case of logical presupposition, in the sedimentation of a prior text, but in the sedimentation of the conventions underlying such activities as the making of requests.

One literary convention is to utter 'Once upon a time' to open up the discourse onto the world of fairytales and bedtime stories. This sets up expectations by establishing the set of conventions associated with a certain set of stories, including and especially the particular relationship which the teller and listener have with the information to be transmitted. Culler discusses an opening sentence which contains no logical presupposition:

Once upon a time there lived a king who had a daughter.

Loaded with literary 'presupposition', the sentence 'relates the story to a series of other stories, identifies it with the conventions of a genre, asks us to take certain attitudes towards it (guaranteeing, or at least strongly implying, that the story will have a point to it, a moral which will govern the organization of detail and incident). The presupposition-less sentence is a powerful intertextual operator' (115). Pragmatically 'presupposed' conventions, which he has emerging from an unexplained locality he calls an 'intertextual space', make up literary genres. To illustrate rhetorical presupposition Culler cites a stanza from Baudelaire's 'Un Voyage a Cythere':

It was not a temple with bosky shades
Where the young priestess, in love with flowers,
Passed, her body consumed by secret flames,
Her robe blowing open in the fleeting breezes

Here I assume the poet is parodying a poetic tradition. Culler picks out 'It was not a temple' and points out that while logically it only presupposes 'It was something', rhetorically it presupposes that someone expected (or, one would conventionally expect) there to be a temple. He goes on to say that this presupposition is intensified by the weight of the rest of the stanza 'and makes the whole stanza the negation of an intertextual citation, the negation of something already in place as a discursive supposition, the negation of the language which poetic tradition might have applied to Cythere' (116). What he is saying therefore is that the rhetorical presupposition draws into the poem a voice from outside it. This external voice is the literary tradition which Baudelaire is parodying.

Presupposition search is no more than a device for looking for likely spots for intertextual elements. In the parodic example he can identify a presupposition; but even without the negation cuing a presupposition, the stanza could still be parodying an existing literary convention. What I assume Culler implies, although he doesn't quite say it, is that the stanza is a parody; it contains two voices which constitute part of the poem as an intertextuality. These two voices are in conflict within the parodic word.[6]

So Culler distinguishes between previous voices and sets of stories, poems etc. sharing established sets of conventions; ie. between presupposed earlier statements (such as the religious discourse presupposed in the Blake poem: 'An immortal hand or eye framed the Tyger's fearful symmetry') and 'presupposed' conventions of genre. These conventions may be conventionally implemented (as in the children's story example: 'Once upon a time') to produce discourse which in Bakhtin's terms is single-voiced. Or they may be implemented oppositionally in a double-voiced way (as in Baudelaire's citation from a probably imaginary mellifluous poem: 'It was not a temple with bosky shades...').

Bloom

The way American literary critic Harold Bloom uses intertextuality is broadly similar to Culler's: 'to dispel the 'commonsensical' [notion] that a poetic text is self-contained, that it has an ascertainable meaning or meanings without reference to other poetic texts ...Any poem is an inter-poem, and any reading of a poem is an inter-reading' (1976: 2). In contrast with Culler, however, he only sees intertextuality in the series of texts by an author and in the specific literary influence of another author - thus effectively reinstating the author as the organising principle. As he limits intertextuality to the relation between a literary text and a specific prior literary text, using it to speculate on the impossibility of writing without tradition, he de-radicalises intertextuality, restoring literary criticism to the study of a traditional canon. The resulting effect, as Culler says, is that 'Intertextuality is the family archive' (108).

Bloom's approach is even more limiting than looking at sources and influences, which the concept of intertextuality includes but far exceeds. As Culler says:

poems do seem to presuppose more than a single precursor poem: what makes possible reading and writing is not a single anterior action which serves as an origin and moment of plenitude but an open series of acts, both identifiable and lost, which work together to constitute something like a language: discursive possibilities, systems of convention, cliches and descriptive systems (110).

Both Bloom and Culler set out to destroy the illusion of a literary text's autonomy. Culler limits intertextual elements in practice to certain 'discursive spaces' which, with the exception of religious discourse, are all literary (the conventions of mellifluous poetry, of bedtime stories etc.) and cut off completely from the non-literary environment. Bloom restores an even more traditional approach, interpreting intertextuality as a series of writings by a given author and the imitation of another author's

82

text. He follows the author principle of classification to the letter and contains the heterogeneity of literary discourse within a self-contained 'literary tradition'.[7]

Summary

The concept of intertextuality as it appears in semiology provides a number of insights into the nature and relationship of texts and subjects. With it, Kristeva explored Bakhtin's view of the novel as 'dialogized heteroglossia'. This conception combined for Bakhtin the views that the 'life of the word is in its transferral from one mouth to another, one context to another, one social collecative to another, and one generation to another' (1973: 167) and that the 'novel as a whole is a phenomenon multiform in style and variform in speech and voice' (1981: 261). Kristeva renamed 'dialogized heteroglossia' as intertextuality: the essential property of a text which makes possible the constitution of subjectivity. Texts position language users in interaction and in the symbolic order. An individual is constituted as a subject in interaction by past practices which enter or 'intersect' it. She characterizes a single text as a textual dialogue, so that it is an indeterminate series of points of intersection of texts and not a fixed structure. It is through the intertextuality of a text, its condition as a textual dialogue, that past practices can be brought into it; and it is in the process of textual dialogue that the language user is constructed. Intertextuality is pervasive and multiplex, at the core of an individual's relation with the culture producing her.

Barthes retains Kristeva's broad perspective, sharing her emphasis on productivity and multiplicity of conventions in his 'slowmotion readings' of realist texts as tissues of codes. The cultural code, a residual category, is conceived as an indeterminate set of metaphorical Books (available to members of a culture) containing all the presupposed beliefs and stereotypes about character- and situation- types not covered by his narrative, suspense, semic and symbolic codes.

For Culler, intertextuality in principle refers to the continuity of a text and its associated field in its "participation in the discursive space of a culture". Texts are not autonomous but dependent for their interpretation on provision of assumed sequentially prior texts and conventions of genre. In practice, Culler chiefly considers the literary context (the exception being the religious discourse in the Blake poem). What is completely absent from his version of intertextuality is Kristeva's perception of it as what makes subjectivity possible. However, Culler's "modest" view of intertextuality offers the analysis of presuppositions as a way of attending to the double-voiced word: writers' oppositional use of genre conventions, dissociation from sets of beliefs to which they are opposed, etc.

In common with Kristeva, Barthes and Culler, Bloom uses intertextuality to dispel the illusion that a single literary text is self-contained. He argues that it can only be understood because of 'tradition', by which he means literary tradition. He does this by identifying specific prior texts by the same author and that author's major literary influence.

These uses of intertextuality are summarized below:

Kristeva:
- Intertextuality as a productivity: the permutation of intersecting semioticpractices in a text embedded in history and society;
- An interpretation of Bakhtin's novelistic dialogic word as 'subjectivity and communication';
- Features covered: the novel as an intertextuality with discursive and scriptual form, meta-linguistic elements interweaving threads of narrative, discourse structure, coexisting novel conventions which contradict one another, the double-voiced word and fragments of external texts, such as citations.

Barthes:
- Intertextuality as a productivity; five codes as "intertexts": hermeneutic, proairetic, semic, symbolic and cultural;
- Used to deconstruct realist texts by exposing the 'structuration process'.

Culler:
- Presupposed previous voices, sets of stories, poems and conventions of genre as 'intertexts';
- Used to suspend a text's autonomy, to identify prior discourse, genre and writer's alignment, e.g. in parody.

Bloom:
- Early drafts of a poem and single precursor's imitated poem as its 'intertexts';
- A reinstatement of a self-contained literary tradition and the author principle.

Intertextuality in linguistics

Beaugrande and Dressler

'Intertextuality' is most extensively used in linguistics by Robert de Beaugrande and Wolfgang Dressler. They present it as the last of seven 'standards of textuality' in their *Introduction to Text Linguistics*, which came out in 1980 (see also de Beaugrande 1980). Under the heading of intertextuality they unite discussion of different types of connection between texts. According to Beaugrande and Dressler, intertextuality 'concerns the factors which make the utilization of one text dependent upon knowledge of one or more previously encountered texts' (10). Beaugrande and

Dressler consider different kinds of intertextual relation, which are distinguished according to the extent to which they are 'mediated'. The notion of 'mediation' as used by Beaugrande and Dressler requires some elucidation. They define it as 'the extent to which one feeds one's current beliefs and goals into the model of the communicative situation' (182). Mediation is assumed to increase according to the temporal distance between the texts being connected and the amount of work required to connect them. For Beaugrande and Dressler, the concept is evidently about the amount of processing involved. This is assumed to be directly related to the distance between the texts being drawn together. Mediation therefore is to do with time, memory and ease of recall. Immediately proximate texts, as a result of this, are considered to be least mediated.

Starting with 'least mediated' connected texts, I shall consider in turn the different types of inter-textual connection which Beaugrande and Dressler include in their discussion.

According to Beaugrande and Dressler, each interactant in a conversation produces a separate text. We can therefore describe a conversation as an intertextuality. In the process of the conversation, each interactant can 'intertextually monitor' mismatches/ deviations in what they believe to be the topic or the governing discourse conventions. In other words, 'intertextual monitoring' is an orientation to what other people have said. For instance, an interactant may query or challenge the relevance of a contribution to conversation in another interactant's text; or may challenge the validity of discourse conventions assumed by another interactant. This intertextual monitoring is necessary for intertextual coherence. Beaugrande and Dressler separate this monitoring of interacting voices (an intertextual phenomenon) from situation monitoring of problems/mismatches in the external setting of discourse, mismatches of beliefs etc (which are not construed as intertextual phenomena). Beaugrande and Dressler view intertextuality as 'a procedural control upon communicative activities' (206). Presumably one could go on to say following from this that in an interaction where the interactants are not familiar with one another's topics, discourse conventions etc., there is a greater amount of processing effort involved and hence a greater degree of 'mediation' than between two good friends who know one another's conversational style very well.

So, Beaugrande and Dressler use the concept of intertextuality here to express the deliberate action of interactants on their jointly produced talk. As I hope is evident from the previous section, intertextuality in semiology is intended to account for far more than this procedural control. Intertextuality extends beyond what language users can be assumed to be aware of or in a position to exert procedural control over. From a perspective from which the subject is a subject-in-process, Beaugrande and Dressler's degrees of mediation have little significance. Given an anti-humanist perspective, all interaction would be called 'mediated'. A person's sense of identity comes from the illusion of being 'unmediated'. Intertextual monitoring is not so much an interactant's conscious act of control as positioning by interactional conventions.

A second phenomenon Beaugrande and Dressler place in their 'intertextuality' category is literary allusion. In text allusion, intertextuality is more mediated than in Beaugrande and Dressler's first sense, given above. The text alluded to is not immediate, but historically distant. Allusion involves deliberate reference an earlier text by reusing a fragment of it. By way of example, Beaugrande and Dressler present allusions in later poems to a fanciful pastoral by Christopher Marlowe. I shall repeat here the opening lines that Beaugrande and Dressler quote. Marlowe's pastoral begins:

Come live with me and be my love,
And we will all the pleasures prove
That valleys, groves, hills, and fields,
Woods, or steepy mountain yields.

The first of the poems Beaugrande and Dressler present as allusions ot this pastoral is Walter Ralegh's rebuttal (on behalf of an untrusting nymph!):

If all the world and love were young,
And truth in every shepherd's tongue,
These pretty pleasures might me move
To live with thee and be thy love.

The second allusive poem is John Donne's pastiche:

Come live with me and be my love,
And we will all the pleasures prove,
Of golden sands and crystal brooks:
With silken lines, and silver hooks.

As Beaugrande and Dressler say, Donne parallels Marlowe's lyrical shepherd with an even more lyrical fisherman, who claims that if his lover bathes in the river the fishes will be so attracted to her that he will be able to dispense with fishing tackle. We can say that, like Bakhtin's double-voiced word, these allusive poems contain two voices, one of which is using the other 'against its will'. Beaugrande and Dressler also quote Cecil Day Lewis's parodic rewrite which begins:

Come, live with me and be my love,
And we will all the pleasures prove
Of peace and plenty, bed and board,
That chance employment may afford.

I'll handle dainties on the docks
And thou shalt read of summer frocks:
At evening by the sour canals
We'll hope to hear some madrigals.

Beaugrande and Dressler contrast the last two lines quoted above with two lines of Marlowe's:

By shallow rivers to whose falls
Melodious birds sing madrigals.

The parodic rewrite undermines the view that 'The lives of shepherds and other working classes are spent in ornate dalliance and merriment, with nature as a purveyor of luxurious toys and trinkets' (188).

All Ralegh and Donne take issue with are the shepherd's proposals. Lewis mocks 'Marlowe's mode of selecting and communicating about a topic'. His parody is oppositional: 'The force of this text is its opposition to the very principles and conventions underlying Marlowe's original' (188).

So, Beaugrande and Dressler present the monitoring of ongoing conversation by interactants (unmediated) and allusion to prior texts (mediated) as two distinct types of connection between texts. They leap straight from immediately paired utterances to literary allusion. However, 'monitoring' and 'allusion' are not as clearcut as Beaugrande and Dressler imply. An interactant can allude to an earlier utterance which is not immediately connected to the current one, but is part of the same conversation. For instance, a speaker, in using a formulation, is both monitoring the other speaker's contribution and alluding to it. In fact, the allusion is part of her monitoring.

Under the heading of intertextuality, Beaugrande and Dressler discuss text-types: 'Extensive mediation is illustrated by the development and use of TEXT TYPES, being classes of texts expected to have certain traits for certain purposes' (182). Actually, they do not discuss text type development at all. They devote their discussion to the difficulties in making a typology of text-types. Text-types are categorized functionally: as narrative, argumentative, scientific, etc. They say that elements of different text-types are possible within a single text, so that a text can contain a constellation of text-types, one of which is dominant (compare this with the multi-genre texts examined by Kress and Threadgold (1988), which I referred to earlier). A book on interaction structures by Eija Ventola (1987), combining discourse analysis and semiotics perspectives, singles out Beaugrande and Dressler's intertextuality concept, when discussing text typology, as useful to account for the relation of the 'instance' of a text to the 'type'. Strangely, the dialogic, interactive, application is ignored.

The remainder of the chapter on intertextuality is given over to the importance of the intertextual 'standard of textuality' for summaries and reports, and in accounts of summary writers' recall of textual content: 'The making of reports and summaries of texts one has read represents another important domain of inter-textuality' (195).

Beaugrande and Dressler, like Culler, express the belief that Kristeva's use of intertextuality is very limited.[8] For an outlook similar to their own on intertextuality, they refer to a paper by Randolph Quirk (1978). Quirk does not use the term himself, but he is discussing a kind of continuity of discourse which can be described as intertextual: 'our effective awareness that beginnings do not exist: we have only continuations' (30). What Quirk is doing in this paper is showing the blurred boundaries between texts and how one text spills over into another, in order to go on to examine how beginning boundaries are marked. He refers to the continuity of conversations shared by friends, to 'established norms' and to topics shared by strangers which are 'known to be conventionally established as common ground in our society' (30).

Neither in Quirk's paper on continuity and the blurring of boundaries nor in Beaugrande and Dressler's chapter on intertextuality are discourse conventions connected in any way with the subjectivity of their users. Beaugrande and Dressler's application of intertextuality is outstanding as an incorporation of interaction (the subject matter of conversation analysis, pragmatics) into textlinguistics. It is interesting to see that other diverse phenomena involving texts 'presupposing'[9] other texts (summary, literary allusion) are put under the same heading of intertextuality as a notion of texts containing multiples of text-types, even though the placement together of relations with earlier texts and multi-genre texts as intertextual phenomenon is not explained. I will end this section with the observation that there are three 'categories' of intertextuality: one involving earlier texts, one concerning dialogue and another involving text-type combination. Note that in the first and second categories, intertextuality is describing the deliberate acts of interactional control, summarising etc, by subjects. In the third, intertextuality is describing existing conventions: 'classes of text expected to have certain traits for certain purposes' (182).

Lemke

For Jay Lemke (1985), like Beaugrande and Dressler, intertextuality is a generalization for the 'connectivity' between texts. Intertextuality is presented in this work as:

an important characteristic of the use of language in communities. The meanings we make through texts, and the ways we make them, always depend on the currency in our communities of other text we recognize as having certain definite kinds of relationships with them: generic, thematic, structural, and functional. Every text, the discourse of every occasion, makes sense in

88

part through implicit and explicit relationships of particular kinds to other texts, to the discourse of other occasions (275).

Lemke uses intertextuality to express both a generic relation between two texts and a relation of one text to a specific previous one. To illustrate the first of these two kinds of relation between texts, the 'text-type' relation, Lemke gives the example of a story which has the organisational structure of an Aesop's fable. This story-text relates generically and structurally to previous text or texts. To illustrate the second kind of intertextual relation, between one text and a specific previous text, Lemke gives the example of the functional relation of a 'rejoinder' to an argument on the previous day. (A single conversation is seen as one text, unlike Beaugrande and Dressler's 'least mediated' intertextuality, where each interactant contributes with a separate text.) This 'rejoinder to yesterday's argument' continues a dialogue, but there is a time lapse. Although a single ongoing conversation is not construed as intertextual, Lemke acknowledges that it is difficult to determine what constitutes one text. This leads her to suggest the likelihood of similarities in the relations between elements of a single text and between intertextually related texts:

When yesterday's argument is resumed today, we are inclined to speak in terms of the relationships of two discourses, tow texts; but when the argument of ten minutes ago is renewed, we may talk in terms of two episodes of a single discourse, two parts of one text. It may well be that the same kinds of relationships exist but across stretches of 'a' text and between 'distinct' texts (276).

In addition to genre and function, other bases for intertextual relations are theme and structure. These kinds of relation, generic, thematic, structural and functional, are complementary, not exclusive: the 'rejoinder' may have (is likely to have) thematic links with 'yesterday's argument', and so on. Hence possible relationships between texts cut across Beaugrande and Dressler's exclusive categories (monitoring ongoing conversation, allusion, text-types and text-type combination, summary).

Lemke uses intertextuality to address the problem of which texts 'go together' and how they do so. In principle, any similarity between texts may be the basis for an intertextual relations. The different kinds of relation between texts - generic, thematic, structural and functional - are the 'basic interlocking modes of intertextual connection' (281). These relate texts sharing a 'thematic system' and also relate texts as actions in sequence. The thematically related texts are more strongly connected if they are also functionally related (e.g. in citation) and even more if they are also structurally related (e.g, in quotation) etc. The sequentially connected texts are more strongly related if they share the same theme etc etc.

Lemke, then, uses intertextuality as a generalisation to cover any kind of connection between texts. In employing the concept, he points out the insufficiency of 'register' to account for relations among texts: 'The notion of register ...does not capture many of the socially most important kinds of relationship among the texts made in a community' (280). In his discussion of how register is used to account for these relations, he distinguishes between what linguists think is important, and what the producers of the language analysed themselves think is important. It is linguists, Lemke says, who view relations between texts in terms of abstract concepts (field, tenor, mode), so that separate occurrences of the same kind of discourse are related. The example given is of two arguments on the same night, one in New York and the other in Toronto: 'two otherwise unrelated pairs of husbands and wives argue face-to-face about whether the husband's mother should be invited for the long holiday weekend' (279). Lemke asks: 'In what circumstances in our community might they be used or presented as a pair?' He suggests that only linguists would make a connection between such utterances by separate pairs of participants in this way (i.e. on the basis of similarities in role relationships, etc). In contrast, the language users themselves would be indifferent to linguistic categories of field, tenor and mode. The kinds of intertextual relation significant to them would be rather different:

What of the relation between the New Yorkers' argument of that night and their argument on the same theme the night before? or two hours before? or a year ago? What of the relation of that night's argument text to the discourse of a phone call between the husband and his mother the day before, or the after? or to a letter from the wife to her sister discussing family problems and written later that evening or to the poem the husband wrote to his mistress the next morning about love and understanding? or to the text of their wedding ceremony? (179).

These different texts are related in that they cite one another, explicitly or implicitly, but they differ in terms of field, tenor and mode.

In making this distinction between linguists' and participants' views of significant relations among texts, Lemke is pointing out that there are relations among texts which are important to actual language users which the concept of register does not cover. In framing the discussion in terms of an opposition between what linguists think and what 'real people' think the case is overstated, however. Although the participants in the two hypothetical argument could not make a link between the two texts produced (obviously, since they could have no way of knowing of the other text's existence), it is not

90

the case, as Lemke implies, that husband - wife arguments about mothers-in-law coming to stay would not be viewed as intertextually related by non-linguists (at the very least, comedians and the writers and viewers of soap operas). The author assumes that in relating them he is engaging in 'metadiscourse' which is 'a legitimate practice in our community', which he presumes is not available to non-academics. However, 'Kitchen sink' drama and sexist practices in comedy and soap opera texts depend precisely upon knowledge of such texts as a type. They are evidence that this kind of connection is made (and perhaps Lemke's anaphoric reference to these two texts as 'the mother-in-law arguments' (280) is evidence that he is drawing upon knowledge of this 'text-type' himself, as much as upon knowledge of situational components of field, tenor and mode).

One aspect of his proposal is an attempted generalisation which is simply confusing. Lemke views the 'intertextual principle' he outlines at work within texts as cohesion: 'One can recognize in this intertextual principle a fundamental mechanism also seen to be at work over short stretches of text' (281). He introduces his proposal for a 'unified inter/intratextual analysis' (289) by noting a broad parallel between her outline of intertextual relations and Ruqaiya Hasan's work on lexical and grammatical cohesive devices: thematic relations between texts can be compared with lexical cohesive tie within a single text; the 'activity-pattern syntax of social action' by which one text connects to another prior to it can be compared with grammatical cohesive ties (281). As it stands. this simply undermines the analytic strength of any distinction between inter- and intra-textual.

More fruitful in my view is his investigation of degrees of explicitness in signalling the relation of one text to a previous one. Verbatim replication is one of the 'traditional notions' of text linkage that he considers. This will serve as the main illustration here. A verbatim repetition is cohesively linked to the original by reiteration. The reiterative items are thematically and structurally related to the items they repeat. A verbatim chunk of one text in another, in the absence of any explicit cue to a functional relation, is plagiarism or (more charitably) coincidental repetition of someone else's words. For the function of a repetition to be made explicit, it requires some device cuing a functional relation. The presence of quotation marks and/ or a reporting clause would indicate the chunk's function as a projection of another's words. So a repetition of part of one text in another is seen to function as quotation or plagiarism/ coincidence according to the presence or absence of some device used to signal a functional relation to another text. (See the section on projection in Ch.5 for detailed attention to quotations, reports and related phenomena.)

Intertextuality is most 'strongly foregrounded' when the two texts are cohesively linked and the functional relations between them is made explicit. Conversely, 'backgrounded' intertextuality refers to the constant bridging between texts in the operation of thematic systems, which are manifested in

91

cohesive relations: 'We thus move from strongly foregrounded intertextuality ...to our normal and continuous operation of thematic systems which bridge between otherwise structurally unconnected texts' (291).

Lemke's treatment has three main strengths. Firstly, the connections between texts are assumed to be actively constructed: 'relations between stretches of text and social actions are not "there" to be discovered already given, but are constructed by us with the available relations and structures of our semiotic systems' which are 'abstract representations of the kinds of relations and structures habitually made by us in our texts and actions' (291). Secondly, it covers more than just overt cuing of a prior text or belonging to the same register: a generic text -type relation. Intertextuality can be present in various forms. Thirdly, dependent on the last point, it draws in the notion of foregrounding. There may be an intertextual relation which is not foregrounded:

> An isolated, possible relationship between stretches of text will be termed a weak relation, and the passages weakly related, until we find either, and hopefully both, that there   are other relationships between the passages that support a coherent or stable meaning relation between them, making them strongly related, and/or that this same kind of relationship recurs between other passages in the text(s), so that we can consider it a strong or foregrounded kind of relationship in between the text(s). (182)

Foregrounding, then, is the key to 'significant intertextual relationships' for Lemke. Foregrounding is the answer he gives to his own question: 'How do we tell, or argue, which of all the possible relations between two stretches of text are the ones in terms of which ...the participants, including ourselves (even as analysts) are making the most significant inter/intratextual meanings?' (282).

Lemke is assuming here that notions of significance are shared by data-subjects and analysts. Why should this be the case? He is also assuming that foregrounded connections are the important ones to look at, that the relations worthy of attention by the analyst are those which are foregrounded. I suggest that, for the critical language analyst, those relations which are not strongly cued, or even mis-cued, may be equally of interest. For, while the foregrounding of prior texts tell us something about the history of the current text as claimed by the writer, prior texts/conventions provide sites for examining the naturalized, taken-for-granted elements of the text, which the writer does not so much claim as assume.

Halliday and Hasan

The concept of intertextuality appears briefly in two books in the Deakin University Open Campus course on language in education: Michael Halliday and Ruqaiya Hasan (1985) and Gunther Kress (1985). Halliday and Hasan use intertextuality in a restricted sense to refer to that aspect of context which is specifically textual. The context of a text includes a set of previous texts. Halliday and Hasan give as an example the way a lesson in a classroom builds on ideational elements of a previous lesson (in the development of topics, in working with concepts which are previously agreed on). In addition to ideational elements, there is also cross-reference to earlier texts in interpersonal and textual features encountered. Halliday and Hasan mention in this respect, types of logical sequencing recognized as valid, and formulaic expression: 'unspoken cross-reference of which everyone is largely unaware' (47). We can relate this 'unspoken cross-reference' to Bakhtin's single-voiced word, the word which is 'unaware' of containing two voices. In this Halliday and Hasan's account differs from Beaugrande and Dressler's, in which intertextuality is ultimately a form of procedural control. In a more pervasive sense of intertextuality than the continuity of topic, repetition of formulaic expressions and so on mentioned above, they also suggest that 'the Classroom' can be seen as one text:

> the entire school learning experience is linked by a pervading 'intertextuality' that embodies the theory and practice of education as institutionalized in our culture. There is a sense in which the classroom is one long text, that carries over from one year to the next and from one stage of schooling to the next.

Halliday and Hasan use intertextuality to capture a sense of continuity in the learner's experience in school. They say that these experiences are linked by an intertextuality which embodies the theory and practice of education. The 'embodiment of theory and practice' sounds very much like 'discourse' in the social theoretical sense of the term. As in Kristeva's use of intertextuality, they are expressing the continuity of practices from one text to another. Unlike Kristeva's development of Bakhtin's writing on the 'literary word', they do not say that every word is a cross-reference to another text, or that a speaker's word is split between the moment of its utterance by the speaker and previous utterances of it, whether the speaker knows and intends this or not.

For Halliday and Hasan, texts form part of the cultural context which determines the form new texts will take. They use intertextuality to capture this dialectical relationship between text and context: 'the text creates the context as much as the context creates the text'. They do not say that the text creates the person as much as the person creates the text.

Kress

Kress's use of intertextuality is also very brief. He employs the term to place a limit on teachers' expectations of pupils' creativity. In Kress's use of the term, intertextuality pervades every text:' Every text contracts ...relations of INTER-TEXTUALITY with a vast network of other texts. Within and out of that network of relation the writer constructs a new text which everywhere bears the marks of its intertextual relationships' (1985: 49). He uses the term to discuss the task of genre-learning; in particular to explain why it is that teachers should not expect genre-learners to be capable of originality and creativity in their writing. Kress distinguishes between authors and writers. Authors have rights of ownership of their texts and claims to creative originality; learners of genre, such as schoolchildren, do not. According to Kress, a writer does not create a text but assembles it on the basis of experience of other texts. She cannot produce a text 'in her own words': 'Writers have the words - and more importantly, the systematic organisation of words - given to them by the discourses and genres of which they have had experience' (49). Schoolchildren, he concludes, should not be expected to be authors.

In Kress's account, intertextual resources are implemented 'neutrally' by the writer who 'assembles' a text: 'The materials available to the writer ...are all those texts which have a relationship of relevance to the particular text which is now to be constructed. Every text constructs such relations of INTER-TEXTUALITY with a vast network of other texts' (49). This 'relationship of relevance' covers intertextual connections both to prior texts and to genres and discourses. Kress states that writers assemble texts using prior texts and knowledge of genre, and that learners cannot produce original work.

Summary

What intertextuality seems to provide for linguists is a view of texts in a complex mesh of relationships with other texts, something like the 'associated fields' of statements according to Foucault, in which discourses in the social theoretical sense come into being. All four of the linguistic usages of 'ntertextuality I have considered contain 'prior text' and 'convention' senses of some kind. Intertextuality is used to highlight the pressure of prior texts on current ones; highlighting intertextual properties stresses the importance of the relation of one text to a previous one. Intertextuality is also used in some way to refer to conventions: to discuss 'presupposed' conventions of genre, to characterize the continuity between texts sharing socially-defined sets of language conventions, or the discontinuity within one text embodying more than one text-type/genre.

Two of the treatments of intertextuality I outlined go into considerable detail. Beaugrande and Dressler's textlinguistic approach offers categories for analysis of different kinds of intertextual connection. The most pervasive and complex conception of intertextuality in linguistics is offered by the most recent contribution outlined. This was Lemke's systemic linguistics treatment. His objective of finding a way of identifying kinds of relationship between texts that are significant to participants, rather than the analysts' constructs of field, tenor and mode, leads him to problematiZe the assumed autonomy of registers and to a detailed discussion of the different kinds of intertextual connection possible and the varying degrees to which they can be foregrounded. Halliday and Hasan and Kress point towards a similar view, but do not develop it at any length as Lemke does.

Below is a summary of linguistic uses of intertextuality:

Beaugrande and Dressler:

- Conversation as intertextual. Used to account for interactants' metadiscoursal actions: their employment of procedures for intertextual monitoring of the texts of others;
- Allusion as intertextual. Used to look at authorial stance (parody etc.) and the relation of summary to original;
- Multi-functional texts as intertextual. Used to account for the mixing of different text-types (narrative etc.) in a single text.

Lemke:

- Generic, thematic, structural and functional relations between texts as interlocking modes of intertextual connection;
- Introduces indeterminacy and degrees of foregrounding of connections, and an 'intertextual principle' in intra-text cohesion.

Halliday and Hasan:

- A text's connection with specifically textual element of context as intertextual. Used to account for continuity of topic and 'unspoken' cross-referencing;
- Totality of a discourse-type as intertextual. Used to discuss the continuity of practices across texts: the embodiment of theory and practice of an institution in a pervasive intertextuality linking specific texts produced in it.

Kress:

- A text's network of relations with other texts as intertextual. Used to set a limit on teacher's expectations of 'creativity' from genre learners.

Three forms of intertextuality

For my overall view of intertextuality I refer to Kristeva's original anti-humanist conception. According to Kristeva, a text is embedded in history and society as an intertextuality. She uses the term to express the concept of a text as the intersection of a heterogeneous array of texts and semiotic practices, in the process of which subjectivity is constituted. Drawing on the range of conceptions and uses in semiology and linguistics reviewed in this chapter, I will establish three forms. For this approach I draw upon Lemke's general claims about an 'intertextual principle' and foregrounding. In his account, intertextual connections are made all the time and differ in the degree to which they are foregrounded.

The first kind of intertextuality covers the connection between two or more interlocutors' texts in interaction. I will call this form of intertextuality covering relations between the proximate texts of interlocutors its *interaction* sense. At the other extreme, intertextual relations of another kind hold between a text and the multiple conventions enacted in it and between its diverse elements. I will call this the *heterogeneity* sense. It relates to the situational context from which language-users draw on discursively constituted knowledge: the institutional and societal dimension of context.[10] Midway between these two extremes, a text may intertextually connect with external texts; that is, with texts outside the current interaction. Texts have an associated field of other texts which they refute, cite, comment on, repeat etc. In Fairclough's model of discourse as social practice, language-users draw on prior texts from the specifically textual element of context relating to interactional history, which he calls intertextual context. I will call this the *prior text* sense of intertextuality.

Interaction

In order to examine how a text is embedded intertextually in history and society, we need to consider how it comes into being in the social practice of discourse. The word 'text', Hodge and Kress (1988: 6) inform us, 'comes from the Latin word *textus*, which means "something woven together".' Spoken interaction consists of two or more interweaving texts, each utterance settling into the 'intertextual' context of the utterance following it, as the interaction proceeds through time. In the production and interpretation of discourse, language users draw upon these texts as resources. Following Beaugrande and Dressler, an intertextual connection is found in face-to-face interaction. In the case of a written text, since the reader is not contributing as a producing participant, the interaction between participants takes place through the writer's text alone. But writer and reader are not the only possible interactants in written discourse. Consider the following 'street interview' taken from *Jackie* magazine, where a 'position statement' followed by an outraged exclamation and a question followed by an enthusiastic response are coherent only if interpreted as adjacency pairs:

EMMA
'I'm down here trying to find a denim jacket - this one isn't mine - it's only on loan! I like The Smiths and The Blow Monkeys, and I hate Howard Jones and Royalty.' Treason! Outrage! The most exciting thing that's happened today? **'This!'**

In the interaction sense of intertextuality, then, face-to-face communication, whether real or imaginary, is inter-textual (following Beaugrande and Dressler's textlinguistic approach). Each speaker produces a separate text; interactants intertextually connect their utterances. So exchanges (Q-A pairs etc.) are intertextually connected; a question uttered by one person becomes part of the answerer's 'intertextual' context. This intertextuality may be meta-linguistic, as in the repetition of someone else's words (such as in the well-known ethnomethodological example 'What d'you mean, "What d'you mean"?') or in formulations, which are rewordings (e.g. 'so what you're telling me is...'). In a discourse analysis approach, note by contrast, a communicative event involving two or more voices is generally seen as a single text. For instance, Sinclair and Coulthard-type discourse analysis imposes a framework of structurally connected speech functions onto interaction. In this type of language analysis, face-to-face interaction is described in terms of intra-textual connections in the sequential progression of verbal actions.

Prior text
Distinct from the immediate sense of intertextuality as the interaction of two people, a particular text may have connections with a specific historically-prior text. We can say that a prior text is 'embedded' in a current one. Perhaps the most obvious manifestation of a text connecting with a prior text is in quotations and reports. Forms of speech representation involve explicit meta-linguistic reference to a prior text external to the ongoing act of communication; the connection of one text to another is foregrounded. Another way an external text is drawn into discourse is through presupposition, as both Fairclough and Culler suggest (Pêcheux refers to similar phenomena as 'the preconstructed'). Fairclough observes that presupposition 'triggers' may signal the placement of some antecedent text in 'intertextual' context. Culler refers to a presupposed earlier statement in his discussion of a Blake poem. As the connection to an antecedent text becomes more attenuated, the words of that prior text become less easily attributable to a producer: a real or imaginary person.

Beaugrande and Dressler's and Culler's treatments of allusion as an intertextual phenomenon fit into this prior text category. In the literary form known as parody, for instance, the target (the text or

97

text-type being parodied) is placed in 'intertextual' context. The target of the parody may be either a specific historically antecedent text, as when Donne parodied Marlowe (see Beaugrande and Dressler section), or an imaginary one, as when Baudelaire parodied a poetic sub-genre in which poems were likely to contain 'a temple with bosky shades' and such like (see Culler section). Baudelaire's poem may not connect with a specific historically prior poem in 'intertextual' context, as Donne's does, but it claims to. As in the case of presupposition, the connection between current and antecedent text is not meta-linguistically cued, and its source is not explicit.

The prior text kind of intertextuality, then, relates to MR of interactional history, real or otherwise. Quotation is its most foregrounded form.

Heterogeneity

So we have looked so far at intertextuality in the weaving together of two texts in interaction and at intertextuality in the relations between a current text and another text in the 'intertextual' context. In the production and interpretation of discourse, language users draw upon other resources. This is where the heterogeneity sense of intertextuality comes in. These resources include knowledge of the types of practice (convention) which determine actual practices (actions). The heterogeneity sense of intertextuality concerns an 'external' connection not to some single supposed discoursal action, of which a prior text is the trace, but to the accumulation of past actions in discourse as a convention. A single text contains diverse conventions, for which readers draw upon MR relating to the institutional and societal dimensions of context. To interpret Baudelaire's poem, for instance, a reader draws upon a wide range of MR for interpretive procedures: knowledge of conventions of poetic genres, of the activity of poetry and a heterogeneous collection of 'world' knowledge not specific to literature.

Beaugrande and Dressler's textlinguistic treatment of multi-functional texts as intertextual phenomena fit in this category; in this view a text may contain a constellation of text-types. Barthes' semiological examination of a text as a mesh of interweaving codes also fits here. Among the diverse conventions which make up a text's heterogeneity, we can include on the one hand discourse-types and genres shaping discourse, and on the other knowledge of conventional kinds of action enacted in them, topics taken up etc. As Fairclough (1989a: 12) observes:

The entities which are articulated and rearticulated in discourse are not all fully-fledged codes or registers; they may be smaller scale entities such as turntaking systems, lexicons which incorporate particular classifications, generic scripts for narratives (for instance), sets of politeness conventions, and so forth'.

98

Conventions which are brought into interpretation inevitably have an intertextual quality. For instance, schemata, frames and scripts that provide 'stereotypical patterns against which we can match endlessly diverse texts' (Fairclough 1989: 164) are accumulations of past practices for text organisation. These have developed over time in intertextual relations constructed across texts to become conventional. A convention is the accumulation of past actions; the enactment of a practice is intertextually connected to all previous enactments of that practice. Providing a common basis for these resources, the concept of intertextuality blurs the boundary between them. It does this by presenting texts as essentially dialogic. Both actual (or imaginary) prior texts and pre-existing conventions contribute to a text's dialogic constituency. In this way, the boundary between overtly dialogic interaction and the conventional is blurred: a social convention comes about as the cumulative result of historical events. Its continuity is created by the intertextual connection of past interactions. See, for instance, the view of 'the classroom' as a single text, in which Halliday and Hasan take 'the classroom' as one, chronologically very long, text built up of a great many smaller texts.

As we have observed, however, the *heterogeneity* sense of intertextuality attends to diversity in types of discourse within a given discourse. Against Halliday and Hasan's impression of historical continuity, which gives an illusion of a single linear progression and development of classroom discourse up to the present day, we need to set diversity and discontinuity. Classroom discourse has been shaped by diverse discourses, including those of the social sciences. In addition to this, on any occasion it is likely to contain elements of yet other discourses, some of which may be from the teacher's viewpoint disruptive. For instance, discourses relating to femininity and consumerism intrude into the classroom in girls' clothing, posture and wearing of cosmetics (and indeed in the magazines read under the desks).

In sum, an interpreter needs to draw upon a wide range of conventions to make sense of a text. These include:

i)   discourse-types determined by orders of discourse;

ii) activity-types, topics and action-structures (represented in schemata, frames and scripts respectively) which may occur across discourse-types within an order of discourse;

iii) sets of conventions for realizing level of formality, the particular classification schemes embodied in lexical choices etc., which may occur across discourse-types.

Conclusion to Part 1

So where does this leave us? All the conceptions of intertextuality set out in some way to undermine the illusion that a text is self-contained. What intertextuality does is introduce history and heterogeneity to the text. The *interaction* and *prior text* senses of intertextuality do this by fracturing the boundaries between text and context. What counts as a single text: does two-party interaction contain one text or two? In reportage, is the text reported part of the text reporting it, or is it a separate text? And similarly in the case of a presupposed text, is it part of the text in which it is embedded, or is it outside it? (The answer to each of these questions is that it is both.) Intertextuality in its *interaction* and *prior text* senses enables us to fracture the boundaries of text, interaction and 'intertextual' context; what counts as a 'single' text is indeterminate. Intertextuality in its *heterogeneity* sense enables us to view a text as a heterogeneous collection of conventions and to view these conventions enacted in discourse from a dialogic perspective as accumulations of past practices.

'Voices' in the text: a text population

Through intertextuality we can look at the subjectivity of language-users. From an intertextual perspective, a text is a "textual dialogue". It consists of a mesh of intersecting 'voices'. In looking at the interaction of texts in the form of face-to-face interaction, we necessarily attend to the interaction of speakers - literal voices here, with no need for scare quotes. Here, looking at text-intersection *is* looking at speaker-interaction, since identification of functional relations between speakers' texts requires knowledge of what the speakers are doing and who they are. That is, we need to know what speech roles are assigned to speakers in exchanges.

Intertextuality presents us with a far more complex textual dialogue than this, however, containing other 'voices' less immediate than those heard in speech itself. In written or spoken discourse, the addressee does not interpret a simple linear sequence of text produced by a single addresser. The text she encounters is a tissue of 'living voices': an intertextuality. The speaker or assumed writer is just one of these 'voices'. Some of these 'voices' will be foregrounded and attributed to a real or imaginary character, others will not. For every prior text there is a presumed originator of it as an utterance: some 'speaking' character who is set up as its producer, whether or not this is made explicit. When the writer is representing the purported words of another, she may distance herself from the character. She may interfere with this 'voice' to various degrees, in terms of faithfulness to the 'original' and her alignment to it as a reporter, i.e. whether she goes along with the words represented or

100

criticizes them. As the connection to an antecedent text becomes more attenuated, as in presupposition, the words of that prior text become less easily attributable to a producer: a real or imaginary person.

A third kind of 'voice' relates to the heterogeneity sense of intertextuality. Subject positions and relations between them are set up by the diverse conventions drawn into discourse that I discussed in the Heterogeneity section above. A single individual is placed in a wide range of subject positions. She is not an autonomous entity who exists independently of these positions and social relations; she is constituted in the act of working within various discourse-types, in enacting conventional kinds of activity, taking up topics, etc. For example, in interaction people take up subject positions specific to discourse-type, 'ventriloquizing' for them. The subject positions available provide conventional 'voices' for people to use. In taking up a subject position at a particular point in discourse, a person speaks in a conventional 'voice': one may speak as a parent, as a judge, teacher etc., drawing upon fashions of discourse associated with family interactions, the classroom, the courts etc.

Any text is necessarily a tissue of voices, containing an indeterminate 'population'. It is not the product of a single author; the author herself is multiple, fragmented, and part of the 'population' of a text. It is likely to contain 'external' prior texts, but these are unlikely to be attributable to a specific, clearly defined set of characters. In summary, these 'voices' relate to the three forms of intertextuality as follows:

Intertextuality	*'text population'*
Interaction	- Interactants
Prior text	- Characters
Heterogeneity	- Subject positions

With intertextuality, then, we can view the complex of intersecting 'voices' with which the reader is involved. It opens up a 'space' in texts. In the next section I suggest that this 'space' may be examined using the concept of coherence.

'Intertextual coherence'

In this final section of part 1, I establish how I use intertextuality and the related notion of 'text population' in conjunction with coherence.

In interpretation, the reader constructs coherence. In the act of reading a text, she is constructing coherence on the basis of the textual cues manifest to her and her own knowledge and expectations. She must make connections between textual elements within it. She must also, as we have seen in chapter 2, make connections between the text she is interpreting and the context in which she is doing so, including the subject positions the context imposes upon her. An interpreter uses what Fairclough has called 'discoursal commonsense' (see chapter 2) to make discourse coherent. In interpretation, she draws upon a wide range of textual and contextual resources. Textual cues, the textual element of MR, provide a focus for attending to the other MR a reader brings in for discourse-interpretation. This in turn provides a way of looking at the construction of subjects in the act of reading.

In chapter 3 I have presented a view of a text as an intertextuality. The concept of intertextuality provides a view of the language-user's relation to text in which she is multiply positioned as a social subject - what is known in the voguish jargon of post-structuralism as the 'dispersion of the subject'. A text is the product of the social activity of discourse. It is not unified and contains external elements. These external elements may not be seen by readers but are nevertheless needed to read a text *as* unified; that is, they are needed for coherence to be possible at all. In terms of this intertextual view, readers are involved in 'textual dialogue'. Reading discourse as coherent requires the construction of inter-textual connections as well as involving the construction of linear, intra-textual coherence. These inter-textual connections draw into discourse the 'voices' that I referred to above as interactants, characters and subject positions. Through 'inter-textual coherence', then, the process of interpretation constructs subjectivity.

PART 2

Practice: critical analysis of the construction of consumer femininity in a two-page feature from *Jackie* magazine

Introduction to Part 2

What I propose to do in this practical half is to carry out an exploratory analysis on a single consumer feature. The sample I have chosen is a 'beauty feature'. This is a two-page consumer feature on lipstick, which I chose because it addresses femininity directly and because it contains elements of different kinds of article - interviews with 'ordinary' people, historical and statistical details about commodities, instructions for their use.

In concluding Part 1 I introduced the notion of a text population. This notion is my attempt to reduce the field of analysis covered by intertextuality, as I have presented it, to manageable proportions. The notion provides the framework for a simple method of analysis which I will present in Part 2. Before presenting the range of features to look for to examine three kinds of 'voice' in my chosen sample I need to give some attention to the journalistic order of discourse: the social and discoursal context of my sample. In the framework itself I shall be looking for points of focus for stimulating critical awareness of the synthetic sisterhood offered by women's magazines.

4

The mass media and *Jackie* in general

Discourse in the mass media

Cavalcanti (1983: 47-48) describes reading as non-reciprocal discourse. The process of discourse takes place on the reader's terms; she can stop whenever she wants to, skip over fragments, re-read others etc. The reader is in control of the discourse. Hodge and Kress (1988: 50-51) make a similar observation about mass media discourse. A television viewer is in the same sense in control of the discourse, being free to switch off, talk over it or listen silently. However, the mass media bestow a position of power on producers, as I will go on to explain.

In contrast with, for example, face-to-face interaction, media discourse is one-sided. Producer and interpreter are sharply divided and distant from one another. So, even though mass media texts are always read or viewed by actual people, because of this distance, as Fairclough (1989: 51) observes, producers cannot 'design their contributions for the particular people they are interacting with'. Addressing a mass audience imposes: i) on mass media producers, the need to construct an 'ideal subject' as addressee; ii) on mass media interpreters, the need to negotiate with the position offered in the ideal subject:

> since all discourse producers must produce with *some* interpreters in mind, what media producers do is address an *ideal subject*, be it viewer, or listener, or reader. Media discourse has built into it a subject position for an ideal subject, and actual viewers listeners or readers have to negotiate a relationship with the ideal subject.

The need to construct an ideal subject bestows a position of power on the producers of mass media texts. They have the right to total control over production, including over what (and how) kinds of representations of events are included. In the construction an ideal subject as addressee, they are in a position to place assumed shared experiences and commonsense attitudes as givens to a mass audience. Actual addressees, in the targeted audience, are likely to take up the position of ideal subject sharing these experiences, attitudes etc. In addition, the producers of mass media texts, unlike their addressees,

106

are professional practitioners. Producers do not work blind in postulating subjects as addressees; mass media discourse is targeted for specific audiences. These have been measured by market research practices: discourse technologies which shape subjects.

The non-reciprocal discourse between producers and audience is not the only form of discourse in the mass media. Producers of mass media texts are involved in two-way discourses in the production process. Magazines are produced in a complex of interactions within the institution of journalism (between editor, staff, company management, printers, etc.), and between publisher and financial backers. Other two-way discourses in the production of magazines involve readers as active participants (see below on audience-participation in *Jackie*).

Mass media and synthetic communities

The ideal subjects postulated by mass media producers are constructed as members of communities. I will briefly attend here to the kinds of community constructed in women's magazines and advertisements. The targeted audience of women's magazines is addressed, simply by virtue of its femaleness, as a single community. As Ferguson (1983: 6) says:

The picture of the world presented by women's magazines is that the individual woman is a member not so much of society as a whole but of her society, the world of women. It is to this separate community that these periodicals address themselves. Their spotlight is directed not so much at the wider 'host' society, as at that host society's largest 'minority' group: females.

This bogus social group has been described as a kind of surrogate sisterhood by various writers (e.g. McRobbie 1978, see next section; Ferguson 1983; Winship 1987). Within this female community, which appears to ghettoize women, magazines are targeted for different socio-economic groups. *Jackie* magazine had a predominantly working-class, young teenage readership.

In advertising, the actual individuals addressed are being offered membership of some specific 'consumption community' (Leiss et al. 1985) or 'totemic group' (Williamson 1978). Advertisements serve to cultivate market consciousness, so that the products themselves are commodities 'asking' for consumption, which are however silent about the material processes and conditions of their production.[1] As well as informing consumers about what is available, they also present to audiences the concept of communities based on the consumption of commodities. Advertisements offer consumers membership of imaginary communities; to belong, we only need to buy and use products. Drawing on the work of Boorstin (1973), Leiss et al. (1985: 53) explain that in the transition from industrial to consumer culture: '"consumption communities"..., formed by popular styles and expenditure patterns among consumers, became a principal force for social cohesion in the twentieth century, replacing the ethnic bonds that people had brought with them to the industrial city'. Similarly, Williamson (1978: 47) observes that advertisements construct totemic groups,[2] based on consumption: 'They create systems of social differentiation which are a veneer on the basic class structure of our society'. Advertisements construct subjects by interpellating actual individuals as addressees who are members of these groups or communities. According to Williamson, mass audiences are interpellated as members of these groups by simulated direct address in advertisements. Her observations here are similar to Fairclough's on the synthetic personalization practiced in a variety of types of discourse used to address mass audiences. In the *Jackie* pages I inspect in chapter 6, producers and readers are set up in a synthesized 'sisterly' relationship in a community based on the consumption of lipstick.

The women's magazine as discourse-type

In the institutional order of journalistic discourse, the mass media is structured into a range of discourse-types. One of these is the women's magazine. This section briefly outlines the historical development and characteristics of this discourse-type. I will focus on elements of particular relevance for the *Jackie* 'beauty feature' analysed in chapter 6 and refer back to Smith's conception of a 'discourse of femininity' presented in chapter 2.

A mixture of instruction and entertainment in publications specifically for women goes back to the late 17th century. A precursor of the modern women's magazine was a publication for aristocratic women called *Ladies' Mercury*, which first appeared in 1693. This publication is generally named as the first women's magazine (White 1970, Ferguson 1983, Winship 1987). It contained a range of elements: fiction, readers' letters with editorial response, fashion articles and plates, educational tracts. In the mid-nineteenth century magazines aimed at a middle-class audience were produced. As Ferguson (1983: 16) remarks, these publications 'offered their readers - the socially climbing wives and daughters of the professional and business classes - guidance about what to buy, wear and do to further their aspirations'. The first women's magazine for a middle-class readership was *The Englishwoman's Domestic Magazine*, which began in 1852. Like its upper-class predecessors, it contained a mixture of fiction and non-fiction, written text and illustration. Unlike them, it dealt with activities and topics relating to women's unpaid work in the domestic domain of the home. The non-fiction element consisted of informative and facilitating features: recipes, instructions for knitting their husbands' socks, articles on the management of servants, and so on.

Another new element was the presence of advertisements. White (1970: 66) reports that women's periodicals in 1800 carried very few. By the end of the century advertising was the main economic support of the magazine industry:

The expansion of the women's periodical press was in fact being underwritten by advertisers from the 1880s onwards, and this dependency greatly enhanced the status of the advertising industry and modified editorial attitudes to advertising copy. The older generation of publishers had consistently frowned on advertising as an obnoxious nuisance and treated it with suspicion and contempt.

As magazines have become dependent on advertising revenue, editors have been 'forced into a position first of neutrality, then of concurrence, and finally of collusion' (115). In the late 1930s, magazines began to carry consumer features, in which advertising is presented as part of the editorial content. The women's magazine as a discourse-type has developed in patriarchal and capitalist social relations.

Some observations made by Winship on the 'tone' of early publications shed some light on changes in the kind of addresser-addressee relationship constructed in magazines. She describes *The Englishwoman's Domestic Magazine* as 'coolly formal and distant in tone' and contrasts it with the 'more relaxed and less intimidating style' (1987: 27) in publications in the 1890's which were aimed at the lower middle class end of the market. It is more than a matter of level of formality, however. The aim of achieving 'an active and intimate relationship' with readers became specific editorial policy in a new publication in 1910 called *My Weekly* (produced, incidentally, by D.C. Thomson). Looking at the preface of the first issue quoted at some length below (from White 1970: 88), we can see that for the editor it involved claims to know and understand the reader and the offer of friendship, in order to encourage readers to correspond. The editor claims:

My editorial experience has left me impressed with one thing in particular and that is the need for what is called the 'personal note' in journalism ...I will try to appeal to readers through their human nature and their understanding of everyday joys and sorrows. For I know well that, in order to get into active and intimate relationship with the great public, one must prove oneself fully acquainted with its affections, sentiments and work ...I understand, too, how that human nature is strangely and pathetically eager for friendship. I mean willingly to become the confidant of readers, young and old, rich and poor, who can safely trust me with their ideas and difficulties.

This change in the producer-audience relationship synthesized spread to other publications and is now a defining characteristic of women's magazines. As Leman (1980: 63) observes, 'direct address, commanding both intimacy and identification still constitutes the principal tone of women's magazines in Britain. The significance of this tone of intimacy and confidentiality is that it attempts to establish some kind of 'sisterly' relationship between magazine and reader'. Leman also notes that 'the notion of team work is an important part of the mythology of the magazines spanning the decades' (77). The producer is often set up in a group identity as an editorial team. For an example Leman quotes *Woman's Own*:

We've enjoyed putting this number together - we hope you'll enjoy reading it (Sept 1937)

The women's magazine is a discourse-type with historical continuity in an accumulated repertoire of practices. White (1970: 299) describes the modern women's magazine as 'a nationwide "Women's Institute", providing an arena in which women can meet, exchange ideas, views and experiences, and derive from it mutual help and support'.

Content and presentation are conventional. Interpersonally, magazines are informal and friendly, constructing the 'tone of intimacy and confidentiality' I referred to above (exceptions, such as in the 'small print' of advertisements, are also conventional). The internal structuring of magazine texts follows an easily recognisable format; the distribution of written text, photographs and illustrations is highly conventional. Turning to content, activities and topics taken up in magazines relate to women's domains of work and leisure. Of particular relevance here is women's work on their own bodies as objects to be looked at, using commodities: a range of activities involving women as consumers who 'feminize' themselves. Magazines for women contain informative and facilitative elements on 'fashion and beauty' products and their use, which appear both in advertisements and in consumer features produced by the editorial. They are sites of the rearticulation of what Smith calls a 'discourse of femininity'.

According to Smith (1988) the kinds of appearance offered to women as ideals to work towards are constructed in the mass media. Through mass media texts, the 'feminizing' practices of the film, cosmetics and fashion industries influence people's standards of appearance. An important element of 'feminizing practices' is the concept of a woman as a visible object requiring work. In advertisements and 'do-it-yourself' sections of magazines for women, women's bodies are frequently itemized as areas requiring separate attention with separate products (e.g. 'Are you doing enough for your *underarms*?' 'How high is your *bikini line*?'). This itemisation has been intensified by an endless proliferation of

110

products by manufacturers and accompanying discrimination of colours, skin types, hair types, and so on.

The women's magazine as discourse-type sets up subject positions for the individuals it impinges on. As I said above, interaction through mass media texts is asymmetrical and puts producers in the powerful position of setting up addresser and addressee. But it is difficult to determine who this empowered producer 'really' is. Who is it that actually wields the power inhering in the construction of ideal subjects in magazines? The employees who put the pages together work under specific editorial control. Any directives from the editor will have been shaped in a more general way by company policies shaping the production of the magazine. Leman (1980: 66) observes:

A set of professional routines is established which are seen as essential, defining characteristics 'inherited' and operated by those involved directly in the production of the magazines. The routines are assumed as 'givens' in terms of journalistic practice, constituting the very fabric of 'woman's magazine' and are rarely acknowledged as the bearers of a particular value system. Decisions made or inherited by those in the front line of production of the magazine are unlikely to challenge the defining conventions which shape the product and structure its ideological message'.

The major determinant is profit. As White (1970: 181) observes, modern magazines are 'run according to strict business methods and are answerable to cost-accountants'. The publishing industry makes profit with magazines through advertising revenue. Manufacturers, in addition to buying advertising space in magazines, also provide publishers with goods and information about their products in return for 'free' advertising in commercial features.[3] Magazines are constructed within the relationship between staff, publisher and manufacturers; more specifically, between those who actually produce the magazines (the editor and her staff, the story writers, photographers and printers), publishing company management and the promotion departments of manufacturing companies. So, the kinds of 'raw material' made available to the copywriter and paste-up artist on the editorial staff are determined not just by their editor but, in the case of *Jackie*, by the relation of DC Thomson & Co. Ltd. in capitalism with manufacturers such as Gibbs Pharmacuticals Ltd. (who make acne cream and advertised regularly in *Jackie*), EMI (who make records and provide 'exclusive' interviews with popstars), etc. The practices enacted in the pages of magazines tend to be naturalized. For instance, practices involving the commodification of femininity and the patriarchal practice of classifying

111

women in terms of their appearance and desirability are likely to appear natural in *Jackie*. The beneficiaries are, among others, cosmetics manufacturers.

The women's magazine as a discourse-type is not homogeneous. In common with advertising, it is shaped by discourses of the social sciences. Publishers offer manufacturers profiles of readerships as consumption groups, for which they have access to sophisticated market research methods. Magazine production is economically dependent on advertising revenue and the women's magazine has developed as a discourse-type hand in hand with the discourse of advertising. White (1970: 206-7) writes of the pressure put on editors by higher management to cooperate with advertisers in stimulating consumption in the 1950s. An (anonymous) employee she interviewed in 1965 relates:

Magazines have been forced to beg for advertising and to make concessions in return that would have been unheard of fifteen years ago. There has been a continual battle between management (run largely by accountants) and Editors, who have the interests of their readers at heart and wish to retain their autonomy. The fight is a losing one. Content is planned with an eye on what will best serve the interests of the advertiser. ...The whole policy of a magazine is nowadays dictated from above where only the advertiser counts. Because of the limitations on space, and the necessity of filling it to the advertiser's advantage, the order has gone out to dispense with 'general interest' features in favour of 'home service', because manufacturers do not like content which cannot be used to sell goods. An editor has to comply, despite the knowledge that readers' interests are much wider.

Women, who have a lifelong concern with the marketplace as wives, mothers etc, are placed in the subject position of consumer in diverse discourses. This subject position of consumer is part of the femininity offered in women's magazines, since 'feminizing practices' involve the use of products. The definition of femininity as a mode of consumption has intensified in these publications since the consumer boom of the 1950s. As Winship (1970: 39) says, 'women reading the ads and consumer features in their magazines have been caught up in defining their own femininity, inextricable, through consumption'.

One area of expansion was the cosmetics industry. Another was the magazine industry itself. *Jackie* magazine appeared in 1964 when Dundee publishers D.C. Thomson & Co. Ltd. picked up on the new 'teenage consumer' market. *Jackie* ceased publication in 1993.

112

Jackie magazine

Jackie has a combination of characteristics of adult women's magazines and girls' romance comics. Hollings (1985) reports that when it first came out it contained fewer romance strips than existing romance comics such as *Marty, Boyfriend* and *Valentine* and gave space to articles on fashion and cosmetics, a regular problem page, etc. Hollings remarks that '*Jackie* proclaimed itself to be the comic for "go-ahead teens", and was concerned primarily with being fashionable and exciting, unlike comics such as *Valentine*, which appeared to be still rooted in the 1950s (28-9). Like other magazines, it contains elements of diverse discourses, the most pervasive of which is advertising. Others include medical discourse in articles and the problem page, on puberty and occasionally pregnancy in recent years, legal discourse in the 'small print' and counselling on emotional development.[4] The publishers' general editorial policy has been described by a former employee, Julie Davidson (1977: 109), as 'Unionist, monarchist, patriotic with a capital UK and push-button Tory on every issue from race to riches'.

Jackie frequently contains features about 'ordinary' people. The editorial staff has apparently real contact with teenagers (not just readers). DC Thomson claim that their communication with actual teenagers is one of the reasons why Jackie has been, and continues to be, so successful (Hollings 1985). There are frequently features consisting of or containing street interviews with people flea-market shopping, etc: their likes and dislikes. These interviewees tend to be slightly above the magazine's targeted age range of 12 to 14.

The editorial also has contact with actual readers through various channels. These include the letters page, the problem page (letters may be tampered with and some may be invented), 'make-overs', occasional 'dreams come true' (e.g. being a primary teacher for a day in 18.3.89), 'giveaways'. All these involve the reader in becoming a writer, an action initiated by the magazine but making the reader an active participant. The editorial staff is dominant, in control of the interaction, its terms and outcome. They are gatekeepers; restricted numbers make writing-in a competitive bid for goods ('make-over', 'wish-fulfilment', 'free gift') or for access to the problem page and letters page. Space puts a restriction on the number of letters appearing in print with a response.

A 'synthetic sisterhood'

McRobbie's main arguments in her CCCS paper on *Jackie* are that the magazine presents its teenage readers with a '*false* sisterhood' and imposes an ideology of femininity which isolates women from one another:

1) The girls are being invited to join a close, intimate sorority where secrets can be exchanged and advice given; and 2) they are also being presented with an ideological bloc of mammoth proportions, one which *imprisons* them in a claustrophobic world of jealousy and competitiveness, the most unsisterly of emotions, to say the least (1978: 3).

She claims that *Jackie* 'addresses "girls" as a monolithic grouping' so that differences in the social conditions experienced by actual girl readers are obscured. Her observations were made about magazines from 1974 and 1975. In chapter 6 I will present a more detailed account of the community synthesized in *Jackie*. Rather than going on to analyse her illustrative examples, I will turn for evidence of this sisterliness to the more recent pages that I've chosen for my sample.

    Jackie presents its readers with an ideology of adolescent femininity, in which the emotional is of paramount importance (14). McRobbie picks out four semiological codes (following Barthes 1967) to characterize this ideology. These are Codes of Romance, Personal Life, Fashion & Beauty and Pop Music. They are drawn from a pre-existing culture of femininity, already impinging on girls' lives, as part of the semiological 'raw material' (12) in the production of *Jackie*. In/through these codes, girls are being addressed as a group with shared interests in romance, makeup, fashion and so on. The codes thus construct a teenage girl grouping: it is their simple existence in the magazine which is the main substantiation for MacRobbie's claim that *Jackie* offers an 'invitation' to its teenage readers to join a bogus social group. Apart from this she refers, in an impressionistic and unsystematic way, to the 'tone' (hesitancy, etc) taken up in the Codes at specific points. More generally, she refers to the informal ''lightness' of tone' (9) characteristic of the magazine and the 'sisterly' social position taken up by the producer. It is her loose observations about the interpersonal dimension - the informal 'lightness' and 'sisterliness' of the magazine - which I shall examine next.

    By 'lightness' of tone McRobbie is referring to those properties of *Jackie* which distinguish it as a magazine, rather than a 'serious' text: the presence of advertisements, use of colour, choice of layout etc. We can include for her in this category the fake slang, 'the language of pop, and of Radio I disc jockeys' (170, i.e. a variety associated with leisure and unseriousness, in the comic strips of the period she examined. She also refers to informality and an unserious attitude towards subject matter, which presumably contribute to *Jackie*'s '"lightness" of tone', although McRobbie does little more than suggest these in passing, forcing her reader to try to draw them out for herself from the occasional fragments of text given as examples.

    The main example of a 'sisterly' relationship is in the problem pages, discussed in the chapter on the Code of Personal Life. The characters set up as the 'counsellors' replying to readers' letters,

Cathy & Claire, are likened by McRobbie to older sisters. Here she refers to the tone of the letters as 'friendly and confidential' and of the replies to them as 'both "jolly" and supportive' (27).[5] In the problem pages in general, she observes 'a tone of secrecy, confidence and intimacy evoking a kind of female solidarity, a sense of mutual understanding and sympathy' (29). She identifies Cathy & Claire as part of girls' feminine education, their function being to advise the less experienced by distributing 'useful feminine knowledge' (29) about how to behave.

McRobbie's references to 'sisterliness' are frequent. My sample text is a beauty page, so for a further example I will look at the 'sisterliness' she observes in the Code of Fashion & Beauty. The beauty pages contribute to the feminine education offered, giving instructions for the 'beauty work' which is an essential part of 'good grooming'. As McRobbie points out, this is necessary for their future entry into the job market. She also notes that in learning self-maintenance, girls are lifting part of the load of domestic reproduction from their mothers. The beauty pages provide a kind of do-it-yourself manual, educating girls in self-maintenance, or 'grooming', which includes becoming a feminine consumer:

Here the girls learn how to apply mascara correctly, pluck their eyebrows and shave their legs. Each of these tasks involve *labour* but becomes fun and leisure when carried out in the company of friends, besides which when the subject is the self, and when 'self-beautification' is the object, narcissism transforms work into leisure. Nonetheless, this labour, carried out in the confines of the home (bedroom, or bathroom) does contribute, both *directly* and *indirectly* to domestic production, itself the lynchpin upon which the maintenance and reproduction of the family depends (41).

The anonymous authors are passing on essential knowledge about using artificial aids to match up to accepted standards of feminine appearance (which are standards of beauty). McRobbie notes 'a tone of hesitancy and apologetics' about the skills being passed on, which she puts down to a double-edged guilt, openly acknowledged, surrounding the inevitable failure to match up to conventions of beauty *without* resort to cosmetics and the dishonesty of achieving it *with* them. In the beauty pages she studied, the skills being passed on concern 'how girls can get the best of both worlds by deceiving men into believing they are naturally lovely, whilst subtly hiding their own flaws'. The authors go about passing on this guilty knowledge by first adopting 'a tone of sisterly resignation evoking comfort and reassurance' (40) and then offering specific actions as a practical solution: actions involving the use of commodities. McRobbie is deeply critical of these pages for offering consumption as the only way of compensating for inevitable failure in the natural beauty stakes, and their lack of any query about 'why women feel ashamed or embarrassed by this "failing"'. This kind of neglect is certainly unsisterly. For the issues of *Jackie* McRobbie looked at, I think it provides a far more convincing argument for their harmfulness than the enticement to competitiveness and mistrust she claims.[6] In the two pages I go on to examine in chapter 6, however, I can detect no shame at all! So much the better.

5

Analytical framework

Analyzing the text population of a consumer feature

I concluded chapter 3 with three forms of intertextuality and a view of coherence as an intertextual phenomenon. I claimed that to read a text as coherent a reader needs to construct intertextual connections with elements outside that text and argued that these connections draw into discourse an indeterminate 'population' of voices, corresponding to the Prior text, Interaction and Heterogeneity forms of intertextuality: i.e. Characters, Interactants and Subject positions. Taking the three forms of intertextuality separately, in this chapter I present a framework for a detailed three-stage analysis of the text population of a mass media text. Stages one and two simply involve picking out traces of prior text and interaction in order to build up a catalogue of characters and interactants in the text population. Stage three is an examination of activity, topic etc. which is intended to draw attention to the multiple subject positions assigned to producer, and correspondingly to the interpreter, and the relationship constructed between them. This chapter provides points of focus for locating members of a mass media text population. I have selected features for examining text populations in the pages of women's magazines, with particular attention to the synthetic sisterly communities they offer.

I begin with prior text as a matter of convenience, since in the inspection of interaction intertextuality I will need to refer to various characters, set up as producers of prior texts, as interactants in simulated interaction. Looking for the characters first simply saves repetition. Examining the series of texts a text belongs to involves attention to its interactional history: previously occurring texts, actual or supposed. As Fairclough (1989: 156) says, 'discourses and the texts which occur within them have histories, they belong to historical series, and the interpretation of intertextual context is a matter of deciding which series a text belongs to'. To take the example of an interview in a magazine: an earlier discourse related to the printed text is the interview itself, whether or not it actually took place. Many other 'subsidiary' texts preceding the printed text, from discussions with the editor to memos to the printers, form part of its intertextual context. In fact, they are not really subsidiary, since the discourses in which they occurred were part of the production process.

117

In the second section of this chapter I will attend to ways of identifying prior texts which are 'embedded' in another text. I use Halliday's work on projection to provide a descriptive approach to the reportage of characters' words or thoughts. Then I present a range of textual features which 'trigger' presupposed prior texts, for which I draw principally on Levinson (1983) and Fairclough (1989).

One way discourse, such as a printed text, may contain synthetic two way discourse; that is, representations of interaction between characters, or between writer and character, or writer and reader. Intertextuality, I have argued, introduces uncertainty over what counts as one text. Hence, in looking at linear sequences of utterances in discourse it is not clear whether we are looking at intra-textual connective values ('internal' connections between elements of one text) or inter-textual connections between texts and external texts in the 'intertextual' context.

In the third section I examine grammatical cues to Speech functions and the speech 'roles' these assign to interactants. For this I draw upon Halliday's description of 'Clause as Exchange'. For specific attention to speech functions foregrounding the producer-audience relationship in mass media discourse, I refer to observations by Montgomery (1988) on 'foregrounding the interpersonal' in the talk of a Radio 1 disc jockey. I then turn to sequences of utterances, by means of which interactants construct coherent stretches of discourse. For this I employ the concept of an adjacency pair from ethnomethodology (e.g. Schegloff 1968, Schegloff and Sacks 1974).

Next I present ways of examining the diversity of a text in terms of the heterogeneity of conventions brought to it for coherent interpretation. As I established in chapter 3, an interpreter needs to draw upon a wide range of conventions to make sense of a text. What I present is a range of focusing points for critical awareness of the complex of subject positions offered to women by magazines and the synthetic sisterhood they construct. I will focus on elements of particular relevance for the analysis of consumer features in magazines for teenagers.

In producing discourse, an addresser always speaks from a social position; she necessarily establishes a social identity for herself and at the same time some relationship with her addressee. In mass media discourse, the positions available for interactants are not interchangeable; as I argued in chapter 4, interaction through mass media texts is asymmetrical and puts mass media producers in the powerful position of setting up addresser and addressee. Magazine discourse contains a repertoire of entertaining and instructive elements: advice on 'personal relationships' in articles and problem pages, romances, letters pages, articles filling in what advertisements leave out about how to use products, etc. These involve participants in activities with expected purposes and topics likely to be recognized by readers. In participating in them, both producer and interpreter take up subject positions (other subject positions are determined by broader societal and institutional considerations).

118

In the fourth section I present a range of features for characterising the multiple subject positions taken up by an addresser and the relationship she constructs with her addressee. Generic scripts taken up in activities provide a focus for analysing the construction of the social identities and relationships of participants. Other points of focus for identifying 'voices' taken up by a producer are frames, classification schemes and grammatical choices, certainty modality and projector's alignment.

I turn specifically to ways of examining a mass media producer's identity as a friend and the synthesized friendly relationship set up between producer and interpreter in mass media discourse. Certain kinds of feature proliferate in advertising and the mass media in general which contribute to synthetic personalisation and the establishment of an informal friendly relationship between the producers of mass media texts and their audience. We have already begun to examine some of these in the section on the interaction sense of intertextuality. The direct address, 'expressive' utterances and interjections discussed there contribute to the simulation of friendly face-to-face encounters in one-way discourse in the mass media. Here I outline other elements that contribute to the synthesis of friendly personae for the writer and like-minded reader. I begin by attending to the pronouns *you* and *we/us*, which are of particular interest in describing simulated friendly interaction in mass media texts. I then propose points of focus for examining how the producer establishes herself as a member of the same social group as her audience. For this I attend to relational and expressive values of vocabulary and refer back to prior text analysis.

Prior text/Character

Projection and cause enhancement

'Speech representation', report of a contents from outside, is realized explicitly in the clause complex by features with connective value which cue an intra-textual connection. These cues, which take the shape of projection structures, requiring verbal or mental process verbs of some kind, are meta-linguistic. Speech representation can be seen as a benchmark (but certainly not any kind of norm) in terms of explicitness in the intertextual quality of a text. Imaginary texts appear within a text, sometimes in speech marks; the writer is writing about prior texts (for simplicity only, I am assuming here that 'speech' representation is written). We can also identify simulated dialogue set up between characters constructed in a writer's text. Speech representation is encoded, in experiential meaning, as a Contents. In an explicit simulation of face-to-face interaction, a writer will tend to introduce a great many metalinguistic elements. The external text and the 'voice' purported to produce it are focused on by the writer and foregrounded for the reader by means of a proliferation of explicit cues to this prior text.

The grammatical relationships set up in clause complexes and in nominal groups are cues to intra-textual connections. My purpose in attending to them here however is not to examine the 'internal' connectivity of texts in itself but to investigate certain kinds of intra-textual connection which set up clauses as prior texts; ie. which have an intertextual connective function. It is in order to find cues to prior texts in intertextual context, and the characters thereby 'conjured into existence' in discourse, that I attend to these grammatical concerns: to relations within clause complexes, and to embedded clauses functioning as elements of nominal groups.

Halliday (1985) distinguishes two fundamental kinds of logical-semantic relationship in clause complexes. These are Expansion, which concerns 'representations of the world', and Projection, concerning 'representations of representations'. For the most part I attend to projection: 'the logical-semantic relationship whereby a clause comes to function not as a direct representation of (non-linguistic) experience but as a representation of a (linguistic) representation' (227-8). After looking at projection, I suggest one kind of expansion which seems to have a projection-like function.

These kinds of relationship are realized by five basic types of clause complex: expansion as either elaboration, extension or enhancement; projection as either locution or idea. They may be realized in either paratactic or hypotactic constructions. Examples of each of these basic types of clause complex are in the table below (they are taken from Halliday's Table 7(2) on p197):

	Paratactic	Hypotactic
Expansion:		
elaboration	John didn't wait; he ran away.	John ran away, which surprised everyone
extension	John ran away, and Fred stayed behind.	John ran away, whereas Fred stayed behind.
enhancement	John was scared, so he ran away.	John ran away, because he was scared.
Projection:		
locution	John said: "I'm running away."	John said he was running away.
idea	John thought to himself: "I'll run away"	John thought he would run away.

Projection structures provide cues to intertextual connections. When explicit, they contain a primary projecting clause and a secondary projected clause. Through Projection, other people's words ('locutions') or thoughts ('ideas') are brought into a text: 'the secondary clause is projected through the primary clause, which instates it as (a) a locution or (b) an idea' (196). When foregrounded, locutions and ideas are projected either by quoting, where the wording of the projected clause is represented, or by reporting, where the meaning is represented but not the wording.[1] (The projected clause in a Report may be finite or non-finite.) Typically, projecting clauses of locutions and ideas contain verbal process verbs and mental process verbs respectively. In each case metalinguistic elements place a text in the intertextual context, setting it up as part of the interactional history of the discourse and its participants. A projecting clause may project a prior text which is either a Statement / Question about information or an Offer / Command about goods&services (see next section for these four distinct kinds of speech function). Some possible variations are presented in the examples below, some of which have been taken from Halliday's chapter:

Verbal

	Quoting	Reporting
Statement	'Oh dear,' he said, 'I am a silly engine.'	She claimed she couldn't do it
Question	'Can I come tomorrow?' she pleaded.	She asked if she could come the next day.
Command	"Collar that Dormouse!" she shrieked.	She told them to silence the Dormouse.
Offer	'Do have a biscuit,' she said.	She urged him to have a biscuit.

Mental

	Quoting	Reporting
Statement	He's going now, she thought.	She knew that he was going.
Question	'Am I dreaming?' Jill wondered.	Jill wondered if she was dreaming.
Command	'Wait here,' she willed him.	She wanted him to wait there.
Offer		She wanted to invite him.

In all the examples of quoting and reporting above, the prior text is explicitly cued in the projecting clause, by a verbal or mental process verb. A prosodic feature (speech marks in written discourse) often marks off the projected text, especially in quotation. In this case some other verb serving the same purpose may stand in for a verbal process verb (as in the example above, 'She'll go "Will you be quiet!"').

The originator of the projected text is 'textually present' as the 'Sayer' or 'Senser' in the projecting clause, realized by a pronoun or Proper Name. It is clear who is responsible for the prior text; who is supposed to have spoken or thought. Sayers and Sensers may be inanimate objects as in the

121

grammatical metaphors: '*my watch* says it's ten past eleven', '*the sign* says turn left here' and '*this pickle* doesn't want to come out of the jar'.

We can say that the intrusion of an external text and its originator is foregrounded by quoting or reporting clause complexes. However, representations of representations are not always structurally foregrounded. External texts may be embedded in nominal groups, in the form of locutions or ideas as Post-modifiers. In such cases the projecting is done either by verbal or mental process verbs in embedded clauses or by members of noun classes that can project: namely, verbal or mental process nouns. Some possible embedded projections are:

Verbal process verbs:
Locution: The character who shrieked 'Collar that Dormouse!' was the Queen of Hearts.
    Her who goes 'Will you be quiet!' is coming.

Mental process verbs:
Idea: The character wanting to be queen was Alice
    Knowing the opposition is the first stage.

Verbal process nouns:
Locutions: the assertion that such an effort is necessary to salvation
    the decree that all tax concessions should be abolished

Mental process nouns:
Ideas: the general feeling was that holders of sterling were about to sell
    her desire to be a queen.

The originator of the prior text projected by a verbal or mental process noun may not be explicitly cued. Only the fourth example contains any textual cue to this necessary connection (in this case, a possessive article) with some character set up as the source. More often we need to rely solely on contextual information to locate the source of the *belief, decree* etc. This kind of construction, where projections are embedded as post-modifiers of verbal or mental process nouns,[2] can be highly mystificatory. It tends to de-personalize, presenting the viewpoint of one set of people as if it were universally held (see especially the third example). It always requires a certain amount of work on the part of the interpreter to see that a prior text is being projected.

Quoting, reporting and the projection of embedded locutions and ideas, then, are set up by Halliday as the same kind of activity: the representation of one text in another. They are all metalinguistic, but vary in the degree to which the projected text and its supposed originator are foregrounded.

Halliday includes a further kind of projection, one which unlike the others cannot be called metalinguistic: statements not of locutions or ideas but of de-personalized 'facts'. Facts may be projected in embedded clauses that are functioning as post-modifiers in nominal groups, as embedded locutions and ideas are. Unlike them, there is no mental or verbal process noun 'doing the projecting'; a projected fact 'involves neither mental nor verbal process but comes as it were ready packaged in projected form' (243). Instead of a mental or verbal process noun, the Head carries a 'fact noun' (e.g. *case, grounds, probability, evidence, rule*). Or, unlike embedded locutions and ideas, the clause may itself be functioning as a Head:

the fact that Caesar was dead
that Caesar was dead   was obvious to all

A fact is the 'idea of a phenomenon', something in people's heads rather than in the world. Fact projections are as it were on the borderline between projection (the representation of people's words and thoughts) and expansion (the representation of things, events), such that 'I can see that the boats are turning' is a representation of fact and 'I can see the boats turning' is a representation of reality (containing an existential presupposition that 'the boats are turning'; see chapter 2). As Halliday says, 'facts are in a sense intermediate between "metaphenomena"' (quotes and reports) and first-order phenomena, or "things"'. (249) The interesting thing about fact projections is that when the projected texts that they put into texts are uncontentious they tend to pass unnoticed (e.g. 'the way fashions in lipstick have changed over the years').

Halliday's treatment of projection covers a wide area. It includes kinds of consideration dealt with elsewhere as presuppositional phenomena. For example, Levinson (1983) gives a range of verbal and mental process verbs in his list of presupposition 'triggers'. These include 'verbs of judging' (verbal process verbs such as accuse), 'factive' verbs (mental process verbs, like regret) and 'verbs of propositional attitude' (mental process verbs e.g. realize). Below are two of his examples of a verb of judging and the presupposition it triggers:

Agatha accused Ian of plagiarism
>> '(Agatha thinks) plagiarism is bad'
Ian criticized Agatha for running away
>> '(Ian thinks) Agatha ran away'

A projection approach is more fruitful. Both these examples contain projecting clauses and locutions. They cue connections with prior texts in the intertextual context ('Ian, you plagiarized!'; 'Agatha, you ran away!'). They also establish the characters Agatha and Ian as Sayers. The projecting clauses contain verbs of reporting; by attending to the choice of reporting verb we can assign certain beliefs to the characters involved ('(Agatha thinks) plagiarism is bad; (Ian thinks) running away is bad').

There is one other kind of clause relation that is worth attention as a possible focusing point for looking at the intrusion of external texts. Some enhancing expansions have a covert projection-like function. In representation of 'first-order phenomena' realized in cause enhancement, the producer may be assuming access to someone else's thought processes and the authority to establish what their motivations were, or will be, in doing something. An enhancement involves the representation of reality; this may be a representation of someone else's reason or purpose. These 'giving of reasons' postulate, but may not specify, a source. The example below is from the reply to a letter in *Jackie*'s problem page from a girl who is apprehensive about 'going out' with a boy because of a scar remaining from a road accident when she was younger. Cause enhancements are often cued by causal connectors, as in the following:

Maybe it's just *because you're getting a little older and a bit more self-conscious about your appearance*? (18.3.89: 30)

The writer here is tentative in her assumption of access to the letter-writer's thought processes. She is helping her to examine these processes. In other cases, the writer may simply 'report' others' motivations (see chapter 6 for examples; in particular, the motivations behind the use of dyes in antiquity by 'ladies').

Within the clause: Verbal/Mental process and Range
Verbal and mental process verbs do not always occur in projecting clauses in clause complexes. There is one other kind of grammatical construction involving them which may set up some 'external' text. Within the clause, Halliday identifies Range as one of the kinds of Participant which can occur with Processes. In the case of verbal processes, the Range element is Verbiage: 'the element expressing the class, quality or quantity of what is said' (137). The following are some of his examples:

He asked a	question
Tell me a	story
She speaks	German

In such cases, verbal process verbs cue the trace of some kind of textual substance in the Range element.

124

On the same principle, the Range element occurring with mental processes can be viewed in this way. A person's thoughts, beliefs, likes or dislikes may be cued within a single clause. The Range element here is Phenomenon rather than Verbiage and deals with what is thought rather than what is said; e.g. 'he likes *fish and chips*'. The boundary between Mental and Behavioural processes is not always clearcut. On the borderline between these two kinds of process are 'processes of consciousness that are being represented as forms of behaviour' (129). One of the examples Halliday gives of a borderline Mental/Behavioural process is '*think* (in the sense of 'ponder')'. These may also have Range elements containing 'texts'; e.g. 'he was thinking of *his next meal*'. Note the similarity between this simple clause element and kinds of mental projection that can appear in clause complexes as projected texts: 'he wondered *when his next meal would be*'; '*What's for tea*, he thought'.

Presupposition

Earlier I presented projection structures as grammatical cues to prior texts in intertextual context. In this section, presuppositional phenomena provide another focus for attending to intertextual context. Unlike projections, presuppositions cannot be accounted for as features of clause complexes. They are not formal properties of texts and may be 'triggered' by a wide variety of textual elements: formal properties which are interpreted on the basis of other MR.

Projections are meta-linguistic (with the 'borderline' case of fact projection) and at their most explicit they foreground the external texts as locutions in projected clauses. By contrast, external texts that are set up as presupposed tend to be backgrounded ideas and may only be detectable when they are encountered by the 'wrong' subject (e.g. 'When you're trying your hardest to impress that hunk in the sixth form...' (*Jackie* 20.9.86)). Presuppositions are a way of setting up shared assumptions and experiences as common ground. This common ground is deniable /contestable, but since it is presented as given it tends to pass unnoticed. The presupposed idea that 'there are times when you are trying to impress that hunk in the sixth form' is presented as uncontentious and attributed to the targeted audience of twelve to fourteen year old schoolgirls. But it jumps out at a reader outside the targeted audience.

But it is not, as it may seem at first glance, just that the presupposed idea is false. In Levinson's (1983) pragmatic approach to the analysis of presupposition, truthfulness is a necessary property of the 'successful' presupposition. He uses the example below to show how a presupposition trigger can 'fail' (Levinson includes factive verbs, verbs of judging etc as presupposition triggers; see above on projection):

125

The student said he hadn't *realized* that Wales was a republic.

He rejects the presupposition 'Wales is a republic' 'because we happen to know it is not the case' (215). To decide whether it is truthful and 'succeeds', he draws upon a universalized notion of background knowledge which he assumes his reader shares (see Talbot 1987). By contrast, for Vestergaard and Schroder (1985) and Stubbs (1983), presupposition and the related concepts of entailment and implicature provide a way of identifying lies set up as implicit content.

Presuppositions provide an interesting point of focus for identifying what is taken as given in discourse. The example below is from a photostrip in *Jackie* about a girl who argues with boyfriends. She worries about it, and a boy addresses her with the following:

I think *your problem* is you haven't met *the right boy before*

This mental projection contains three presupposed ideas: two existential presuppositions ('you have a problem', 'there is a right boy') and a temporal contrastive ('you've met the right boy now'). It is not enough to consider whether 'it happens to be the case' that the girl has a problem, whether there are such things as right boys and, if so, whether she's met him. More to the point are questions such as: where do the presuppositions come from, what kinds of subject do they postulate, what is the significance of such ideas being placed in readers' intertextual context, who benefits from their taken-for-granted quality? Some teenage readers were asked what they thought of this utterance.[3] Perhaps attending to the presupposition cued by *before*, they said the male character was 'setting himself up', which would explain why he places this presupposition in the intertextual context. The presupposed ideas also come from the anonymous author and reflect the sense of responsibility and concern over relationships elsewhere, in the 'problem pages' of girls' and women's magazines.

Fairclough (1989:158) observes that the use of presupposition provides producers of mass media discourse with an 'effective means of manipulating audiences through attributing to their experience things which they want to get them to accept'. In advertising, one way of promoting a commodity is to establish the need for it by placing this need in intertextual context, as in the following advertisement for hair remover: 'Are you doing *enough* for your underarms?' The producers are attributing the presupposed idea that 'you are (or you should be) doing something for your underarms' to potential consumers.

Presuppositions can be placed in intertextual context by being contested in the negation of positive assertions, as in the following extract from *Blue Jeans* in Fairclough (1989: 158-9) (we have seen part of it already in chapter 2):

126

No amount of make-up and hair stuff will turn you into a glamorous chick if your gnashers aren't in good condition. It's nothing to be proud of if you haven't been to the dentist for the past five years - you're only asking for trouble. Treatment *isn't* the equivalent of listening to Nana Mouskouri records and your dentist *isn't* there to give you nightmares and inflict unnecessary pain on you... (24.5.86)

Fairclough asks what the motivation is for making all these negative assertions (since the same points could have been made positively) and observes:

> The writer is evidently using negatives as a way of implicitly taking issue with the corresponding positive assertions *(treatment is the equivalent of a week of listening to Nana Mouskouri albums,* etc.). But that would be a rather peculiar thing to do unless their assertion were somehow connected with this discourse. What the writer in fact seems to be assuming is that these assertions are to be found in antecedent texts which are within readers' experience.

A similar point is made by Vestergaard and Schroder (1985: 26-27) concerning negative claims made about products in advertising texts; for example, the claim that a moisturing cream is 'not greasy or sticky'. Similarly, a negative assumption may be placed in the intertextual context. A producer may use emphasis in a positive assertion to contest a consumer's pessimistic assumption (e.g. 'You *can* achieve a long lasting look!' presupposes that 'you think you *cannot*').

Presuppositions are cued by a wide variety of textual features. I will not attempt to cover them exhaustively, but refer only to features occurring in the sample text in chapter 6. The definite article in 'the right boy' cues the existential presupposition 'there is a right boy'. 'You have a problem' is more accurately described as an 'attributive' presupposition, as I have represented it in an attributive relational clause. The possessive article *your* cues a presupposed attribute. A 'temporal contrastive' presupposition is cued by *before*. (Another example, suggested by Levinson, is *any more*, as in 'They don't make gobstoppers any more'.) The presupposed idea in the 'hunk' example is in a subordinate temporal clause marked by *when*. Various adverbials cue presuppositions which might be called entailments: *not/ often, always, all the time, enough* (e.g. *not often* 'presupposes' *sometimes*). Other cues to presuppositions are comparative adjectives *more, subtler, other* etc (e.g. 'More for your money at...'; 'other brands don't match up').

Interaction/Interactants

Speech functions and speech 'roles'

Halliday (1985: 68) examines the Interpersonal component of meaning-potential at clause level under the heading of 'Clause as Exchange'. This provides an interactive perspective on grammar:

> the clause is ...organized as an interactive event involving speaker, or writer, and audience. ...In the act of speaking, the speaker adopts for himself a particular speech role, and in so doing assigns to the listener a complementary role which he wishes him to adopt in his turn. For example, in asking a question, a speaker is taking on the role of seeker of information and requiring the listener to take on the role of supplier of the information demanded.

In the clause as exchange, we can identify grammatical realisations of relational and expressive meaning in speech functions. Halliday identifies four basic kinds of speech function: Offers, Commands, Statements and Questions. These differ according to the type of exchange, the role of the clause in it and the 'commodity' exchanged. By the 'role' of the clause in the exchange, Halliday means the basic relationships of giving-receiving and demanding-complying that are realized in speech functions. In an exchange of the 'goods & services' type, the commodity exchanged is a proposal, which may be realized as Offer or Command; in the 'information' type, what 'changes hands' is a proposition, realized as Statement or Question. This is summarized in Halliday's figure below:

Role in exchange:	Commodity exchanged: (a) good s& services	(b) information
(i) giving	'offer' Would you like this teapot?	'statement' He's giving her the teapot
(ii) demanding	'command' Give me that teapot!	'question' What is he giving her?

Of course, form and function are not always matched. The textual realisation of some action in grammatical mode may not match the action being performed: commands may have the textual form of questions ('is the window open?') etc. Halliday's example of an Offer in the Figure above is realized by the interrogative mode.

Since 'giving', 'demanding' etc. are actions performed by people and speech functions are merely traces of these actions, I take what Halliday designates as the 'role' of a clause in an exchange to be rather the experiential value we can assign to it. I reserve the term 'role' for the function/position in the exchange which that specific Contents assigns to its producer/ interpreter. By looking at the basic kinds of speech function realized in the clause, we have begun to examine grammatical features as cues to the identities and social relationships between people in interaction: i.e. as cues to Interactants' 'roles'.

These four primary speech functions, as Halliday says, are 'matched by a set of desired responses: accepting an offer, carrying out a command, acknowledging a statement and answering a question':

		initiation	expected response (& discretionary alternative)
give	goods&services	offer	acceptance (rejection)
demand	goods&services	command	undertaking (refusal)
give	information	statement	acknowledgement (contradiction)
demand	information	question	answer (disclaimer)

In addition to inspection of primary speech functions, sometimes a finer analysis of the function of an utterance will be needed. Turning specifically to mass media discourse, some useful observations have been made by Montgomery (1988: 94) on the spoken one-way discourse of a Radio 1 disc jockey. Montgomery observes the frequency in radio talk of 'response-demanding' utterances (Questions and Commands) and 'expressives' e.g. Congratulating, Apologising, Commiserating, Criticising:

...what's the gossip today?
...can you see that?
...stop that it's dirty!
...poor dear with a name like that
...it's plagiarism fellas come on that's two day old story

These contribute to the simulation of two-way discourse: 'To treat the audience as if they were in visual contact with the speaker, available for greeting and capable of responding to the discourse, is to construct a sense of reciprocity even in its absence'. 'Expressive' and response-demanding utterances are common in *Jackie* magazine. Two examples are a criticism in a horoscope: 'What a rat you've been recently. Isn't it time you stopped thinking about yourself and treated the people around you a bit better? (18.3.89: 17)' and an editorial greeting: 'Hi again, you lot!' (20.9.86:2). They are also common in advertising, as in the simulated personal address with Questions in this headline from a car advertisement:

The best thing in your life?

Is he four years old, the image of his Dad and destined to captain England?
(with accompanying photograph)

Other features contributing to 'a sense of reciprocity' in radio discourse that Montgomery examines are short shifts of speech role within the speaker's Statements as infomation-giver (which he refers to as shifts in 'speaker alignment'). These involve short interjections in spoken discourse - occurring in separate tone units - which he calls Interpolations. Interpolations are often response-demanding or 'expressive' utterances. Here are two of his examples:

Statement: ..er Lisa   Lisa Counter
Interpolation: (heh)   (poor dear with a name like that) ...

Statement   Uranus in Sagittarius
Interpolation: (please please)
(Statement):   is urging and even compelling you to
                    sever a few ties
Interpolation: (oo that could be painful couldn't it)

Below are three fragments from *Jackie* (18.3.89). The bracketed remarks in them seem to be simulations of such interpolations:

...now's the time to throw away any old broken bits of make-up you have lurking in your drawers (!) and treat yourself...

'Grimm's Tales' features Rik in a luminous cabin telling (would you believe it) Grimm's Tales (hence the title!)

Hmmm, I must admit I just adore that mauve vest! (Hur hur!)

Adjacency pairs

Kinds of utterance that occur in pairs (Question-Answer, Statement-Comment, Greeting-Greeting, Complaint-Apology and so on), which contribute to the orderly organisation of talk, are intertextually connected. The two utterances connect together, forming a small two-part exchange in an adjacency pair. The two separate components of the adjacency pair have 'internal' connective properties: the first pair part *sequentially implicates* the second pair part; the second pair part is *conditionally relevant* to the first pair part.

Why have it both ways? Because structures of this kind may be simulated in one-way mass media discourse. When we are attending to spoken discourse, it is more usual to take the texts that speakers weave together as one text. But when representations of interaction appear in written discourse this becomes difficult to do, since we need to consider them both as elements of one text and as separate speakers' texts. Consider the following samples of written discourse printed in *Jackie*. They were taken from a page full of reconstructed interviews with shoppers at Greenwich Market[4] and display the connective properties of single texts. We can interpret them with ease as a single coherent stretch of discourse, but each connected utterance is a separate text:

Statement: I'm down here trying to find a denim jacket - this one isn't mine - it's only on loan! I like the Smiths and The Blow Monkeys, and I hate Howard Jones and Royalty.
Comment: Treason! Outrage!
Question: The most exciting thing that's happened today?
Answer: This!

Statement: I'm only here by mistake - I got off the bus too early on the way to a friend's house. I am very pleased though, 'cos I've stumbled on a pair of ski pants which actually fit me!
Comment: Hmmm.
Question: A teensy bit large aren't they?
Answer: 'Course not.
Statement: My ambitions are to travel the world and to go on an archaeological dig...

Since these are reconstructed interviews, the utterances I have identified as Statements can also be interpreted, despite the absence of Questions, as Answers. In simulations of interaction in written discourse a 2nd pair part only may be present, conditionally relevant to an absent-but-assumed 1st pair part. In the magazine interviews above, absent-but-assumed first pair parts are the Questions the interviewer at Greenwich market is supposed to have asked her informants. Alternatively, a 1st pair part may sequentially implicate reader-response, as in the examples of response-demanding earlier.

Heterogeneity/Subject positions

Social identities

Scripts. Participants' expectations about how interaction will proceed provide cues for discourse coherence. These can be represented as scripts, which, as the theatrical metaphor suggests, are representations of people's expectations about parts taken up by participants and how relationships will be conducted. Fairclough (1989: 163) describes them as follows:

They typify the ways in which specific classes of subject behave in social activities, and how members of specific classes of subjects behave towards each other - how they conduct relationships. For instance, people have scripts for a doctor, for a patient, and for how a doctor and a patient can be expected to interact.

Scripts are organisational features of discourse of a stereotypical kind and relate closely to features covered in the sections on interaction intertextuality; e.g. a script for interviewing sets up expectations about the kinds of adjacency pair likely to occur and how speaker 'roles' will be distributed. The street interview example above was laid out as a script. Here is an example from a consumer:

MOUTHING OFF
We give you a few lip tricks on how to achieve the perfect pout...
1. When applying foundation take it over your lips, too, to give a good base.
2. Outline your lips first of all with a lip pencil in a shade as close as possible to your lip colour.
3. Fill in your lips with lipstick, using a lip brush for a more professional finish.
4. Blot your lips on a tissue then apply another coat and blot again for extra staying power.
5. Finally, smile and make the most of those luscious lips!

To interpret the text beneath the heading 'MOUTHING OFF' as a single coherent whole we need to draw upon a conventional script: a probable sequence of actions with a certain kind of producer and recipient. In this script the producer is a facilitator, giving a sequence of Commands consisting of directives for the reader's benefit. These are often realized textually as imperatives, as here: 'take... Outline... Fill in... Blot..' etc.. The activity places the producer in the subject position of 'facilitator', initiating the reader into femininizing practices. More broadly, the producer who takes on this 'voice' is a member of *Jackie*'s editorial staff, a journalist whose job is to entertain teenagers and an employee of DC Thomson Ltd.

Frames and classification schemes. Examination of a text as a Contents is part of identifying who its producer is; i.e. what she writes about is part of who she is. Frames are cognitive representations of kinds of Contents and consist of stereotypical notions relating to topics likely to be taken up: 'A frame is a representation of whatever can figure as a topic, or 'subject matter', or 'referent' within an activity' (162-3). The topic-frame in the 'mouthing off' example above is a particular practice with cosmetics. This is cued by a photograph of someone using a lip pencil, followed by the Statement in the orientation: 'We give you a few lip tricks on how to achieve the perfect pout...'.[5] Other knowledge needed relates to the itemisation of the face for separate acts of 'beauty work' and the reader's desire 'to achieve the [presupposed] perfect pout'. We can use frames to account for such implicit assumptions not in presupposition 'pools'.

Similarly, in another text from the same consumer feature the topic is a hairstyle, for which an interpreter needs to draw upon a mental representation, a frame. But we need to draw on other, implicit, frames as well, as in this extract from the text: '*Trying to grow your hair* but getting to that horribly

132

straggly stage?' Here it is assumed that growing one's hair is something one actively tries to do (rather than it happening of its own accord, whether we want it to or not!).

In the above example, it is also presupposed that there is a stage which is 'horribly straggly', for which an interpreter must assume that in this active pursuit of hair-growing one goes through a series of stages. An implicit mental representation drawn upon is taken-for-granted knowledge of 'hair-growing stages'. We can examine such configurations of knowledge by attention to classification schemes. A text may establish systems of classification that may not have been previously encountered but are needed to make sense of the text. Kress (1985) gives the following example of a text that forces its readers to think of new classificatory areas:

Club rules
1 Parents must accompany and take responsibility for their children at all times, unless the child is in the water in an instructed class...
2 Being absent more than three consecutive sessions without explanation to the membership secretary means automatic expulsion.
3 No outside shoes will be worn when in the pool area.
4 Please respect the facilities and equipment, and take particular care with untrained children.
(quoted in Kress 1985: 61-62)

Here new categories are coined through modification with adjectives: *instructed class* opens up a possible set of other classes (*uninstructed, partially instructed, well instructed?*); *untrained children* (*trained, partially trained?*); *outside shoes* (*inside shoes?*). The club rules reposition the parents' views of what constitutes a class, of their children and of their own footwear in new systems of classification in the Waterbabies Club.

Similarly, in advertising, the consumer features of magazines and so on, schemes of classification are set up for us, marking out the world we live in. In women's magazines, classification schemes which proliferate relate to the kinds of appearance or 'looks' offered as standards by the fashion industry and the itemisation of the body as a visible object requiring work. Readers are encouraged to discriminate facial shapes, skin tone and 'problems', hair colour, hair-growing stages, etc. These classificatory areas may be new to readers; encountering them forms part of their initiation into feminizing practices. Each of the areas itemized requires a different product and different treatment. Other important classificatory areas which are essential for a feminine education are the range of commodities needed to approximate the 'looks', for which practitioners need to acquire the ability to make fine discriminations of colour, shape, texture, etc.

Topics, implicit assumptions and classification schemes common in consumer features are concerned particularly with feminizing practices, commodity attributes, multiple choice and availability, consumer-fashion styles and changes.

Grammatical choices. To further examine the 'voices' taken up by a writer, and pinpoint her shifts from one to another, we can look at the functional relations in clauses. The types of Process, Participant or Circumstance in which topics are realized may be characteristic of certain discoursal activities. To give a simple example, there is a tendency for historical narratives to have time circumstantials in adjuncts. Kinds of grammatical choices frequent in advertising copy reflect the focus on a commodity and its availability, rather than the processes of its production. Very often a product may simply be represented with a photograph, captioned with name, stockist and price, without any grammatical relationship formally established between them at all. In clauses, attributive relational processes are common, as in the following from *Jackie* (18.3.89: 35) and the *Radio Times* (8-14.7.89: 92). The Participants in each clause are a product, as the Carrier, and some desirable quality or qualities, as the Attribute:

	Carrier	**Relational process**	**Attribute**
	They	have	no added perfume or colour
so	they	're	ideal for even the most sensitive skins.
	These handy little items	are	perfect for serving food or snacks, as general containers, or as decorative objects.

Another kind of functional relation frequent in advertising and related discourses is Existent | Circumstance. Other features to look for are representations of fashion changes and innovations as acausal and agentless events.

Certainty modality. Modality is attached to speech functions. An aspect of a producer's social identity is her degree of certainty; i.e. whether she is categorical, emphatic or tentative about what she says. These degrees of certainty are expressed in modality. Degree of certainty may be realized by a variety of formal features: principally modal auxiliaries, mood adjuncts and tense. The simple present and simple past carry the modality of categorical certainty. A producer who uses this categorical, 'committed' form is claiming authoritativeness. This commitment may be stressed for emphasis. Emphasis of the modal auxiariary *can* (as in 'it *can* be done') has a similar effect. Examples of a variety of modal elements indicating lesser degrees of certainty are the modal operators *probably, possibly,* modal adjuncts such as *in all probability.* I include projecting clauses which are conventionally interpretable as markers of uncertainty about a statement (i.e. *I think; I don't know if*) as features marking producer's tentativeness or 'hedging'. I also include two other markers of tentativeness identified as hedges (Holmes 1984): *sort of* and *about*. Here are some examples of certainty modality from Jackie:

certainty: 'You know, you would *probably* look great in this Elida Gibbs T-shirt! ..New Harmony hairspray *has* new improved hold and *is* just what you need to get your hair looking super good! So how do you fancy winning one of these T-shirts, a selection of Elida Gibbs products and a really informative booklet called 'Head Start' which *gives* you a guide to hairstyles? (18.3.89)[6]

Alignment as projector. The choice of reporting verb contributes to establishing the social identity of the interactant who projects prior texts. The quoter's or reporter's choice of projecting verb may tell us something about her attitude towards the projected text or towards the person responsible for it. For example, projecting a character's verbal proposition with claimed distances the reporter from reportee. An example of such distancing can be seen in the *Sun* article below: news coverage of a successful court conviction for sexual harassment in the workplace. It is the victim Lisa's projected text which is distanced, not her employer's (the capitalisation is in the original; I have highlighted the projecting verbs in italics):

He *offered* to INCREASE Marnie's salary, help BUY her a flat, and TAKE her to Gibraltar. And Lisa *claimed* she LOST her job after refusing his advances. (19.4.89)

A producer can indicate her attitude towards a projected text or the person responsible for it by other means, such as modification of Sayer/Senser (e.g. '*polite* girls say please!') or realisation of Range (e.g. 'he gave some *excuse*').

Synthetic personalisation and friendship

Pronouns. Synthetic personalisation very often includes direct address of a bogus individual as 'you', so that the audience is constructed as millions of identical 'you's (similar observations about direct address and the use of personal pronouns are made by Fowler et al. 1979). In the extract below, the 'exclusive' *we* identifies the editorial as a team personally addressing *you*, the reader:

We give *you* a few liptricks on how to achieve the perfect pout... (*Jackie* 18.3.89: 35)

Sometimes the use of *you* in simulated direct address is interspersed with its use in an indefinite sense to refer to 'people in general': *you* meaning *one*. The extract below begins by establishing a 'universal' experience, for which the indefinite you is used; then shifts to the synthetic-personal *you*:

> The clock strikes eleven, your tummy rumbles, *you* reach for... CHOCOLATE, of course! Since *we* have no sense of calories here on Extras *we*'re going to take *you* on a tour of some of the most chocolatey bars around! (*Jackie* 18.3.89: 5)

In the first sentence you could be replaced by the 'inclusive' *we*: 'The clock strikes eleven, our tummies rumble, we reach for ...CHOCOLATE, of course!' In the second sentence it could not.

In using the 'inclusive' *we* a writer makes an implicit claim to the right to speak for the reader. This use is common in newspaper editorials, but is less common in Jackie than the editorial team's 'exclusive' *we*.[7]

Since social relationships set up subject positions, the relational and expressive dimensions of meaning are closely related. In attending to the relational values of *you* and *we*, we necessarily attend to their expressive values.

Relational and expressive values of lexis. Relational and expressive values of vocabulary contribute to setting up social relationships and identities; they provide points of focus for examining how a producer constructs herself as a friend in mass media discourse. In *Jackie* magazine, for example, there is a variety of levels of formality. Choice of informal lexical items contributes to setting up a friendly 'chatty' relationship with the reader. The use of informal words (referred to by McRobbie as 'fake slang', e.g. 'great stuff', 'billions and squillions of giveaways', 'choccy', 'dosh', 'vids') is one way a writer may do this (at the other extreme is the formality of the 'small print' e.g. 'kind courtesy', 'default', 'liquidation'). Another is punning word-play (e.g. 'Hair's the latest!') presumably intended to amuse readers. Setting up a particular social relationship also involves setting up identities for the participants in it. For instance, as expressive elements, the informal words construct the producer as someone who uses 'teenage vocabulary'. The *Jackie* writer's use of informal terms that teenagers might be supposed to use establishes her as someone who 'speaks the same language': female and a member of the same general age group and social class.

Punctuation. Jackie abounds with prosodic features, particularly exclamation marks. These tell us something about the writer's identity in that they express some feeling towards the content (e.g. they frequently add enthusiasm to headings: 'Socksess story!' 'Spring into action!' 'Hobby holidays!'). They also help to set up a friendly relationship with the reader. Similarly, scare quotes may be used by a writer to distances herself from a contested term or special usage from some other discourse, or to indicate that she thinks the reader will not be familiar with it.

Prior texts attributable to the reader, us or commonsense. By minimising social distance and making implicit claims to common ground a producer establishes herself as a member of the same social group as readers. In *Jackie*, aimed at a targeted readership of twelve to fourteen-year-old girls, this amounts to the construction of a 'sisterly' identity for the editorial. We can pinpoint claims to common ground by returning to the analysis of prior text intertextuality to see if any prior texts purport to be shared. We can start by looking out for any explicitly shared prior texts, and then attend to others with vague commonsensical attribution (presuppositions and fact projections). For example, in the extract below the *Jackie* writer presents an existential presupposition that is attributable to 'common sense' or 'everybody':

> Compliment [sic] all the great ethnic fashions around just now with a soft romantic style like this one from Schwarzkopf. (18.3.89: 35)

She is setting herself up as the kind of person who takes for granted the presupposed idea that 'there are great ethnic fashions around'. She is also setting up the reader as a like-minded 'fashion-conscious' person. A significant contribution to the writer's establishment of an identity for herself and a friendly, 'close' relationship with the reader is achieved through her claims to common ground, to her assumption of shared knowledge and experiences. In the establishment of this common ground, a 'likeminded' reader is also constructed. Other prior texts attributable more specifically to the addressee add to the writer's impression of 'knowing the reader'. The writer's establishment of a 'sisterly' identity is wrapped up in her construction of an ideal reader and we can say little about the constructed writer without also considering this reader. Prior texts to look out for then are fact projections and presuppositions attributed to the reader, to 'us', or simply to 'commonsense'.

Analysis of a sample consumer feature

Introduction

The sample I have chosen is a 'beauty feature' about lipstick. The two page beauty feature is a combination of advertising and editorial material and is made up of a number of texts. I shall treat it as a collection of five, grouped under a shared heading:

Header: a title and subheading accompanied by a photograph of a mouth with lipstick and a mouth imprint in lipstick (a 'kissprint')

A. Column: a 400 word column of text on the 'kissprint', the origins and historical development of lipstick

B. Testimonials: photographs of four young women with captions giving names and ages, and quotations from interviews about their lipstick use

C. Instructions: instructions on how to apply lipstick; in stages, with photographic illustration

D. Facts&figures: a selection of snippets of marketing information on lipstick

E. Illustrated history: a history of lipstick fashions in terms of six female celebrities, containing six photographs and four segments of text.

The 'beauty feature' is reproduced in full in an appendix. Texts A to E are quoted at the beginning of the relevant section. I have numbered the paragraphs in each text. When I need to refer to individual sentences within a paragraph I will use secondary numbering; so that for example the first sentence of the first paragraph of the column can be referred to as A1.1

First, some brief observations about the photographs. In the lipstick users' Testimonials they are snapshots; in the Instructions, the Header and the Illustrated history they are studio photographs, composed by professionals. Work by media practitioners on the construction of femininity has gone into the visual component of C, the mouth-and-lipstick photograph in the header, and the celebrities in

E. These images of femininity have been constructed by people with professional skills in close-up photography, retouching, the use of greased glass, etc and others with professional skills in the use of cosmetics, in hairstyling and so on. The well-groomed sheen of the film stars, for instance, shows the importance of the photographic studio and the make-up artist for the cultivation of media personalities. Their constructed 'public' images are for media consumption and they have a weight of expertise behind them. Another iconic[1] visual image decorating the feature is a pictorial representation of a disembodied mouth. It is reproduced seven times; the largest of these is floating above the column of text. A1 identifies it as a 'kissprint', and as an advertiser's construction.

I have selected this consumer feature because it contains a range of different elements, and for its attention to history and representing femininity. The *Jackie* editorial is constructed as an entertainer who bestows 'useful feminine knowledge' of which the reader is beneficiary. In the *Jackie* beauty pages, as I will go on to show, producers and readers are set up in a synthesized 'sisterly' relationship in a community based on the consumption of lipstick. I do this by detailed examination of the text population - the characters, interactants and subject positions 'inhabiting' the feature - using the framework for analysis of prior text, interaction and heterogeneity intertextuality given in chapter 5.

For each text I first establish the cast of characters, discussing the contents of the prior text produced by each character and the feature cuing it. This analysis draws out the population of the text; it does not necessarily involve the location of actual source texts used by the copy-writer who put the feature together. An actual text used in the production of the LIPSTICK FACTS AND FIGURES, for example, was the source of the marketing details. This is not cued by any of the features relating to quotation, reportage, presupposition or cause enhancement.

Secondly I attend to interactants in producer-audience interaction and in representations of dialogue in the texts. In one-way discourse between mass media producers and audiences we only see one 'side' of exchanges. Only the writer's initiations appear in the text. In the 'beauty feature' text, speech functions in the clause as exchange are predominantly Statements. These assign to the writer the role of giver-of-information and the corresponding role of information-recipient to the reader. I will list the producer's utterances *other* than such straightforward information-giving Statements in examining the producer-audience interaction in the different texts. These are in the column, testimonials and instructions. In the one-way discourse between producer and audience, response-demanding utterances (Questions and Commands) and interpolated utterances tend to contribute to synthetic personalisation and a synthetic friendly relationship. Exceptions to this are the Commands conventionally used in instruction-giving. At this stage, I simply identify the writer's utterances which appear to be interpolated or have the specific speech function of Command (the writer does not address the reader directly with any questions in this feature). I will refer back to them, as conventional elements in scripts, in the analysis of subject positions. I then examine representations of dialogue involving some of the characters introduced in the prior text analysis. Some of the projected texts take up places in adjacency pairs. Dialogue is synthesized between a variety of characters - reader-advertiser, experts-writer, interviewer-interviewee - as I go on to show. I attend to the adjacency pairing of speech functions in synthesized two-way discourse in the column and the testimonials.

Thirdly, I examine subject positioning. The producer (and correspondingly the interpreter) in this mixed text has multiple identities; she is never in a single subject position. In addition to positions assigned to her as employee of D.C. Thomson & Co. Ltd. and as journalist placed on the editorial staff of *Jackie*, she takes on 'roles' specific to the different activities she engages in as aspects of her social identity. This part of my inspection of the text population is necessarily looser and more discursive than the straightforward isolation of interactants and characters. Under the heading of Heterogeneity for each text I will put a general discussion of content, drawing on the suggested features as applicable. I will make some general observations here first.

The journalist who produced the 'beauty feature' is entertaining and informing readers. The feature consists of an assortment of activity-types and related topics, for the purposes of pleasure- and information-giving, from a larger repertoire of activity-types in the order of discourse related to the institution of journalism. A dual 'role' of informer-entertainer is common to the scripts for all the different activities that have left traces in the pages of *Jackie* (which is not the same as activities that have gone into their production; see chapter 4). Subject positions taken up by the editorial staff member are interviewer, advertiser etc. These are set up specific to script: facilitator in a conventional script for instructions in C; interviewer in a script for interviewing in B and historian in scripts for historical accounts in A and E. As well as examining the specific activities being enacted and their related frames and scripts, I will also attend to the producer's lexical and grammatical choices, and to her attitude towards certain prior texts. The other feature I suggested in chapter 5 for examining producer-identity was certainty modality. The editorial is knowledgeable, and certain in her knowledge. She sometimes speaks in the modality of emphatic certainty, using the simple present with emphasis in A6.1 and the modal auxiliary can with emphasis in C. In fact most of the modal elements indicating uncertainty in the particular pages of *Jackie* analysed here are in the Testimonials.

I will reserve all discussion of a specific 'pair' of subject positions taken up by the producer - editorial-as-friend - until later. This, and the corresponding identity and synthetic relationship of friendliness with the producer that this offers the interpreter, is the focus of a separate section.

A. Column

1.1 Ask any clever advertiser how to suggest femininity with a product, and he'll probably tell you 'a kissprint.' 1.2 Lipstick on a collar, a glass, his cheek – they all suggest that a woman was there. 1.3 When men think of make-up, they think of lipstick.

2.1 It's hardly a modern invention – women have been adding artificial colour to their lips for centuries now. 2.2 Before the days of lipstick as we know it, ladies used vegetable or animal dyes like cochineal - beetle's blood - to colour their lips.

3.1 The reason behind it wasn't simply to make themselves more beautiful - superstition lingered that the devil could enter the body through the mouth, and since red was meant to ward off evil spirits 'lipstick' was put around the mouth to ward off his evil intentions!

4.1 These days there are more complicated (and ruder!) theories. 4.2 Experts in human behaviour say that it's all to do with sex (what else?!).

5.1 Other 'experts' claim that the shape of your lipstick can reveal a lot about your character – i.e. if you wear the end flat you're stubborn, if it's sound and blunt you're fun-loving etc. etc. – but don't seem to take into consideration the fact that each brand of lipstick is a different shape to start with and it's easiest just to use it accordingly. 5.2 So much for the experts!

6.1 What *is* interesting is the way that fashions in lipsticks have changed over the years. 6.2 When lipcolour first came into fashion at the beginning of this century, dark colours and the style of 'drawing' on little pursed lips meant that women looked cutesy and doll-like. 6.3 Later on, in the forties, film stars wanting to look 'little-girl'ish continued this, while the newer breed of dominant women opted for a bolder look, colouring right over the natural 'bow' in the lips. 6.4 By the sixties 'women's lib' was in style and most girls abandoned lipstick altogether, or used beige colours to blank out the natural pink of their lips, and concentrated on over-the-top eye make-up and face painting instead.

7.1 Now, in the eighties, there are more colours available than ever before – right down to blue, green and black! 7.2 'Glossy' lips, popular fro a while in the seventies, are out again, and the overall trend is for natural pink tints, with oranges and golds in summer, on big, full lips.

8.1 Large cosmetic manufacturers will have upwards of 70 shades available at a time, introducing a further three or four shades each season to complement the fashion colours of that time. 8.2 And with some companies churning out batches of lipstick at a rate of 9,000 an hour, that's an awful lot of kisses to get through...!

Prior texts/ characters

In the first paragraph of the column there are three projected texts which are explicitly attributed to characters: namely, the reader, a hypothetical advertiser and lipstick traces:

The reader

Verbal Process | Receiver || Projection ('Ask any clever advertiser how to suggest femininity with a product' 1.1)

'any clever advertiser'
Sayer | Verbal Process | Receiver || Projection, and speech marks ('he'll ...tell you "a kissprint"' 1.1)
'Lipstick on a collar' etc

Sayer | Verbal Process || Projection ('Lipstick on a collar, a glass, his cheek - they all suggest a woman was there' 1.2)

Men's thoughts about cosmetics are cued as a text in a Range element by a borderline Mental/Behavioural process:

'men'
Senser/Behaver | Mental/Behavioural process | Range ('they think of lipstick' 1.3)

There is another Range element in paragraph 1, which can be viewed as an external text of unspecified origin. This is cued by a Verbal process verb within the text attributed to the reader:

Verbal process | Range '...suggest femininity'

A character in paragraph 1 who is not given 'lines' to say is the woman in sentence two who is set up in some kind of cliched scenario about marital infidelities (leaving traces of lipstick on men's collars etc. in 1.2). In this sentence, it is the smudges of lipstick that are presented as the 'speaking' characters, not the woman herself, whose presence they 'speak' about: the grammatical subject of the verbal process verb *suggest* is 'Lipstick on a collar, a glass, his cheek - they all'. These eloquent smudges signify (presumably to 'everybody') not just the presence of a woman, but some amorous relationship with a man. In 1.2, the writer postulates an inanimate lipstick smudge as a Sayer. The Sayer is a collection of inanimate marks, not capable of speech at all. This is a grammatical metaphor; following Halliday, we can suggest a more 'congruent' wording:

Carrier	Relational process	Attribute	
Lipstick on a collar, a glass, his cheek - they all	are	evidence	a woman was there

Lipstick smudges can only *suggest* metaphorically.

In paragraphs 2 and 3, writer, reader and some early lipstick-wearing 'ladies' are set up as characters:

Before the days of lipstick as we know it, ladies used vegetable or animal dyes like cochineal - beetle's blood - *to colour their lips.*
The reason behind it wasn't simply *to make themselves more beautiful* - superstition lingered that the devil could enter the body through the mouth, and *since red was meant to ward off evil spirits* 'lipstick' was put around the mouth *to ward off his evil intentions!*

142

In the first sentence of this extract, writer and reader are assumed to have a shared conception of what lipstick is, set up in an embedded projection postmodifying 'lipstick':

'we'
[[Senser | Mental Process | Range]] ('as we know it' 2.2)

Turning to the 'ladies', the writer does not quote or report these early 'users' supposed own words or thoughts, but presents their motivations in four cause enhancements and a fact projection. They used lipcolour in order '*to* colour their lips', but not simply in order 'to make themselves more beautiful'; '*since* red was meant to ward off evil spirits', they used them in order '*to* ward off his [the devil's] evil intentions!' The Head word 'superstition' is a 'fact' noun postmodified by a projection. It cues a reported belief that 'the devil could enter the body through the mouth':

'ladies'
Cause enhancement: 'to colour their lips' (2.2); 'to make themselves more beautiful', 'since red was meant to ward off evil spirits', 'to repel his evil intentions!' (3.1)
Fact projection: 'that the devil could enter the body through the mouth' (3.1)

Two sets of characters reported by the column-writer are some unspecified psychologists in paragraph 4 and some 'folk-psychologists' in paragraph 5:

'Experts in human behaviour'
Sayer | Verbal Process || Projection ('Experts in human behaviour say that it's all to do with sex' 4.2)
'Other "experts"'
Sayer | Verbal Process || Projection ('Other 'experts' claim that the shape of your lipstick can reveal a lot about your character' 5.1)

In paragraph 6, the thoughts of two other sets of characters are drawn in; namely, 'film stars' and 'dominant women':

... dark colours and the style of 'drawing' on little pursed lips meant that women looked cutesy and doll-like. Later on, in the forties, film stars *wanting* to look 'little-girl'ish continued this, while the newer breed of dominant women *opted* for a bolder look, colouring right over the natural 'bow' in the lips.

The Head word 'stars' is postmodified by a want projection. The 'dominant women' are the Senser/ Behaver of a Mental/ Behavioural process verb. Both prior texts concern style of appearance, or 'looks':

143

'film stars'
[[Mental process || Projection]] "'wanting to look "little-girl"sh'
'the newer breed of dominant women'
Senser/Behaver | Mental/Behavioural process | Range 'The newer breed of dominant women opted for a bolder look' (6.3)

Other lipstick users' preferences and motivations – 'most girls in the 60's', at the end of the same paragraph - are set up by a Mental/Behavioural process verb, in a Range element, and by a cause enhancement giving the purpose underlying a mode of action:

...most girls abandoned lipstick altogether, or used beige *colours to blank out the natural pink of their lips*, and *concentrated* on over-the-top eye make-up and face painting instead.

'most girls' in the sixties
Senser/Behaver | Mental/Behavioural process | Range 'most girls ...concentrated on over-the-top make-up and face painting'
Cause enhancement: 'to blank out the natural pink of the lips' (6.4)

Cosmetics manufacturers appear briefly as text-producing characters in paragraph 8, where the writer announces their motivations as manufacturers of fashion products in a cause enhancement:

'cosmetic manufacturers'
Cause enhancement: 'to complement the fashion colours of that time' (8.1)

There are a number of prior texts of the presupposition and fact projection type which are difficult to attribute to specific characters as origin. Two of them - negations of prior assumptions about the modernity of lipstick and its uses - can perhaps be attributed to the reader, but the rest appear to be simply 'ordinary' commonsensical expectations:

The reader?
Negation of assumptions: that 'lipstick is a modern invention' (2.1); that 'women have always used lipstick for the sole purpose of making themselves more beautiful' (3.1)

commonsense
Temporal clause presupposition: 'men think of make-up' (1.3)
Comparative presupposition: 'there were less complicated and rude theories in those days' (4.1)
Fact projections: postmodifying Head word 'fact' ('each brand of lipstick is a different shape to start with' 5.1); postmodifying Head word 'way' ('fashions in lipsticks have changed over the years' 6.1)
Presupposition (emphasis): 'what experts have to say about lipstick is not interesting' (6.1)
Existential presupposition: 'There was a newer breed of dominant business like women' (6.3)

144

These presupposed historical details about 'breeds' of women, the projected facts of fashion change, lipstick shapes etc. are set up as common knowledge. Such commonsensical knowledge in backgrounded prior texts is very common and appears in every section, particularly in presuppositions.

Interaction/ interactants

Producer - audience. The writer begins by directly addressing the reader with a Command: 'Ask any clever advertiser' (1.1). She interpolates her own Statements twice:

```
Statement:    '..ladies used animal dyes like cochineal
Interpolation:                              - beetle's blood -
 (Statement):                                              to colour their lips'  (2.2)

Statement:    'These days there are more complicated
Interpolation:                              (and ruder!)
 (Statement):                                              theories.' (4.1)
```

Representations of dialogue. The opening sentence places the reader in an imaginary dialogue with a male advertiser. This dialogue consists of a two part Question-Answer exchange, in which the reader asks the advertiser for some information and he provides it:

Reader-advertiser
Question: '...how to suggest femininity with a product
Answer: ..."a kissprint"'

The reported Statement by 'Experts in human behaviour' in 4.2 is set up as the first pair part of a Statement-Comment adjacency pair. The second pair part is the writer's bracketed remark, an ambiguous Comment which may be either an Acknowledgement or a Contradiction:

Psychologists-writer
Statement: '...it's all to do with sex
Comment: (what else?!)'

This comment is marked off prosodically like an interpolation.

The reported Statement by 'Other experts' in 5.1 is also set up as the first pair part of a Statement-Comment adjacency pair. The second pair part Comment is again the writer's. It consists of a rewording of the Statement followed by criticism:

Folk-psychologists-writer
Statement: '...the shape of your lipstick can reveal a lot about your character

145

Comment: - i.e. if you wear the end flat you're stubborn, if it's round and blunt you're fun-loving etc etc - but [you] don't seem to take into consideration the fact that each brand of lipstick is a different shape to start with and it's easiest just to use it accordingly. So much for the experts!

Like the writer's ambiguous Comment on the psychologists' Statement, the first segment of this Comment is marked off prosodically like an interpolated remark.

Heterogeneity/ subject positions

The 400-word column is the largest written text in the feature. The largest 'kissprint' appears immediately above the first paragraph, in which this image is discussed. The remainder of the column is a narrative on the origins and historical development of lipstick, its availability and range. I examine each paragraph in turn, drawing out aspects of the writer's social identity established in each: i.e. the way she is constructed in various personae, each with feelings and attitudes.

In B1 the topic-frame is the pervasiveness of the symbol for femininity, i.e. the kissprint, in advertising discourse. It begins with the hypothetical dialogue between the reader and an imaginary advertiser about the 'kissprint': 'Ask any clever advertiser how to suggest femininity with a product and he'll probably tell you "a kissprint".' The editorial claims to speak on behalf of 'any clever advertiser'. The hedge adds tentativeness to the writer's otherwise certain knowledge; namely, the modal operator *probably* attached to her report of advertisers' likely approach to marketing feminine products. At this point she is a purveyor of symbols, an advertiser's spokesperson (and her assumption that advertisers are men is androcentric). She is implicitly classifying advertisers: 'clever' advertisers are those whose response to the reader's question would be the one she proposes. In constructing this dialogue between reader and advertiser, the editorial is claiming a certain expertise: knowledge of advertisers' likely approach to marketing products for female consumers. I shall therefore call her not just advertiser's spokesperson here but advertiser. The writer also implicitly claims access to the thoughts of men in general on cosmetics, and has some fairly stereotypical notions of what lipstick represents. In paragraph 1 she establishes the kissprint as both symbol and index.

Paragraph 2 is the beginning of a narrative on lipstick past and present produced by the historian. The topic shifts to the antiquity of lipstick technology, from a symbol in paragraph 1 to a material substance and its use in 2. In 3 the topic is the reason for the development of lipstick technology (for the reported motivations of early lipstick wearers, see prior text analysis). By contrasting the writer's wording of Types of artificial colour for lips past and present, we can see that what people in this vague historical period used is not considered to be real lipstick, but some primitive forerunner:

Ancient/superstition: 'artificial colour' 2.1; 'vegetable or animal dyes like cochineal - beetle's blood' 2.2; 'lipstick' in scare quotes 3.1

Modern/fashion: 'Lipstick' 1.2, 1.3, 5.1, 5.1, 6.1, 6.4, 8.2; 'lipstick as we know it' 2.2; 'lipcolour' 6.2

The editorial-as-historian in paragraph 3 is downgrading the past (and perhaps in 2; since in the pre-consumerist undemocratic past, lipstick was only used by 'ladies'). The fact noun superstition in 3 has expressive value: the projected belief is not the editorial's and provides a source of amusement.

4.1 introduces the topic shift in paragraphs 4 and 5 to 'theories' about lipstick. In the editorial's interpolated Comment she makes clear her position of critic: 'These days there are more complicated (and ruder!) theories'. Two 'theories' are presented in the projected Statements attributed to psychologists and folk-psychologists, identified in the prior text analysis. In reporting these Statements, which bring in discourses of psychology and folk-psychology, the editorial-as-critic also interacts with the reportees, responding to their Statements, as we have seen in the interaction analysis:

'Experts in human behaviour say that it's all to do with sex (what else?!). 4.2
Other 'experts' claim that the shape of your lipstick can reveal a lot about your character - i.e. if you wear the end flat you're stubborn, if it's round and blunt you're fun-loving etc etc - but don't seem to take into consideration the fact that each brand of lipstick is a different shape to start with and it's easier just to use it accordingly'. 5.1

The distance she maintains from her reportees here is part of her social identity, establishing her dissociation from specific discourses. She may be either endorsing or ridiculing the Statement from psychological discourse, since her Comment '(what else?!)' in 4.2 is ambiguous. However, in 5.1, her dissociation from folk-psychology is clear. She distances herself from their text with the reporting verb 'claim'. Then in her Comment she draws in frames relating to knowledge, as a lipstick-user, of lipstick as a product to criticize the folk-psychologists' classification of lipstick-users into personality-types. She uses this 'critique' as the basis for dismissing both in 5.2: 'So much for the experts!' An aspect of her identity, then, is mistrust of experts giving scientific, or pseudo-scientific, statements.

A shift in topic focus is strongly foregrounded in the first sentence of paragraph 6. Clefting and italicisation, for contrastive stress, cue a presupposition that what has preceded was uninteresting (which we have already noted is set up as 'common knowledge'): 'What *is* interesting is the way that fashions in lipstick have changed over the years'. 6.1 It is presupposed that what 'the experts' have to

147

say is not interesting, but that changes in lipstick use in terms of fashion are (since the Contents of the presupposition is not specified, it may also refer to the historical passage earlier). The editorial's anti-intellectualism here contrasts with her respect for businesses, which are presented as benign (se the marketing details text). What follows is a narrative on lipstick fashion changes, put in historical sequence by a series of time circumstantials in adjuncts over the next four paragraphs.[2] The historian represents lipstick fashion either as self-governing and undergoing spontaneous changes or as a matter of the free choice of individuals. Fashion change is an acausal process, for example, in the fact projection (6.1) and presupposed idea (6.2):

'the way that *fashions in lipsticks have changed...*' (6.1)
'when *lipcolour ...came into fashion...*' (6.2)

There are more examples of the representation of consumerism and fashion as acausal below. An example of lipstick fashion changes being represented as though governed by individual choice is in the following clause with the functional relations of Senser/Behaver| Mental/Behavioural Process| Range: 'the newer breed of dominant business-like women opted for a bolder look' 6.3. Fashion is the 'free choice' of individuals in the Contents of B, D and E below.

In discussing fashion changes in styles for wearing lipstick, the editorial, as fashion historian, refers to skills relating to the application of lipstick. She draws on a variety of frames and classification schemes relating to feminine practices. These include practical knowledge of Methods, a catalogue of Lip Types, Lip Features and Lipstick Colours (some of these appear in paragraphs 7 and 8; I have included them here for clarity):

Methods: '"drawing" on little pursed lips' 6.2; 'colouring over the natural "bow" in the lips' 6.3; 'beige colours to blank out the natural pink of their lips', 'over-the-top eye make-up and face painting' 6.4
Lip Types: 'little pursed lips' 6.2; '"Glossy" lips', 'big, full lips' 7.2
Lip Features: 'the natural 'bow''' 6.3; '''the natural pink' 6.4
Lipstick Colours: 'dark colours' 6.2; 'beige colours' 6.4, 'blue, green and black!' 7.1; 'natural pink tints', 'oranges and golds' 7.2; 'shades' twice, 'fashion colours' 8.1)

In 6.2, the editorial-as-historian is interpreting the meaning of visual features according to a set of conventions for women's 'looks' in feminine discourse. She outlines a set of Women's 'looks'/character-types:

'cutesy and doll-like' 6.2; 'lovable and "little-girl"sh', 'a bolder look' 6.3

148

I think we can reasonably assume that the editorial is non-feminist. The Women's Liberation Movement, pejoratively referred to as 'women's lib' in scare quotes, is presented as a sixties' fashion option:

          Carrier   **Attribute**
'By the sixties "women's lib" was in style...' (6.4)

In bringing her history of lipstick up to the present day in paragraphs 7 and 8, the historian becomes fashion correspondent, drawing on frames representing fashion attributes of lipsticks (see lists of lip types and lip features above). This subject position is closely related to that of advertiser. Availability and multiple choice are topics characteristic of advertising discourse and they are often realized in the functional relations of Existent| Circumstance and Carrier| Attribute, as here:

Existent| Circumstance e.g. 'there are more colours available than ever before' 7.1
Carrier| Attribute e.g. 'the overall trend is for natural pink tints, with oranges and golds in summer, on big, full lips' 7.2

These representations of commodity availability and consumerist fashion contain processes which are acausal and agentless, like the process-types already observed in paragraph 6. Another agentless and acausal process is '"Glossy" lips ...are out again' in 7.2.

Extent of variety and seasonality are the topic-frame of the last paragraph, 8. The activity of advertising assigns the subject position of advertiser to the editorial again; the interpreter is correspondingly constructed as a potential consumer or interested party. In this transition from historian, to fashion correspondent, to advertiser, there appears to be an implied contrast between the exclusivity and quaintness of lipstick use in the dim superstitious past and in the 'democratic' marketplace available to you, the fortunate modern reader. 'Large cosmetics manufacturers' are represented by the advertiser as the Carrier in an Attributive relational clause:

                  Possession as   **Manner as**
Carrier   **Attribute**   **Attribute**
'...manufacturers will have upwards of 70 shades available at a time'

The motivations of these manufacturers, presented in a cause enhancement ('to complement the fashion colours of that time') are not commented on.

In 8.2, in contrast with the more customary practices of advertising discourse, mass production becomes visible, in functional relations of Actor| Goal and a Material process verb in the first clause: 'And with some manufacturers churning out batches of lipstick at a rate of 9,000 an hour, that's an awful lot of kisses to get through ...!' The items realising Actor and Goal are 'some companies' and 'batches of lipstick' respectively; lipstick is exposed as a mass-produced commercial product. By drawing on terms used in mass production ('batches', "'a rate of 9,000 an hour') and an informal word for the process ('churning out') in the first clause, the editorial sets the final sentence in contrast with the consumerist fashion discourse earlier. There is a shift in voice in this final sentence. This shift is potentially face-threatening, but the writer has two ways for making it palatable. Three informal lexical items ('churning out', 'awful', 'get') and punctuation contribute to the 'chatty' way mass production is introduced, assigning a friendly identity to the writer (there is detailed discussion of the editorial-as-friend in a later section). In the last clause the editorial brings back the link established in the opening sentence of the column between lipstick and the kissprint as index: lipstick use is associated with affectionate relations. Consumption is established as pleasurable, thus minimising the face-threat in setting up the respective positions of manufacturer and consumer.

B. Testimonials

1. MARGARET (15)
'I wear it all the time, because I always wear make-up. My favourite shade's a sort of brown-and-red mixture – I usually buy Boots 17 or Max Factor lipstick. I got my first one when I was 10, for Xmas – it was a sort of pink colour. I think it was just for me to play with'
2. EMILY (12)
'Usually I just wear lipstick when I'm going out, but sometimes for school. I like pinks, oranges and plain glosses. I was about 7 when my mum gave me a bright red lipstick to experiment with – I think I've worn it ever since!'
3. CLARA (wouldn't tell us her age!)
'I always wear red – dark red – and usually from Mary Quant or Estee Lauder. I don't know if I can remember my first lipstick – wait! Yes I can! It was called "Choosy Cherry" by Mary Quant – everyone used to ask me if I was ill when I was wearing it!'
4. RHONA (18)
'I like pinks and deep reds. I don't wear it all that often. My first lipstick? I stole it from my sister's drawer – I was about 12 – dying to look grown-up even then!'

Prior texts/ characters

Four individuals are quoted. The quoted texts are identified by the presence of speech marks. I assume that actual interviews constitute part of the historical context of this section of the beauty feature. (As I observed in chapter 4, interviews are one of the subsidiary channels for two-way discourse with actual individuals.) Whether or not actual interviews took place, the interviewees have been constructed as characters - they are set up textually for the reader. (As a matter of fact, the actual occurrence of these interviews, and indeed the existence of the purported individuals as interviewees, is irrelevant; at this stage in the analysis, at least).

The quoted texts are the constructed testimonials of named lipstick-wearers. Within them, Mental process verbs proliferate, cuing either projected clauses or Range elements as texts. The presupposed ideas presented as givens are biographical details. The quoted texts contain self-reports by the interviewees, constructed of course by the writer. The writer establishes these people as characters with feelings and attitudes towards things. Presupposed ideas concerning the possession and use of a commodity are given the same commonsensical status as other kinds of biographical detail also established in presuppositions, one of which really is shared by everyone; namely, Emily's 'my mum gave me a bright red lipstick to play with', which presupposes that she had a mother:

Margaret
Senser | Mental Process || Projection 'I think it was just for me to play with' (1.3)
Cause enhancement: 'because I always wear make-up' (1.1)
Presupposition (entailment?): 'if you wear make-up, you wear lipstick' (1.1)
'Attributive' presuppositions: 'I have a favourite shade' (1.2) 'I had a first lipstick' (1.3)
Temporal clause presupposition: 'I was 10' (1.3)

Emily
Senser | Mental Process | Range 'I like pinks, oranges and plain glosses' (2.1)
Senser | Mental Process || Projection 'I think I've worn it ever since!' (2.2)
Temporal clause presupposition: 'I habitually go out' (2.2)
'Attributive' presupposition: 'I have a mum' (2.2)

Clara
Sayer | Verbal Process | Receiver | Range 'Clara (wouldn't tell us her age!)' (3)
Senser | Mental Process || Projection 'I don't know if I can remember my first lipstick!' (3.2)
Senser | Mental Process | Range 'I can remember my first lipstick' (3.2)
'Attributive' presupposition: 'I had a first lipstick' (3.2)
Temporal clause presupposition: 'I used to wear it' (3.3)

Rhona
Senser | Mental Process | Range 'I like pinks and deep reds' (4.1)
Mental Process || Projection 'dying to look grown-up' (4.4)
Presupposition (entailment?): 'I wear it sometimes' (4.2)
'Attributive' presuppositions: (+anaphora) 'I had a first lipstick' 'I have a sister who had a drawer with lipstick in it' (4.4)

The self-reports and presupposed ideas of these lipstick-wearers establish the normality of lipstick use from an early age, of being a regular user with developed preferences, of first lipsticks being memorable, etc. The presupposed idea 'I had a first lipstick' is in three of the four interviewees' texts. They are all responding to the same questions in interaction with the interviewer (see next section). Here we need to suppose that the presupposed 'first lipstick' they attribute to themselves in

151

each testimonial was preceded by a presupposed 'first lipstick' the interviewer has already attributed to them in her question.

The testimonials construct a bunch of people with shared 'newsworthy' experiences about their lipstick use. The reports and presuppositions establish common ground. The writer constructs characters who share biographical details in terms of consumption with the editorial-as-interviewer and the reader. The testimonials from consumers contribute to the establishment of a lipstick-using community; a community in which having a mother and having a lipstick are set up as the same kind of thing, in which a first lipstick is something universal and memorable in women's lives and to be shared with other women. This is not an actual community but an imaginary consumption community; the consumption of a commodity is all that is needed to become a member of it.

There are other characters inhabiting the interviewees' lipstick centred world who have left traces of texts; namely, Clara's *everyone* who responded to the first lipstick she wore:

'Everyone'
Sayer | Verbal Process | Receiver || Projection ('everyone used to ask me if I was ill' 3.3)

Interaction/ interactants

Producer - audience. An interpolation by the writer appears in the caption to Clara's contribution: '(wouldn't tell us her age!)'. Apart from the captions, the writer's utterances to the reader are all reconstructed interviewee-responses. They will be examined below as representations of interaction.

Representations of dialogue. The four interviewees' contributions are prior texts which the writer is quoting, simulations of utterances in an earlier interaction. For this reason, rather than identifying them as Statements, I take it that the interviewees are giving responses to questions posed by an interviewer. The speech functions, then, are mostly Answers. On the basis of the first interviewee's Answers, the Questions would have been something like this: 'How often do you wear lipstick?' 'What's your favourite shade?' 'When did you get your first one?'

There are two other speech functions which contribute to the simulation of spoken interaction between respondent and questioner. One of these is Rhona's Question in 4.3. Taken as an action with connective value in the exchange it can be seen as an element of two adjacency pairs. It is identifiable as the first part of a Question-Answer pair. The next sentence is the Answer and completes the exchange:

Question: 'My first lipstick?
Answer: I stole it from my sister's drawer...'

In other words she answers her own question. Her question can also be interpreted as a rhetorical strategy for responding to a question from the interviewer, an utterance which has not appeared on the page:

Interviewer and *Rhona*
Question: [When did you get your first lipstick?]
Answer: My first lipstick? I stole it from my sister's drawer - I was about 12...

There is an imperative in Clara's text ('wait!'). The utterance it appears in is not really a Command, but the preface to a Comment on her own self-report in the previous sentence:

Statement: 'I don't know if I can remember my first lipstick
Comment: - Wait! yes I can! It was...'

Four lipstick-wearers give information about themselves. The testimonial producers - Margaret, Emily, Clara and Rhona - are strongly foregrounded. As an interactant, the interviewer is backgrounded.

Heterogeneity/ subject positions
In her interaction with the reader, the producer indicates that she is quoting prior discourse by other people. The 'ordinary' lipstick-wearers are strongly foregrounded; the writer, in her persona of interviewer, is present only as a 'shadow' cast by questions (except for the editorial's 'us' in the caption of Clara's text). The editorial constructs these young women as the producers of their own texts. These interviewees' 'own words' are structured by the interests of the editorial-as-interviewer, who has set the agenda.

The content of the testimonials is information about the interviewees themselves, which we have already attended to in some detail in the analysis of prior texts. So there is really no need to spend much time examining topic, classification scheme etc. in order to find out what kinds of social identity they have as producers. They are consumers, and have an assortment of experiences and preferences relating to the consumption of a commodity: lipstick.

The interviewees do not always use the certainty modality of experts, as the editorial does. The editorial has certain knowledge, the interviewees do not, even though they could presumably be categorical about their own experiences. The only things the lipstick wearers are categorical about are their colour preferences. There are more modal elements than in other sections of the feature. The particular items used for certainty modality serve to indicate tentativeness, to avoid making categorical statements about the information given:

153

| 'sort of' | 1.2, 1.3 | 'about' | 2.2, 4.4 |
| 'I think' | 1.3, 2.2 | 'I don't know if' | 3.2 |

All but one of the modal elements indicating tentativeness are in the testimonials. (Inclusion of intensity and frequency modality as well makes the contrast even sharper.) This hedging is probably contributing to the simulation of informal speech. It is interesting to note that tentativeness, a characteristic of so-called 'women's language' (Lakoff 1975), is a feature of these constructed interviews with 'ordinary' women.

The four people are supposedly the producers of these testimonials, not the editorial, who is simply quoting them. This part of the beauty feature contains some of the features that I proposed in the framework chapter for attending to synthetic personalisation and the synthesis of a friendly close relationship between a producer and a mass audience of young people: 'commonsensical' presupposed ideas, 'teenage vocabulary', frequent use of exclamation marks. The prior texts tend to have a vague commonsensical attribution. As they consist of biographical details of young women, they establish common ground with the reader. There are two lexical items that are worth noting for their contribution to constructing a youthful identity for Rhona; namely, 'grown-up', which is a child's word for an adult, and the informal word 'dying'. Another point of focus I suggested was the use of the pronouns *you* and *we/us*. These are absent, but the pronoun *I* is frequent (19 in all; it doesn't appear anywhere else). The four testimonial-givers are personalized.

C. Instructions

LIP TRICKS!
Choosing the right shade of lipstick is easy – making it stay on is a bit more tricky. But by applying lipcolour correctly, you can achieve a long-lasting look!
1. Outline the lips with a toning lip-pencil – this will elp stop your lipstick from 'bleeding' around your mouth (a touch of Elizabeth Arden's Lip-Fix Crème, £4.95, provides a good base to prevent this, too).
2. Fill in using a lip brush loaded with lipstick – a lip brush gives you more control over what you're doing, and fills in tiny cracks more easily.
3. Blot lips with a tissue, dust over lightly with face powder, apply a second layer and blot again.

Prior texts/ characters

The 'Lip tricks' instructions carry three presupposed ideas. One, concerning uncertainty about using lipstick, is attributed to the reader; the others, concerning choice and ownership of lipstick, can only be attributed to some vague 'commonsense':

The Reader
Presupposition (emphasis): 'you think you can't achieve a long-lasting look!'
commonsense
Existential presupposition: 'There is a right shade of lipstick'
'Attributive' presupposition: 'You have a lipstick'

Interaction/ interactants

Producer - audience. Each stage of the instructions for applying lipstick begins with a Command, requiring a mode of action as a response:

[stage 1]	'Outline the lips with a toning pencil...
[stage 2]	Fill in using a lip brush...
[stage 3]	Blot lips with a tissue,
	dust over lightly...
	apply a second layer...
	blot again'

Heterogeneity/ subject positions

The Instructions text contains the DIY element, filling in what the paid ads often leave out about consumption; in this case, how to do the beauty work with your lipstick once you've bought it.

The friend who knows who the reader is also an advertiser. As noted already, her emphasis ('you *can* achieve a long-lasting look!') cues a negative assumption in the reader's mind. This bit of advertising discourse can only reassure the reader by first setting her up as a failure, or perhaps just a faint-hearted pessimist.

The three numbered stages for applying lipstick are illustrated with photographs. The topic-frame is the application of lipstick. Other implicit frames needed to coherently connected together the three stages concern the sequential ordering of photographs and the itemisation of the body. The editorial-as-facilitator follows a script for instruction-giving. She gives step-by-step commands, conventionally using unmitigated directives and material process verbs. She is constructed as a skilled professional beautician bestowing 'useful feminine knowledge' on initiates, giving expert advice on how to apply lipstick 'correctly'. In the process she is teaching a specialist vocabulary of painting/craft work: 'fill in', 'loaded', 'brush', 'tiny cracks', 'blot', 'dust', 'bleeding' (with scare quotes as cue for unfamiliar technical use).

These subject positions or 'personae' are not clearcut. For example, the editorial-as-facilitator in the DIY section is fulfilling the important function of teaching the skills needed to use products. She makes conventional use of Commands in providing numbered instructions for the application of

155

lipstick: '1. Outline... 2. Fill in... 3. Blot...' etc. In the same section she is still an advertiser, promoting a product; namely, Elizabeth Arden's Lip-Fix Creme.

D. Facts and figures

1. LIPSTICK FACTS AND FIGURES
2. Rimmel, the largest-selling 'budget' brand of cosmetics, sell over 5 million lipsticks every year, at an average price of 94p each – that's a staggering $4,700,00 plus spent on coloured kisses from Rimmel alone!

3. Out of all the lipsticks sold 47% are 'pink' shades – Rimmel's top seller is 'Pink Shimmer'.

4. Lipstick is basically made up of oils and animal fats, particles of raw colours and pigment held together with waxes, and added perfume.

5. The average price of a lipstick is £1.39.

6. Women wear more lipstick now than ever before, though the trend is towards subtler shades, rather than the brilliant reds favoured by previous generations, to reflect the 'natural' look of the 80's.

7. The biggest business in make-up is with young women. On average, every woman in Britain under 24 buys 20 make-up items each year, including four lipsticks and one lip pencil or crayon. For over   35's however, the figures plummet to just 6 items per year, of which only one will be a lipstick.

8. (Statistics by kind courtesy of SDC and Rimmel.)

Prior texts/ characters

Backgrounded texts in this section concern the condition of lipstick as a commodity subject to fashion change. Presupposed ideas are presented as commonsense. One of them is contained within a clause giving the motivation underlying a recent fashion trend. This is difficult to attribute to anyone in particular and appears to be reporting what 'everyone' knows to be the case:

commonsense
Existential presuppositions: 'there is a largest-selling "budget" brand of cosmetics' (2); 'there are such things as trends' 'brilliant reds were favoured by previous generations'; 'The 80's look is "natural"' (5); 'there is an average price of a lipstick' (6); 'there is a business in make-up' (7)
Comparative presuppositions: 'women used to wear less lipstick', 'shades used to be less subtle' (5)
Cause enhancement: 'to reflect the "natural" look of the 80's' (5)

This text contains a selection of smaller texts, snippets of marketing information on lipstick. The title lexicalizes the topic frame of the small fragments. Its seriousness contrasts with the punning titles elsewhere. It is not classing other texts in beauty feature as non-fact, but marking this text off as the trace of a different activity, in which the editorial has the persona of market-researcher.

These segments require considerable expertise for interpretation. Consumers, participants in activities in consumerist discourse, need to be able to select and discriminate. This includes comparing prices: the discerning reader-consumer can contrast the overall average price given in 6 with the cheaper average price of the lipstick brand being promoted, which was given in 2. The writer here is an advertiser promoting a specific company's products.

In 7 the market researcher identifies the chief consumers of cosmetics ('young women') and the consumption patterns of 'average' (hence normal?) people. She states the quantity consumed annually by 'under 24' and 'over 35' age ranges, classifying women into monolithic consumption groups in the process. All targeted readers are therefore included.

The formality and technicality of vocabulary for lipstick ingredients in 4 contrasts with the historian's reference to 'beetle's blood' in A. The source of 'raw colours and pigments' is not specified; notably there is no reference to cochineal, presumably one of the pigments used. The editorial harbours contradictory attitudes towards lipstick ingredients, apparently. In 8 the formulaic politeness of 'kind courtesy' indicates a respect for business experts, which contrasts with the ridicule of scientific experts in A. Copyright laws make the acknowledgement of source for statistics etc. a legal requirement. This is not for the teenage reader's benefit (the reader is given no indication of what 'SDC' is).

E. Illustrated history

1. Clara Bow, the 'It' girl of the 1920's who first set the fashion for wearing make-up – she wore her lipstick in a perfect Cupid's Bow.

2. By the 1940's, female film wore their lippy to reflect their own characters. Jean Harlow, the platinum blonde pin-up girl, went for absolute kissability with a lip-line as unnatural as her eyebrows – while no-nonsense dramatic actresses like Bette lDavis and Joan Crawford preferred the wide-mouthed 'stiff upper lip' look.

3. By the 60's, innocence was IN – models like Twiggy abandoned lip colour altogether, and all the emphasis was on the eyes instead.

4. Into the 80's, and Madonna brings back bright lip colour with the most famus pout since Marilyn Monroe.

The photographs of media 'personalities' in E introduce six lipstick-wearers; they are uncaptioned, but their names appear in the text. Although visually prominent, these women are not quoted; they are not given prominent 'voices'. Prior texts are cued by a cause enhancement, reporting the purpose underlying the action of wearing lipstick, and a mental process:

> **Female film stars of the 40's**
> Cause enhancement ('to reflect their own characters' 2.1)
> **Bette Davis & Joan Crawford**
> Senser | Mental Process | Range ('Bette Davis and Joan Crawford preferred the wide-mouthed "stiff upper lip" look' 2.2)

The writer reports the thought processes of two actors best known for screen roles in the 40's, Bette Davis and Joan Crawford. Another possible candidate is Jean Harlow, who '*went for* absolute kissability' (2.2). The thoughts and motives attributed to them relate to the wearing of lipstick. Apparently, the purpose behind lipstick-wearing for female film stars of the 40's in general was (in order) 'to reflect their own characters'. There seems to be some confusion between 'character' and 'look'.

As in the other parts of the feature, the illustrated history of lipstick fashion carries a variety of commonsensical presupposed ideas. These concern types of 'look', types of 'girl' and various phenomena relating to the world of fashion:

> **commonsense**
> Existential Presuppositions: 'There was an '"It" girl' (1.1); 'There is a fashion for wearing lipstick' (1.1); 'There was a platinum blonde pin-up girl' (2.2)
> Comparative Presupposition: 'Her eyebrows were unnatural' (2.2)
> Existential Presuppositions: 'There is/was a wide mouthed 'stiff upper lip' look' (2.2) (entailment?) 'There was an 'emphasis' on something' (3.1) (entailment?) 'There are such things as 'famous pouts' (4.1) 'Marilyn Monroe had a famous pout' (4.1).

Heterogeneity/ subject positions

This text is a history of lipstick fashions in terms of six female celebrities, with studio photographs. The historical 'phases' covered are very similar to those in the recent history part of the column. The editorial has the subject position of historian, producing a combined history of cinema and lipstick (as in the column, Narrative sequence and Progress is a clue to this: 'By the 1940's..' 2.1; 'By the 60's..' 3.1; 'Into the 80's' 4.1.

In the first section, she identifies an origin for modern lipstick fashion, naming a single progenitor: Clara Bow, 'the "It" girl of the 1920's'. The historian presents the preferences and motivations of wearers without comment. For instance, she does not intrude into the narrative, as she might well have done, with any bracketed criticisms or sarcastic remarks such as '...went for ultimate kissability (what else?!)'. The celebrities' actions, thoughts and motivations are represented, but as part of the writer's own specialist knowledge: information that she, the informed expert, is imparting for the reader's enjoyment. Part of her expertise are her abilities, as in A, to discriminate between different Mouth-types and to categorize celebrities into different 'looks'/ character-types:

Mouth-types. 'Cupid's Bow' 1.1; 'unnatural', 'wide-', '"stiff upper lip"' 2.2; 'pout' 4.1
'Looks'/character-types. 'the platinum blonde pin-up girl', 'absolute kissability', 'no-nonsense dramatic actresses', 'the wide-mouthed "stiff upper lip" look' 2.2; 'innocence' 3.1; 'the most famous pout since Marilyn Monroe' 4.1.

As with the representation of fashion change in terms of free choice elsewhere, the changes narrated here are presented as the result of the options of celebrities as individuals. In fact, they have been generated by the Hollywood 'glamour factory'. Differences and changes in fashion 'looks' are set either in terms of personal whims of celebrities, or, another characteristic of consumerist fashion discourse, in acausal and agentless processes, as with the following Attributive relational clauses:

Carrier		Attribute
innocence	was	IN
all the emphasis	was	on the eyes 3.1

According to the second paragraph, female film stars of the 40's wore lipstick for purely personal reasons: 'By the 1940's, female film stars wore their lippy *to reflect their own characters*'. In the same paragraph, the editorial-as-historian reports the thought processes of two characters, Bette Davis and Joan Crawford: 'Bette Davis and Joan Crawford *preferred* the wide-mouthed "stiff upper lip" look'. However, the photographs of these characters are the work of a studio. They are not snapshots, as the photographs of the interviewees are in the testimonials. The styles of appearance or 'looks' displayed in the illustrated history are products of huge amounts of professional activity. These 'looks' are not personal preference but big business. As in A, changes and variations in lipstick 'looks' are accounted for in terms of personal preferences in 'self-expression' through appearance, belying the extent of professional involvement in 'looks'.

The friendship of producer and interpreter

In this section I examine one specific social identity taken up by the writer, namely that of the reader's friend. Most of the features I listed under Producer-audience interaction contribute to simulating a friendly face-to-face encounter: the direct address with a command in A, the interpolations. Writer and reader are synthesized in a friendly relationship. Like 'Cathy & Claire' and the 'beauty editor' in MacRobbie's account, the producer is the distributor of 'useful feminine knowledge'. As an older sister might do, she demonstrates the application of lipstick and 'gossips' about it. Here I attend to her use of the pronouns 'you' and 'we/us' in her simulation of friendly interaction with the audience, how she shows she knows who the reader is and how she establishes herself as a member of the same social group.

Pronouns.

The producer is pronominalized as an editorial team twice: 'we' in the Header and 'us' in the Testimonials. 'We' appears in the orientation in the Header ('We kiss and tell the whole story behind lipstick!'). This establishes the anonymous group voice as a friendly gossip. There is also an inclusive 'we' in the Column, referring to both writer and reader. Personal reference to the reader as *you* is a common feature of the 'synthetic personalization' practiced in the mass media. Instances of pronominal reference to the reader as if she were an individual addressee can be found in the Instructions and in the opening sentence of the Column (C3,4,5; A1.1).

Relational and expressive values of lexis.

The informality of a few lexical terms ('cutesy' A6.2, 'lovable' 6.3, 'churning out', 'awful', 'get through' 8.2, 'lippy' E2) contributes a little to the construction of a youthful, female identity for their writer, matching the targeted audience by approximating the sort of vocabulary that teenagers might be supposed to use among themselves. In the beauty pages there is none of the 'fake slang' reported by McRobbie, although something similar can be found in other parts of the magazine (e.g. in readers' letters and editorial responses on the letters page).

The copywriter engages in punning word-play in the feature heading: 'LIPS INC!',[3] and the heading of C: 'LIP TRICKS!'

Punctuation. A social identity is set up for the addresser. We have already seen that she is constructed as a person with feelings and with attitudes towards things. The frequent exclamation marks have some expressive value contributing to this, attributing to the writer some kind of friendly, enthusiastic emotional state.

The writer's use of scare quotes contributes to setting up the familiar and the normal for readers. They often signal what is assumed to be an unfamiliar term or divergence from (what is assumed to be) 'normal' usage. Examples of this use of scare quotes I suggest are 'bow' A6.3, ''drawing' 6.2, 'bleeding' C4. Thus with 'bleeding', for example, the writer constructs a reader who does not normally use, and is possibly unfamiliar with, this term in its painting and craftwork sense of 'seeping over a line'.

Prior texts attributable to the reader, 'us' or commonsense.

In the column and the instructions the writer negates assumptions attributable to the reader, concerning the modernity of lipstick and pessimism about using it successfully. She is the reader's friend and knows what she thinks, or rather claims to. The writer minimizes the social distance between herself and readership, claiming common ground and a social relation of closeness. She uses various means to set herself up as a member of the same social group as her teenage readers. One way in which she claims common ground with the reader is by producing the embedded report attributed to an inclusive 'we' in A2.2. This takes the shape of post-modifier to a Head noun: 'lipstick as we know it'. More frequently, common ground is claimed in embedded texts for which no reportee is explicitly cued, so that they are attributable only to some vague 'common sense' or 'everybody'. This common ground claimed by the writer can be set up in various ways; in presuppositions, for example, which place assumed beliefs or experiences in the reader's intertextual context, or in embedded fact projections. By presenting the embedded fact projections or presuppositions attributable to 'common sense' or 'everybody', the writer is setting herself up as the kind of person who takes the projected facts or presupposed ideas for granted. She is also setting up the reader as a like-minded person. So for example it is taken as an agreed fact in A6.1 that *fashions in lipstick have changed over the years.* The shared knowledge that the writer assumes relates to historical details about 'breeds' of women, kinds of 'look', to fashion changes, to choice and ownership of lipstick, details relating to lipstick as a commodity subject to fashion change, and so on.

Conclusion to the beauty feature analysis

Sisterhood in consumption: the consumption community of lipstick wearers

In McRobbie's work on *Jackie* magazine she claims that the publication offers its readers membership of a 'false sisterhood': 'The girls are being invited to join a close, intimate sorority where secrets can be exchanged and advice given' (1978: 3). Reinterpreting this notion, the text population of the feature I have inspected contains a feminine consumption community consisting of free individuals whose identities are established in consumption. It is a 'false sisterhood' which offers readers membership; to join, they need only consume. Members of this community are the media celebrities, the testimonial givers, other wearers (such as 'most girls in the 60s' in the column), the monolithic groups of women consumers 'under 24' and 'over 35' in the facts & figures text and the friendly editorial. Synthetic personalization and the need for adult femininity catches readers up in this bogus community. The subject position of consumer is presented as an integral part of being feminine.[4] In the beauty feature womanhood is a pattern of consumption. Teenagers aspire to adulthood. What girls aspire to be as women is presented for them as a matter of what kind of look they will 'opt' for. Character and 'looks' are conflated; the terms appear to be used interchangeably in the column and the illustrated history. Identity, it would seem, is skin deep.

An unsisterly sisterhood?
McRobbie also claims that the sisterhood offered to teenagers by the magazine is 'unsisterly', because it *'imprisons* them in a claustrophobic world of jealousy and competitiveness' (3). Can the consumption community in the beauty feature be described as unsisterly?

Well yes, but not for the reasons McRobbie suggests, but because the community is totally bogus and ultimately manipulates the reader. The magazine discourse-type is controlled and delimited by accountants, manufacturers etc. The beauty feature is not a piece of sisterly advice or an exchange of sisterly secrets; it is covert advertising: a consumer feature. Its producers' aim, apart from to fill two pages in the magazine cheaply, is to promote lipstick as a commodity. The advice it does provide for readers - that is, the instructions for professional application of lipstick - is curiously inappropriate for the age range. These instructions seem to be calculated to encourage experimenters to consume extravagantly, by playing at being film star and beautician rolled into one.

Girls need peer group membership; they turn to other girls for friendship and to learn how to behave like a teenage girl. Consumer femininity is a real part of adolescent patterns of friendship. The consumer feature however offers no real human relationship. The testimonials are an example of how, at puberty, girls are drawn into synthetic consumption communities of commodity users. Whether based on actual interviews or invented altogether, they are manipulative. Cosmetics use is presented as a natural part of a woman's identity, making demands on their discernment, their creative energies and their time. In reading the feature, girls are 'associating' with business people. Fashion and beauty alone

162

are newsworthy. The only practices cultivated relate to being a competent consumer; in fact they are encouraged to ridicule the scientific/ analytical.

The sisterhood offered in the consumer feature is also 'unsisterly' because it is patriarchal. The feature makes a small contribution to the shaping of the 'paradigms for women's production of appearances' (quoted from Smith in chapter 2) that are formed for women by manufacturing, advertising, fashion and magazine industries. In the paragraph on the kissprint as a symbol of femininity (the first paragraph of the column) the symbol is provided by a male character. It is a man who is the authority on femininity. There are other characters, inanimate lipstick smudges which only communicate metaphorically, who are indexical signs of a woman's presence. These are located on a man; to be feminine is to be (hetero)sexual. Feminine identity is achieved in consumption and in relationships with men. The editorial, the friendly 'older sister' writing for *Jackie* magazine, betrays her young readers, tying up their self-definition with external patriarchal standards of femininity, all in order to plug a product.

7

Conclusion

Summary

Working from the outset with an anti-humanist view of the language-using subject, what I have undertaken to do in the theoretical part of this study is to build a model of discourse in which language users are constituted as social subjects. I have argued that prevailing conceptions of the language user as rational actor, role player and bearer of intentions embody a view of people as far too self-conscious, calculating and strategic about their actions and as far too detached and distant from the conventions they enact. Against these prevailing conceptions I have presented a view of language users as social subjects whose identities are constituted in their acts of engaging in discourse. After setting out a dual view of discourse as both action and convention, I examined two attempts to use linguistic analysis to focus on the constitution of identity. At this point I noted in particular certain tendencies in discourse change observed by Fairclough: sophistication of discourse technologies, synthetic personalization and the proliferation of the subject position of consumer. I proposed coherence as a fruitful focus of attention. I went on to look for an approach to analysis that would specifically attend to the multi-voiced or 'dialogic' quality of discourse. This led to a detailed examination of the concept of intertextuality in semiology and linguistics. I concluded the theoretical half of the study by pushing the conception of coherence to the limit. I proposed that coherence is an intertextual phenomenon: to read a text as coherent we need to supply 'external elements'. To focus on 'intertextual coherence' in analysis, I proposed the notion of a text being 'populated' by three kinds of 'voice'.

In the practical half I set about examining the subjectivity offered readers by a sample text. I did this by examining its fragmentary quality and the multiple voices readers interpret in making sense of it. I began with attention to the order of discourse in which the chosen sample 'consumer feature' is embedded. This involved examination of the women's magazine discourse-type and more specifically the proposal that the magazine *Jackie* offers its readers membership of a synthetic sisterhood. I then presented a range of features as focusing points for locating a text population, choosing elements of particular relevance for scrutiny of mass media texts in general and advertising-related features addressed to women in particular. Turning to the actual analysis, I took Prior text intertextuality first, scouring through the data looking for verbal/mental processes, presuppositions, etc. On the basis of these I listed characters to be found in the text, including 'commonsense' and the reader, users of the product being promoted, etc. I followed this first stage with attention, when applicable, to foregrounded producer-audience interaction and simulated dialogue between characters. For the Heterogencity part of the text population analysis I had a range of different kinds of feature for attending to the diverse personae taken up by the editorial who produced the sample pages. This stage lent itself most readily to a line-by-line inspection of each text, with a separate section devoted entirely to synthetic personalization and friendship. In this way I slowly built up a picture of the text population of each text in the 'beauty feature'. The examination of the text population uncovered a synthetic sisterhood, a consumption community based on a single commodity - lipstick - to which girls are offered membership by the friendly sisterly editorial.

Applications

The way of focusing on subjectivity I have proposed can be incorporated into teaching materials - hopefully it will make a real contribution to stimulating learners' critical awareness of tendencies in discourse change: the increased use of synthetic personalization as a manupulative device and the proliferation and naturalization of the subject position of consumer. I do not recommend a full blow-by-blow analysis but selective attention to the different kinds of members of text populations to sensitize readers, enabling them to see the kind of relationship they are forced into as mass media readers, the kinds of assumption practitioners are foisting on them and, not least, the multiple subject positions of text producers. The illusion of a text having a source in a single writer is important to focus on because this illusion is one of the things that obscures the functioning of discourses in social organisation to position people - both on the producing and the receiving ends of interaction - in relations of power. The positions and relations set up for writer and reader in discourse take on an obvious quality. The possible multiple, and even contradictory, positions available for subjects may be obscured, giving the impression of unitary subjectivity. This illusion is shattered by identification of a whole range of subject positions set up for writer and reader.

I have attempted to formulate a set of simple questions in 'plain English' in a chapter entitled 'The construction of gender in a teenage magazine', appearing in *Critical Language Awareness* (Fairclough, ed. 1992).[1] However, the task of taking up the notion of text population in order to put it into operation in the classroom is better in the hands of professional producers of teaching materials and teacher trainers. Hilary Janks is one such practitioner who has added text population analysis to a pack of teaching materials in which subjectivity is a central theme (*Language Matters*, Unpublished ms.).

I intend to use the dual view of discourse as action and convention in an examination of how fiction contributes to social reproduction and social change. Intertextuality and the notion of text population will be useful here, to help me to examine works of fiction as heterogeneous mixes of diverse discourses, to pinpoint the devious means by which authors force their readers' complicity or expose their prejudices, and so on.[2]

The notion of 'text population': an assessment

In putting substance, in part 2, onto the generalisation with which I concluded part 1 - that coherence involves supplying 'external elements' and requires an intertextual perspective - I undoubtedly stepped beyond what one would expect the notion of coherence to cover. 'Text population' was my attempt to reduce the vast and unmanageable field of analysis offered by intertextuality to manageable proportions and to find simple, clear focusing points for analysis. However, I feel that the notion was only partially successful as an attempt to put an anti-humanist view into operation for critical analysis of discourse focusing on subjectivity. Heterogeneity, the most diffuse and a residual category, was the part I had most difficulty with, because I had set my sights on a simple checklist approach which proved very difficult. Clearly, the particular data looked at determines the details of the kinds of feature that will go into this category. I tried out the inspection of a text population on the synthetic sisterhood in a magazine consumer feature. In principle, it is applicable to any discourse, requiring an initial investigation of the order of discourse before settling on the details of what features to look for.

There is a sense in which the three forms of intertextuality go full circle which I feel I have not expressed. Interaction is only possible because of convention; all interaction is the enactment of conventions. I had some difficulty in deciding where to put the boundary between interaction and heterogeneity elements. I initially included synthetic personalization features in Interaction. But, after becoming aware of the historical construction of this synthetic personalization as a key element of women's magazines, I decided to highlight the conventional quality of informality and friendliness in addressing mass audiences by dealing with it under the heading of Heterogeneity.

The analysis took a long time to take shape because the data appeared *natural* to me. When I first turned to *Jackie* magazine I was to some extent looking for 'easy' data, having been previously working with taped spontaneous conversations. In fact it was far from easy, and required a lengthy excursion into cultural studies for any critical understanding of the context at all. Initially I was scarcely aware of the subject position of consumer the magazine offers and ignorant of the economic determinants of magazines and their consequences. I have learnt a great deal and I hope that as a consequence I can help others to do the same.

Examination of the text population of magazine features can help us to become critically aware of our identities as gendered consumers. With the help of the notion of text population we can become more self-conscious, as readers and viewers, of the interaction we engage in with media practitioners, by for example pinpointing direct address in the media. We can become more aware of the motivated choices mass media producers make in selecting particular items of vocabulary etc. to achieve an impression of friendship, distant formality etc. and perceive the shifts from one persona to another. We can glimpse the process by which our subjectivities are constructed, moment-by-moment, in interpreting mass media texts, how our identities are constituted in the act of working within diverse discourses, the extent to which what we take for granted is placed in our heads by mass media practitioners. In short, examination of text population can stimulate our awareness of the media impinging on our selves.

LIPS IN

Ask any clever advertiser how to suggest femininity with a product, and he'll probably tell you 'a kissprint'. Lipstick on a collar, a glass, his cheek — they all suggest that a woman was there. When men think of make-up, they think of lipstick.

It's hardly a modern invention — women have been adding artificial colour to their lips for centuries now. Before the days of lipstick as we know it, ladies used vegetable or animal dyes like cochineal — beetle's blood — to colour their lips.

The reason behind it wasn't simply to make themselves more beautiful — superstition lingered that the devil could enter the body through the mouth, and since red was meant to word off evil spirits 'lipstick' was put around the mouth to repel his evil intentions!

These days there are more complicated (and ruder!) theories. Experts in human behaviour say that it's all to do with sex (what else?!).

Other 'experts' claim that the shape of your lipstick can reveal a lot about your character — i.e. if you wear the end flat you're stubborn, if it's round and blunt you're fun-loving etc etc — but don't seem to take into consideration the fact that each brand of lipstick is a different shape to start with and it's easiest just to use it accordingly. So much for the experts!

What is interesting is the way that fashions in lipsticks have changed over the years. When lipcolour first came into fashion at the beginning of this century, dark colours and the style of 'drawing' on little pursed lips meant that women looked cutesy and doll-like. Later on, in the forties, film stars wanting to look lovable and little-girl'ish continued this, while the newer breed of dominant, business-like women opted for a bolder look, colouring right over the natural 'bow' in the lips. By the sixties 'women's lib' was in style and most girls abandoned lipstick altogether, or used beige colours to blank out the natural pink of their lips, and concentrated on over-the-top eye make-up and face painting instead.

Now, in the eighties, there are more colours available than ever before — right down to blue, green and black! 'Glossy' lips, popular for a while in the seventies, are out again, and the overall trend is for natural pink tints, with oranges and golds in summer, on big, full lips.

Large cosmetic manufacturers will have upwards of 70 shades available at a time, introducing a further three or four shades each season to complement the fashion colours of that time. And with some companies churning out batches of lipstick at a rate of 9,000 an hour, that's an awful lot of kisses to get through . . .!

MARGARET (15)
"I wear it all the time, because I always wear make-up. My favourite shade's a sort of brown-and-red mixture — I usually buy Boots 17 or Max Factor lipstick. I got my first one when I was 10, for Xmas — it was a sort of pink colour, I think it was just for me to play with."

EMILY (12)
"Usually I just wear lipstick when I'm going out, but sometimes for school, I like pinks, oranges and plain glosses. I was about 7 when my mum gave me a bright red lipstick to experiment with — I think I've worn it ever since!"

CLARA (wouldn't tell us her age!)
"I always wear red — dark red — and usually from Mary Quant or Estée Lauder. I don't know if I can remember my first lipstick — wait! yes I can! It was called "Choosy Cherry" by Mary Quant — everyone used to ask me if I was ill when I was wearing it!"

RHONA (18)
"I like pinks and deep reds. I don't wear it all that often. My first lipstick? I stole it from my sister's drawer — I was about 12 — dying to look grown-up even then!"

LIP TRICKS!
Choosing the right shade of lipstick is easy — mak
But by applying lipcolour correctly, you can achiev

1. Outline the lips with a toning lip-pencil — this will help stop your lipstick from 'bleeding' around your mouth (a touch of Elizabeth Arden's Lip-Fix Creme, £4.95, provides a good base to prevent this, too.).

2.
loo
bru
ove
in t

3. Blot lips with a tissue, dust over lightly with face powder, apply a second layer and blot again.

LIPSTICK FACTS AND FIGURES

Rimmel, the largest-selling 'budget' brand of cosmetics, sell over 5 million lipsticks every year, at an average price of 94p each — that's a staggering £4,700,000 plus spent on coloured kisses from Rimmel alone!

The average price of £1.39.

Out of all the lipsticks sold, 47% are 'pink' shades — Rimmel's top seller is 'Pink Shimmer'.

Lipstick is basically made up of oils and animal fats, particles of raw colours and pigments held together with waxes, and added perfume.

The bigg
with you
is t
tha
prev
notu

The bigg
with you
every w
buys 20
includi
pencil
howe
6 pie
will l

(Statistics by kind courtesy of SDC and Rimmel.)

168

INC!

...d tell the whole story behind lipstick!

...shade of lipstick is easy — making it stay on is a bit more tricky.
...colour correctly, you *can* achieve a long-lasting look!

...s with a toning
...will help stop
...'bleeding'
...th (a touch of
...Lip-Fix Creme,
...good base to

Clara Bow, the 'It' girl of the
1920's who first set the fashion
for wearing make-up — she
wore her lipstick in a perfect
Cupid's Bow.

2. Fill in using a lip brush
loaded with lipstick — a lip
brush gives you more control
over what you're doing, and fills
in tiny cracks more easily.

By the 1940's, female film stars wore their lippy to reflect their own
characters. Jean Harlow, the platinum blonde pin-up girl, went for absolute
kissability with a lip-line as unnatural as her eyebrows — while no-nonsense
dramatic actresses like Bette Davis and Joan Crawford preferred the wide-
mouthed 'stiff upper lip' look.

...a tissue, dust
...face powder,
...ayer and blot

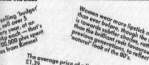

AND FIGURES

...selling 'budget'
...sell over 5
...very year, at an
...40 each — that's
...700,000 plus spent
...es from Rimmel.

Women wear more lipstick now
than ever before, though the trend
is towards subtler shades rather
than the brilliant reds favoured by
previous generations, to reflect the
natural look of the 80's.

The average price of a lipstick is
£1.39.

...sticks sold, 47%
...s — Rimmel's top
...mmer'.

The biggest business in make-up is
with young women. On average,
every woman in Britain under 24
buys 20 make-up items each year,
including four lipsticks and one lip
pencil or crayon. For over 55's,
however, the figures plummet to just
6 items per year, of which only one
will be a lipstick.

...lly made up of oils
...particles of raw
...ents held together
...added perfume.

...urtesy of SDC

By the 60's, innocence was IN
— models like Twiggy
abandoned lip colour
altogether, and all the emphasis
was on the eyes instead.

Into the 80's, and Madonna
brings back bright lip colour
with the most famous pout since
Marilyn Monroe.

169

Notes

Chapter 1

1. This provides a partial answer to a problem addressed by many feminists, formulated by Belsey (1985: 45) in the question: 'Why, since all women experience the effects of patriarchal practices, are not all women feminists?' It may seem obvious to feminist scholars that femininity is a patriarchal construction which places women in the invidious position of being sexualized, but this is by no means the case for the majority of women, who are simply trying to be themselves.

2. I use the 'generic' she throughout, while retaining he as it occurs in quotations. I trust this will not be confusing and I apologize in advance for any feeling of exclusion experienced by male readers in encountering the female 'generic'. However, such readers will perhaps come to appreciate the exclusion women experience every time they open a book. This could stand on its own as my reason for using this 'generic' she. But my true reasons are more personal and selfish; namely, to combat the experience of feeling outside or at best only peripheral to academic discourse and to help me to write in that discourse. It is far easier for me to associate myself with an imaginary reader, learner, discourse analyst etc who is assumed to be female than one who is assumed to be male. If in so doing I provide any male readers with a novel and informing experience of being left out of the discourse, well so much the better!

Chapter 2

1. This term comes from Husserlian phenomenology. It is frequently used by Kristeva, who is quoted below.

2. To stick more precisely to Kristeva's account, she says that semiology already contains this anti-humanism in that it has discovered a general social law, governing the process of producing meaning, which a given social practice is a particular expression of. A social practice is defined by, among other things, a semiotic system. So the given social practice is articulated doubly, in signifier - signified, a doubleness that has an arbitrary relation to its referent. As Kristeva says, 'all social functioning is marked by the split between referent and symbolic and by the shift from signified to signifier coextensive with it' (25).

3. I use the neuter pronoun 'it' for the decentred subject. If I designated the subject as 'she' or 'he', I would be assigning gender to it inappropriately. Gender itself is not fixed; people are positioned as gendered subjects.

4. The distinction that sociolinguists make between communicative competence and actual performance is descended from the Chomskian distinction. It clearly perpetuates the schism between the speaking subject and the conventions she/it employs, which I suspect is precisely the problem with both Chomsky's competence/performance distinction and the langue/ parole distinction from which it descends.

5. Goffman (1974) himself describes the speaking subject as a "player in a ritual game" 239.

6. Similarly, Goffman's 'Facework' reads at times like a poker-player's guide.

7. showing that something is not natural but constructed by showing that it contains its own opposite ('contradicts itself').

8. This noun-turned-verb is particularly appropriate here!

9. Despite the fact that it is part of the good grooming necessary for entry into the jobmarket.

10. Smith (1988: 38) defines text as follows: 'By texts I mean the more or less permanent and above all replicable forms of meaning, of writing, painting, television, film, etc. The production, distribution, and uses of texts are a pervasive and highly significant dimension of contemporary social organization'.

11. Pêcheux (1982: 14) criticizes formal semantics of being unaware of its own ideological content. As he says: 'the cold spaces of semantics conceal a burning subject'. The target of his criticism is the kind of circular classification practiced by Katz (e.g.1972). Pêcheux points out that the classification of meaning in formal semantics relies upon tautological definitions such as 'a bachelor is an unmarried man'. Such definitions present meanings as givens and tell us nothing about their production or origin. *Language, Semantics and Ideology* is 'dedicated' to the 'hero' of a French comic song, Monsieur de la Palice. The humour of this song lies in its tautologies, such as '..he never lacked for anything / So long as he had plenty'. Pêcheux proposed that this character should be the patron saint of semanticists. He parodies the tautological definitions of formal semantics with a tautology, or 'lapallisade', of his own: 'if a man is not married that is because he is a bachelor' (14). 'Bachelor', we are intended to realize, does not have a meaning 'in itself':

a word, expression or proposition does not have a meaning 'of its own' attached to it in its literalness; its meaning is constituted in each discursive formation, in the relationships into which one word, expression or proposition enters with other words, expressions or propositions of the same discursive formation (112).

The meaning of a word changes as it shifts from one discursive formation to another. In contrast with formal semantics Pêcheux does not conceive of language as a set of 'givens' (a grammar, a lexicon defined by 'lapallisades', etc). For him, meanings and meaning relations are defined in terms of ideological orientation. Meaning is produced by positioned subjects.

This way of looking at issues of meaning relations in terms of ideological orientation sprang from the work of a research group at the Centre National de la Recherche Scientifique. In this project, a text extract was presented to two groups (a page from the Mansholt report). Each group was told that the extract had a different origin (i.e. a different orientation) and asked to summarize it. They found that items were interpreted differently according to whether the summariser thought they were politically 'right' or 'left'. The resulting summaries were treated as just two separate texts, a 'left' corpus and a 'right' corpus. Propositions in the original were each represented by two distinct 'paraphrastic domains'. The results provided evidence that items only have meaning from a standpoint, i.e. they always have some orientation, and this is dependent on the source to which they are ascribed. (Note that Pêcheux' claim is more far-reaching than that of Harris (1952) on whose early work on text analysis this Mansholt report research was based. Harris's claim was that meanings are specific to individual texts. Pêcheux claims that it is a discourse formation which fixes meaning across a group of texts with the same orientation.) Thus Pêcheux and associates were undermining the conception of a 'universal semantics', a semantics where meanings are assumed to be shared: 'no universal semantics will ever be able to fix what should be understood by planning, political change, radical reform, government action and so on because words, expressions and utterances change their sense according to the position from which they are uttered (1978: 265).

In this account, subjects are positioned in discourse formations. It is a discourse formation which fixes meaning across each group of summaries. The two alternatives, left and right, are in opposition.
12. I'm simplifying here, Pêcheux also coins another term: transverse-discourse. It doesn't seem worth the complication of the extra terminology here.
13. This is what makes change a theoretical possibility, so the model is not deterministic. Subjectivity is constituted moment-by-moment in discourse; it is by definition not fixed and is open to change. Social subjects are both constrained and capable of individual creativity. Language users must take up pre-determined subject positions in producing and interpreting discourse, thus being constituted as subjects in interaction. However, discourse practices (including the possible subject positions set up for people who bring discourse practices into being by enacting them, and the distribution of these subject positions) may be creatively transformed. This is possible because the relationship between discourse and discourse-type is not one-directional and mechanistic. In a given discourse, interactants may draw upon several different discourse-types and combine them creatively. Through this 'creative extension-through-combination of existing resources' (31), actual discourses can transform discourse-types, leading to the creation of new discourse-types. Change also takes place in societal and institutional orders of discourse. Although determining actual discourse, an order of discourse is affected by it: every discourse contributes to either change or continuity in the social structures in which it is embedded. As Fairclough (1989: 37) says: 'As well as being determined by social structures, discourse has effects upon social structures and contributes to the achievement of social continuity or social change'.

A language user can be in varying relations to discourse and the conventions enacted in it. Subjects in discourse are under the subjection of both the power of others and their own identities, constituted in relations of power. The constitution of the subject in the act of producing and interpreting discourse is not deterministic. A language user can be in varying relations to discourse as a producer. She may be drawing upon discourse-types 'automatically', in a non-creative way, in discourse production and interpretation, thereby straightforwardly reproducing discourse-types and the subject positions associated with them. As a producer, she may creatively combine discourse-types in novel ways in order to reinforce existing positions and relations of power between them. Alternatively, she may be drawing upon discourse-types in order to creatively undermine them.

There are, then, three possibilities open to her. She may be uncritically reproducing conventions, in which case there is no change. Or she may creatively manipulate conventions in order to either uphold or undermine them. CLS is intended to counter specific kinds of change upholding existing conventions within the societal order of discourse.

14. Fairclough is using 'strategic discourse' in the sense in which it is used by Habermas. Habermas distinguishes between 'communicative' and 'strategic' discourse to differentiate between a genuine desire to communicate through discourse (an orientation to understanding) and the desire to dominate through discourse (an orientation to success).

15. A particular body of work not given specific attention which I must note is that of Teun van Dijk and associates.

16. Marilda Cavalcanti (1983: 31) makes a similar observation with regard to the use of prior knowledge as a last resort in text-linguistic approaches to text comprehension.

17. a distinction between the 'inside' and the 'outside' of a text. From an intertextual perspective, there are elements of both kinds of connection in sentences containing presuppositions (the non-sequential connection is with an assumption; the sequential connection is with a prior text).

18. In Thibault's Problem page text, the 'Agony aunt' picks out the presupposition you have to be brave to try sexual intercourse in her reply, contesting it with the explicit assertion: There is nothing brave about trying sex.

Chapter 3

1. Beaugrande & Dressler (1980), whose application of intertextuality for textlinguistics I examine in 3.1 below, refer to an article by her in *Linguistique et Litterature* (1968).

2. discussion of the same work of Bakhtin's is also in Kristeva (1970: 87-96)

3. This paper originally appeared in *Semiotike* (1969), which Culler refers to. Incidentally, in another book, *Le Texte du Roman*, written about the same period but not published until 1970, there is a highly schematic diagram (about 'generators' of the novel) in which 'citations and plagiarism' are entered under 'intertextuality'. Culler does not mention this book.

4. cf. Derrida's discussion of supplement-marking to indicate the simultaneous presence of contradictory arguments as an intertextuality in *Of Grammatology*.

5. I find the distinction between them unclear; presumably the literary are a sub-set of the pragmatic. But I am discussing the critical theory concept of intertextuality as presented by Culler here, not inventorizing types of presupposition.

6. By drawing in an external voice - the kind of poem being parodied - the wily Baudelaire contrives to have his cake and eat it, referring to an eroticized female form while claiming he does not write about that sort of thing in his poems.

7. I am unwilling to cast Bloom's work in an unfavourable light - he has his own good reasons for this position with regard to intertextuality, to follow which would deflect the present writing too far into literary issues. As a champion of the Romantic movement (Shelley in particular) he differs from the dominant Eliot/Leavis verson of literary history by placing it firmly in the dissident tradition. One of the features of this is that he stresses, quite rightly in my view, the strategic norm-'transcending', Nietzschean power of will in poetic creation - specifically countering the respect for a constraining but venerable literary convention voiced so loudly and so often by the followers of Eliot/Leavis.

8. They refer here to a single paper: Kristeva (1968) 'Problemes de la structuration du texte', *Linguistique et Litterature* 12: 55-64

9. De Beaugrande (1980) defines intertextuality as a presuppositional phenomenon.

10. Kristeva uses intertextuality to describe the intersection of semiotic systems. We can extend the scope of conventions drawn into 'textual dialogue' to include visual systems of signification (again, see Fairclough (1989: 28) for inclusion of visuals in language).

Chapter 4

1. Advertisements present for their audience the marketplace in which subjects are 'equal' as consumers (that is, a £1 coin of mine has the same exchange value as a £1 coin of yours) and 'free' (to buy or not buy, and to choose between different products) (Vestergaard & Schroder).

2. She takes the concept of 'totemism' from Levi-Strauss (1966).

3. From the publisher's viewpoint, these are 'freebies' and publicity leaflets for 'courtesy ads'.

4. Advice on social relations even finds its way into ads, after a fashion: e.g. 'Don't let spots spoil your social life!'

5. Barker (1989: 102) observes that *Jackie*'s predecessors were more overtly dictatorial (notably *Marilyn*, which ran a feature entitled 'Mum knows best').

6. Barker (1989: 108-9) finds her justification for this claim very tenuous.

Chapter 5

1. Halliday does not attend to the representation of words and thoughts in terms of 'faithfulness' to an original.

2. Verbal and mental process nouns may be modified by expansion rather than projection. Halliday notes a possible ambiguity in the report that he was submitting, in which the beta clause could be either an elaborating clause or projected information. The same applies to verbs; here structural ambiguity is most likely with non-finites, e.g. 'he promised to make her happy', where beta may be an enhancing clause or a projected offer.

3. I showed the 'photostrip' containing this line to a researcher at Oxford, Liz Frazer, who was working with teenage girls in discussion groups.

4. with accompanying photographs. The reconstructions appeared under headings, something like this:

EMMA

'I'm down here trying to find a denim jacket - this one isn't mine - it's only on loan! I like The Smiths and The Blow Monkeys, and I hate Howard Jones and Royalty.' Treason! Outrage! The most exciting thing that's happened today? **'This!'**

BIANCA

'I'm only here by mistake - I got off the bus too early on the way to a friend's house. I am very pleased though, 'cos I've stumbled on a pair of ski pants which actually fit me!' Hmmm. A teensy bit large aren't they? **''Course not. My ambitions are to travel the world and to go on an archaeological dig...'**

5. and not the heading: 'MOUTHING OFF'. This seems to be a characteristic of headings in consumer features. Others in the same feature are 'SPRING INTO ACTION!', 'WATERBABIES!', 'TOTALLY TROPICAL!' and 'HAIR'S THE LATEST!'. Although vocabulary in headings does generally have a connection of some kind with a classification scheme also set up in the text beneath it (e.g. 'mouth' in 'MOUTHING OFF' connects with 'lip' through lexical cohesion), it is the first sentence which verbally introduces the topic: 'We give you a few lip tricks on how to achieve the perfect pout...'. The topic is not mouths or talking too much/ indiscretely ('mouthing off' being an informal expression for this?), but lipstick and a sequence of various actions involving it. Sometimes the semantic relation established is very tenuous: eg 'Waterbabies!' connects with the title given to a range of products, 'Seascape'. As cues to frames, one might say the headings are 'unhelpful'; sometimes they introduce a Contents absent in the text below: e.g. 'Spring' is not mentioned in the text headed as 'Spring into action!'; the pun in the header brings in a seasonal fashion frame. In academic texts, a heading has to contain information directly relevant to the main topic frames (usually a noun phrase identifying it). In other discourses, this is a redundancy to be avoided. Graphic design students, for instance, are taught to avoid repeating the same information in different semiotic systems; a heading should have additional signification. cf. the connotations of an image in advertising examined by Williamson (1978).

6. The *Jackie* writer's use of intensity modality in intensifiers contributes to the establishment of an informal friendly relationship with her readers in this sample (and many others). Examples of modal elements indicating intensity here are 'just', 'really'. However, this form of modality is not a significant feature of the data analysed in chapter 6.

7. Sometimes it is not clear whether *we* is being used inclusively or exclusively. There may be ambivalence surrounding the social identity of the group and whether the reader is a member of it. Consider the following example in the front-page headline of a free local paper:

'GIVE *US* MORE POLICE' PLEA

LANCASHIRE has come out fighting in the latest round of its battle for more policemen.

...

...

The group, led by police authority chairman Councillor Mrs Ruth Henig, travelled to Whitehall following the latest snub to their request for more officers.

The Police Committee was seeking seven more sergeants for training and 89 more foot patrol officers. (*Preston Red Rose Advertiser* 21.7.89: 1)

Confronted with the headline, we need to work out who are included among the pleaders for more police. Looking at the body of the text, the first candidate is 'LANCASHIRE'. The actual spokesperson only appears in the fourth paragraph. The reader seems to be set up as member of social group along with spokeperson for Police Committee and its other members, and the Lancashire police force.

Chapter 6

1. I am using this term in Eco's sense. Eco distinguishes three kinds of sign: the iconic, where the connection between sign and referent is one of resemblance; the indexical, where there is a factual/causal connection; and the symbolic, where sign and referent are conventionally associated.

2. note the complexity of adjunct embedding and chaining in this historical narrative; time as 'location' in history as well as 'duration'.

3. I assume an intended polyvalency here: lips (plural) and abbreviation of incorporated; lip (singular) and abbreviation of synchronisation. (This ambivalence is enhanced by what appears to be a fortuitous error in the registration of the two pages: there is a letter space gap between 'LIP', on the left hand page, and 'S', on the right hand page.)

4. the facts & figures text seems to be providing readers with early training in housekeeping; comparing prices is something every thrifty housewife needs to do!

Chapter 7

1. The analysis of the friendship offered in the advertorial has since appeared as 'Synthetic sisterhood: false friends in a teenage magazine' in Hall and Bucholtz, eds. (1995).

2. This appeared as *Fictions at work: language as social practice in fiction* (Longman 1995).

References

Althusser L. 1971 'Ideology and ideological state apparatuses (Notes towards an investigation)'. In *Lenin and Philosophy and Other Essays* (Ben Brewster trans.) London: New Left Books.

Bakhtin M.M. 1973 *Problems in Dostoevsky's Poetics* New York: Ardis

Bakhtin M.M. 1981 *The Dialogic Imagination* (M. Holquist, ed.; trans. C. Emerson and Holquist) Austin/London: University of Texas Press.

Barker, M. 1989 *Comics: Ideology, Power and the Critics* Manchester: Manchester University Press.

Barthes R. 1967 *Elements of Semiology* Jonathan Cape

Barthes R. 1970 *S/Z* Paris: Seuil

Barthes R. 1972 'Textual Analysis of Poe's 'Valdemar'', in Young R. 1981 *Untying the Text* London: Routledge and Kegan Paul.

Beaugrande R. de 1980 *Text, Discourse, and Process: Toward a Multidisciplinary Science of Texts* London: Longman

Beaugrande R. de and Dressler 1980 *Introduction to Text Linguistics* London: Longman.

Belsey, C. 1985 'Constructing the subject; deconstructing the text'. In Newton J. and Rosenfelt (eds.) *Feminist Criticism and Social Change* New York/London: Methuen.

Bloom, H. 1976 *Poetry and Repression* New Haven: Yale University Press.

Boorstin D. 1973 *The Americans: The Democratic Experience* New York: Random House

Brown P. and Levinson 1978 'Universals in language usage: politeness phenomena'. In Goody E. (ed.) *Questions and Politeness: Strategies in Social Interaction* Cambridge: C.U.P.

Brown G. and Yule 1983 *Discourse Analysis* Cambridge: Cambridge University Press

Brownmiller S. 1984 *Femininity* New York: Paladin

Cameron D. 1985 *Feminism and Linguistic Theory* London: Macmillan

Cavalcanti M. 1983 *The Pragmatics of FL Reader-text Interaction: Key Lexical Items as Source of Potential Reading Problem* Lancaster: Unpublished Ph.D.

Chomsky N. 1957 *Syntactic Structures* The Hague: Mouton.

Chomsky N. 1965 *Aspects of a Theory of Syntax* Cambridge, Mass.: M.I.T. Press.

Chomsky N. 1968 *Language and Mind* New York: Harcourt, Brace, Jovanovich.

Clark R., Fairclough, Ivanic and Martin-Jones 1987 *Critical Language Awareness* CLSL Working Paper Series 1. Lancaster.

Cohen L. 1984 *Small Expectations: Society's Betrayal of Older Women* Toronto: McCelland and Stewart.

Courtine J.J. 1981 'Analyse du Discours Politique (le discours communiste adresse aux chretiens)', *Langages* vol. 62

Coward R. 1984 *Female Desire. Women's Sexuality Today* London: Paladin.

Coward R. and Ellis 1977 *Language and Materialism* London: Routledge and Kegan Paul.

Craig R.T. and Tracy (eds.) 1983 *Conversational Coherence: Form, Structure, and Strategy* New York: Sage

Culler, J. 1981 *The Pursuit of Signs: Semiotics, Literature, Deconstruction* London: Routledge & Kegan Paul.

Davidson, J. 1977 'Speak softly and say yes please.' In Harris, P. pp.105-116.

Downes W. 1984 *Language and Society* London: Fontana.

Dreyfus H.L. and Rabinow 1986 *Michel Foucault: Beyond Structuralism and Hermeneutics* Harvester Press.

Fairclough N.L. 1988 'Michel Foucault and the analysis of discourse' CLSL Research Papers 10. Lancaster University.

Fairclough N.L. 1989 *Language and Power* London: Longman

Fairclough N.L. 1989a 'Language and Ideology'', *English Language Research Journal* Vol.3. M. Knowles & K. Malmkjaer (eds.) University of Birmingham.

Fairclough N.L. (1992 *Discourse and Social Change* Cambridge: Polity.

Fairclough N.L. (ed.) 1992 *Critical Language Awareness* London: Longman

Ferguson M. 1983 *Forever Feminine: Women's Magazines and the Cult of Femininity* London: Heinemann

Firth J.R. 1950 'Personality and language in society', *Sociological Review* 42

Foucault M. 1972 *The Archaeology of Knowledge* (trans. A. Sheridan) London: Tavistock.

Foucault M. 1975 *The Birth of the Clinic. An Archaeology of Medical Perception* (trans. A. Sheridan) London: Tavistock.

Foucault M. 1981 *The History of Sexuality. Volume 1: An Introduction* (trans. R. Hurley) Harmondsworth: Penguin.

Foucault M. 1984 'The Order of Discourse'. In Shapiro M. (ed.) *Language and Politics* Oxford: Blackwell.

Foucault M. 1984 'What is an author?' In Rabinow P. (ed.) *The Foucault Reader* Harmondsworth: Peregrine.

176

Fowler R. 1988 'Notes on critical linguistics'. In Steele R. and Threadgold (eds.)

Fowler R., Hodge, Kress and Trew 1979 *Language and Control* London: Routledge & Kegan Paul.

Giddens A. 1976 *New Rules of Sociological Method: a positive method of interpretive sociologies* London: Hutchinson.

Giddens, A. 1987 *Social Theory and Modern Sociology* Cambridge: Polity.

Giglioli P. 1972 *Language and Social Context* Harmondsworth: Penguin.

Goffman E. 'On facework'. In Blount B. (ed.) 1974 *Language, Culture and Society: a book of readings* Winthrop

Haberland H. and Mey 1977 'Editorial: linguistics and pragmatics', *Journal of Pragmatics* 1 pp1-12

Habermas J. 1984 *Theory of Communicative Action, volume 1: Reason and the rationalisation of society* (trans T. McCarthy) London: Heineman.

Hall K and Bucholtz (eds.) 1995 *Gender Articulated: Language and the Socially Constructed Self* New York: Routledge.

Halliday M.A.K. 1985 *An Introduction to Functional Grammar* London: Arnold.

Halliday, M.A.K. and Hasan 1976 *Cohesion in English* London: Longman.

Halliday M.A.K. and Hasan 1985 *Language, Context, and Text* Victoria: Deakin University Press.

Haroche C.L., Henry and Pêcheux 1971 'La semantique et la coupure Saussurienne: langue, langage, discours', *Langages* 24: 93-106

Harris P. 1977 *The DC Thomson Bumper Fun Book* Edinburgh: Paul Harris Publishing.

Harris Z. 1952 'Discourse Analysis', *Language* vol.28, no.1

Hatim B. & Mason 1990 *Discourse and the Translator* London/New York: Longman.

Henriques J. et al. 1984 *Changing the Subject* London: Methuen.

Henry P. 1975 'Constructions relatives et articulations discursives', *Langages* 37: 81-98

Hodge R. and Kress 1988 *Social Semiotics* Cambridge: Polity.

Hollings J. 1985 'The portrayal of women in romance comic strips 1964-84.' Unpublished BA dissertation: University of Reading.

Holmes J. 1984 'Hedging your bets and sitting on the fence: some evidence for hedges as support structures', *Te Reo* 27: 47-62

Hymes D. 1971 'On communicative competence'. In J.B. Pride and Holmes (eds.) 1972 *Sociolinguistics* Harmondsworth: Penguin.

Ivanic R. 1988 'Critical language awareness in action', *Language Issues* Vol.2 No.2 pp2-7

Jameson F. 1972 *The Prison House of Language* Princeton, New Jersey: Princeton University Press.

Janks H. *Language Matters* Unpublished ms.

Jarrett D. 1984 'Pragmatic coherence in an oral formulaic tradition: I can read your letters/ sure can't read your mind'. In Tannen (ed.)

Katz J. 1972 *Semantic Theory* New York: Harper & Row.

Kress G. 1985 *Linguistic Processes in Sociocultural Practice* Victoria: Deakin.

Kress G. and Threadgold 1988 'Towards a social theory of genre', *Southern Review* 21

Kristeva J. 1969 *Semiotike: Recherches pour une semanalyse* Paris: Seuil

Kristeva J. 1970 *Le Texte du Roman* The Hague: Mouton

Kristeva J. 1973 'The system and the speaking subject', *Times Literary Supplement* 12 October 1973 pp.1249-52 (reprinted in Moi T, ed. 1986)

Kristeva J. 1980 *Desire in Language: A Semiotic Approach to Literature and Art* (L.S. Roudiez (ed.); trans. T Gora, Jardine and Roudiez) Oxford: Blackwell.

Lacan J. 1966 *Ecrits* Paris: Seuil

Labov W. 1970 'The study of language in its social context', *Studium Generale* 23:30-87

Lavers A. 1982 *Roland Barthes: Structuralism and After* London: Methuen.

Leech G. 1983 *Principles of Pragmatics* London/ New York: Longman.

Leech G. and Short 1981 *Style in Fiction* London: Longman.

Leiss W., Kline and Jhally 1986 *Social Communication in Advertising* London/New York: Methuen.

Leman J. 1980 '"The advice of a real friend" Codes of intimacy and oppression in women's magazines 1937-1955'. *Women's Studies Quarterly* Vol.3, pp.63-78.

Lemke J.L. 1985 'Ideology, intertextuality, and the notion of register'. In Benson, J.D. & W.S. Greaves (eds.) *Systemic Perspectives on Discourse* volume 1. Norwood, New Jersey: Ablex

MacKinnon C.A. 1982 'Feminism, marxism, method, and the State: An agenda for theory', *Signs* 7, #3 Spring 1982

McRobbie A. 1978 'Working class girls and the culture of femininity'. In Women's Studies Group, CCCS (eds.) *Women Take Issue* London: Hutchinson

McRobbie A. 1978 'Jackie: an ideology of adolescent femininity'. University of Birmingham: CCCS Occasional paper

Moi T.(ed.) 1986 *The Kristeva Reader* Oxford: Blackwell

Montgomery M. 1988 'D-J talk'. In Coupland N. (ed.) *Styles of Discourse* London: Croom Helm

Pêcheux M. 1978 'Are the masses an inanimate object? In Sankoff D. (ed.) *Linguistic Variation: Models and Methods* London: Academic Press

Pêcheux M. 1982 *Language, Semantics and Ideology: Stating the Obvious* (trans. H. Nagpal) London/Basingstoke: Macmillan

Pêcheux M. and Fuchs 1975 'Mises au point a propos de l'analyse automatique du discours', *Langages* Vol.37 pp7-80

Quinn, N. and Holland 1987 'Culture and cognition'. In Holland, D. and Quinn (eds.) *Cultural Models in Language and Thought* Cambridge/ New York / Melbourne: Cambridge University Press.

Quirk R. 1978 'Focus, scope and lyrical beginnings', *Language and Style* 11: 30-39

Rabinow P. (ed.) 1986 *The Foucault Reader* Harmondsworth: Peregrine.

Schegloff E. (1968) 'Sequencing in conversational openings'. In Gumperz J. and Hymes (eds.) 1972 *Directions in Sociolinguistics* New York: Holt, Rinehart and Winston.

Schegloff E. and Sacks (1973) 'Opening up closings'. In Turner R. (ed.) 1974 *Ethnomethodology* Harmondsworth: Penguin.

Sebeok T.A. (ed.) 1986 *Encyclopedic Dictionary of Semiotics* Berlin: Mouton.

Shank and Abelson 1977 *Scripts, Goals and Understanding* Hillsdale, New Jersey: Lawrence Erlbaum.

Sinclair J. and Coulthard 1975 *Towards an Analysis of Discourse* Oxford: Oxford University Press.

Smith D. 1988 'Femininity as Discourse'. In Roman L.G. and Christian-Smith (eds.) *Becoming Feminine: The Politics of Popular Culture* London/NY/Philadelphia: Falmer Press.

Sperber D. and Wilson 1986 *Relevance* Oxford: Blackwell.

Steele R. and Threadgold (eds.) 1988 *Language Topics II* Amsterdam: Benjamins.

Stubbs M. 1983 *Discourse Analysis: The Sociolinguistic Analysis of Natural Language* Oxford: Blackwell.

Talbot M.M. 1987 'The pragmatic analysis of presuppositional phenomena in Levinson's *Pragmatics*', *Acta Linguistica Hafniensia* 20 pp.173-187

Tannen D. (ed.) 1984 *Coherence in Spoken and Written Discourse* vol XII New Jersey: Ablex.

Thibault P.J. 1988 'Knowing what you're told by the Agony Aunts: language function, gender difference and the structure of knowledge and belief in the personal columns.' In Birch D & O'Toole (eds.) 1988 *Functions of Style* London/New York: Pinter.

Threadgold T. 1987 'The semiotics of Volosinov, Halliday, and Eco', *American Journal of Semiotics* vol 4, 2 pp.107-142

Threadgold T. 1988 'Changing the subject'. In Steele R. and Threadgold (eds.)

Ventola E. 1987 *The Structure of Social Interaction* London: Frances Pinter.

Vestergaard T. and Schroder 1985 *The Language of Advertising* Oxford: Blackwell.

Walkerdine V. 1985 'On the regulation of speaking and silence: subjectivity, class and gender in contemporary schooling.' In Steedman C, Urwin and Walkerdine (eds.) *Language, Gender and Childhood* London: Routledge & Kegan Paul .

Wardhaugh R. 1985 *How Conversation Works* Oxford: Blackwell.

Weedon C. 1987 *Feminist Practice and Post-Structuralist Theory* Oxford: Blackwell.

White C. 1970 *Women's Magazines 1693-1968* London: Michael Joseph.

Widdowson H. 1979 *Explorations in Applied Linguistics* Milton Keynes: Open University Press.

Winship J. 1987 *Inside Women's Magazines* London/New York: Pandora.

_____

19012669R00110

Printed in Great Britain
by Amazon